We lay down on the bed, this time with our clothes on.

"Is it that you just don't want to do it?" I said. "Because we don't have to. It doesn't matter."

Lyle frowned. "Well, the thing is, I'm just not sure I'm in love with you."

I felt relieved. "That's okay. I'm not sure I'm in love with you."

"That's what I mean."

"I don't care if you love me or not."

"You should."

"Why?"

"That's your birthright, Jody, to be loved."

IT'S OKAY
IF YOU DON'T
LOVE ME

Norma Klein

FAWCETT JUNIPER • NEW YORK

For Lou

1

"Coward."

We were standing at the net, on opposite sides. I was holding my tennis racket, but Lyle just stood there, kind of leaning on his, squinting at me since he always takes the sunny side and never wears sunglasses. I admire that. I always wear not only sunglasses but my magic green plastic sun visor. It seems like it's magic in that ever since I got it, a few months ago, my tennis game, which I have to modestly admit is pretty good, has been even better. But I do have this thing about hating the sun in my eyes, especially when I serve. Basically I shouldn't let Lyle always take the sunny side. I know he does it because he wants to be chivalrous and all that, and maybe since so far we've only rallied, it's not that crucial.

"What's wrong with rallying?" he said, smiling at me.

"There's nothing wrong with it, but it's more fun to play a set."

"Just for the competitive thing?"

"Yeah."

He looked dubious.

"Look, what do you have to lose? Will it wreck your pride or something if I win?"

He smiled again. I really like his smile. Lyle is a real non-New Yorker. Maybe I shouldn't say that to mean he's nice, since I'm a New Yorker myself, but there's something about his manner that you could spot a million miles away and say: This person did not grow up in New York City. He's tall and sort of gangling, with greenish eyes and I guess what you'd call dirty-blond hair, and he has this warm, very friendly smile. He talks sort of slowly, like he was choosing his words very carefully, unlike me. I just kind of blurt things out. "You seem to have your heart set on this," he said.

"Right, I do. . . . Only let's switch sides the regular way."

"Won't the sun bother you?"

"Well, if it bothers *me*, it'll bother *you*. You don't even have sunglasses."

"I don't mind it so much."

8

"I don't care. I don't want any handicaps."

He turned, and I called, "M or W?"

"I thought it was Rough or Smooth."

"We always say M or W for Men or Women."

"Then I guess I pick M."

I twirled the racket. "Okay, let's see. . . . Hmm, I serve."

I wasn't sure that was so auspicious. My serve is the most unperfected part of my game. When it's working, it's okay, but lately I don't seem to have as much control as I used to. "I'll take a couple."

"Take as many as you want."

The first two were out, a wonderful beginning, but I hate standing there taking a million practice serves, so I just said, "Okay, I'm ready."

I don't want to go into a blow-by-blow account of our whole set because that might be sort of dull, especially for anyone who doesn't play tennis. The essence of it is that I lost. Disastrously. Horribly. In fact, if you have to know, the score was 6-love, which means I didn't get one measly game. Lyle was fantastic! You'd say how come I couldn't tell from rallying with him. Well, my first excuse is you can't always tell just from rallying with someone. There are lots of people—like my friend Marion— who hit hard low shots when they rally and then crack up completely in a game. Or they'll hit it right at you. That's sort of what I expected with Lyle. He didn't seem so much the competitive type.

And in a way he wasn't, which made it even worse. You could tell he really didn't *want* to win, that it was making him embarrassed. But he had a great serve, which I could barely get back and every single time I came to net, he'd either lob it over my head or smash it past me. After about the third game I felt really disheartened. I know you're supposed to never give up, but the sheer dumbness of the thing overwhelmed me. Here, *I'd* insisted we play a set, when *he* was perfectly content to rally, and now I was making a complete ass of myself, not even getting near the ball. I had too much pride to just say in the middle, "Let's stop," so I floundered around hopelessly for the next three games. When we'd change sides and pass each other on the side of the court, he'd smile, sort of sheepishly.

I'd just glower.

Luckily just as he put away the final point, a couple walked on the court for the next hour. I looked at my watch. It was four. We were playing at Riverside and 120th, which is a place I like because you can look out at the river. Even on a hot day there are cool breezes. After you play, it's nice to sit under a tree for a while. We walked off the court and plunked down on the grass, our rackets next to us.

"So, why didn't you tell me?" I felt depressed enough to kill myself on the spot.

"Tell you what?"

"That you were so good!"

"You never asked me."

"Nope, that doesn't work. . . . My God, if *I* was that good, I'd tell the world. I mean, I'm *not* that good, as you see, but I would still *tell* people. I'd warn them."

"Okay, maybe I should have. . . . I thought I did tell you that I'd played a lot in Ohio."

Lyle comes from Ohio. He just moved here a few months ago. I met him at Sloan-Kettering, this laboratory where we both worked over the summer. He's going into his last year of high school, like me, and they have a program for seniors who are interested in science; you work as a kind of technician. It was a terrific job, and I even got paid, though I'd have done it for free just for the experience. Lyle worked at a lab down the hall from the one I was in, and we really didn't get to know each other that well, but once at lunch—which everyone ate in this cafeteria downstairs—he said something about not knowing how to get a tennis permit, and we got to talking about it. I went with him one day to the Arsenal, where he got one. Today's the first day we've played. Our jobs ended a week ago, and school starts pretty soon. He's going to Bronx Science. I go to a private school called Talbot that I've gone to since I was in third grade.

"When did you start playing," I asked, "when you were three?"

11

"I was eight. My mother was pretty good and she taught me."

"Like Jimmy Connors, huh?"

Lyle was looking at me curiously. "Why did you want so much to play a set?"

"Why shouldn't I have?" I felt defensive. I always feel defensive about being interested in and caring so much about sports. I've read in all these magazines that Jewish girls aren't supposed to be interested in sports, that they're afraid they'll get their hair messed up, stupid stereotypes like that. But I've always liked sports, even ones like basketball and baseball. It's true our school doesn't have that much of a sports program, but even so, I've always enjoyed it and been one of the best.

"No, there's no reason you shouldn't. I just meant, well, couldn't you tell from rallying that I was fairly good?"

I sighed. "I guess I should have. But I hoped you might be the type that would go to pieces in a game."

He laughed. "Do I look like that type?"

"You can't always tell by looking at someone." I was still feeling rotten.

"Jody, don't feel bad."

"Why not? It's my inalienable right to feel really lousy."

"No, it's not. First of all, you're a very *good*

player. You're the best girl tennis player I've ever played with."

Not knowing me very well, Lyle didn't realize that to me that kind of compliment is like a punch to the vital parts. "Yeah, but you said you went to an all-boys school, so how many girls have you played with?"

"I've played with some. . . . You're really good, you must know that. It's just your serve is much too shallow, and you don't let yourself hit out in games the way you do in rallies. You seemed to get very nervous and kept blooping it back, instead of really swinging into it."

"Maybe. But even if I hadn't done that, you'd have won anyway."

"Is winning the only thing that counts?"

"Yes!"

He smiled. "*I* don't think so. We must have different philosophies of life. Look, I really enjoyed the rallying. I don't see why we can't go on doing that."

"But you're so much better. Why should you want to rally with me?"

"Because in rallies you get everything back, you hit really hard. Listen, I was hitting my hardest shots at you when we rallied, and you got every one back. It was a really good workout. And if you want me to show you a few things about serving, I'd be glad to."

"Sure," I said glumly.

"You're much better than a lot of *guys* I've played with. Anyway, apart from all that, it does happen that I'm probably half a foot taller than you and maybe thirty or forty pounds heavier, so even if we were equally good, that would give me a slight edge."

"How tall are you?"

"Five eleven. How tall are *you?*"

"Five five."

"And you weigh around a hundred and ten?"

"Sort of." Really I weigh a hundred and fifteen, but a hundred and ten sounds better.

"So, doesn't it stand to reason that I have a slight advantage, just physically?"

"Yes, only—I hate that!" I said fiercely, yanking up a piece of grass.

"Why? What do you hate?"

"It's so *unfair*," I said. "Why do men have to be bigger than women? It's one of those completely unnecessary things."

"Maybe it was necessary biologically."

"It wasn't! How? You mean so they could go out and get wild animals to eat and stuff like that?"

"Partly."

"Okay, maybe men had to be *somewhat* strong to do that, or whoever was going to do it had to be somewhat strong, but why couldn't women have

14

been just as strong? I mean, it didn't *help* to have them weaker."

"It may have been sexual selection . . . stronger men were more appealing to women."

"But why? Don't you see, it could've just as well been the other way? Why didn't Nature or God or whoever planned the whole thing plan it so men found *strong* women attractive? Or why throw in differences at all?"

"Do you wish men and women were exactly the same? That there was no difference?"

"No, I guess I can accept sexual differences. Though, well, if I'd been God, I'd have done it a little differently."

"How would *you* have done it?" He looked a little teasing, but not in a mean way.

"Well, I think I'd have made it so either a man or a woman could get pregnant. Nobody would know when they made love who would end up pregnant."

"That *would* lend a certain element of surprise," Lyle said, smiling.

Whenever I say things, Lyle looks at me with this kind of puzzled expression, like he's never met anyone like me before. I hope I don't seem like some kind of freak to him. I looked right back at him. I hate being stared down by someone.

"If you had just beat me, would you be feeling happy now?" he asked.

I nodded.

"Why do you *care* so much about winning?"

"Everyone does! Don't you, really and truly?"

"Not *that* much."

"Maybe that's because you're not Jewish. Jews always want to win, to be the best."

"Not in sports, though."

"They just didn't go into sports, because they couldn't be the best."

"Are *you* Jewish?"

"No, I'm a Zen Buddhist."

"How could I have told?"

"Because I'm a certain type. In New York girls like me are a dime a dozen."

"What type?"

"Sort of aggressive, but insecure. We all end up being doctors and lawyers and being analyzed for nine million years."

He didn't say anything. "So, will you still play tennis with me?"

"Sure."

He leaned back and looked across the river. "I hope I'm going to like New York. Well, it's only a year."

"What do you mean, it's only a year?"

"Well, next year I'll be in college. Won't you?"

"Oh, sure, right. It's hard to believe it's so close. Where're you going to go?"

"Well, my father went to Yale, so I guess I'll apply there. And maybe Princeton and Haverford. I have to get a scholarship, though."

"How come?"

He didn't answer for a moment. "My parents died six months ago. They were in a car crash. That's why I'm here. I'm living with my sister. She's married." He broke off.

"Oh." I didn't know what to say. I felt really dumb having gone on about the tennis that way.

After a few minutes he said, "I guess it'll work out. It's only—their apartment is sort of small, and they just had a baby, so it's not so ideal in terms of space. I could've stayed in Ohio and lived with the family of my best friend, Kent, but Renee wanted me to come stay with them. Her husband's got a job here."

"Didn't your parents leave any money? Is that why you need to get a scholarship?"

"Oh, they left some, but not a lot. My father taught biology at a small college, and the salaries weren't too high, and my mother gave flute lessons."

I tried to imagine what that would be like, having no family left except Eric. Of course, our family is a little different, but still I could see it would be sort of horrible. "Would you rather have stayed in Ohio?"

"It might've been easier in some ways."

"Have you always lived there?"

He nodded. "Well, actually when I was a baby, my parents lived in Boston, but they moved to Ohio when I was four, so I don't much remember anything else. Have *you* always lived in New York?"

"No, we were in San Francisco for a while when I was little, only it didn't work out that well. Mom was just twenty-four or so. She says she was much too young when she got married. So one day she just split and took off for California, not even knowing anyone or anything. I guess that was kind of the point—to go somewhere where she didn't know anyone."

"What about your father?"

"Oh, he stayed behind in Scarsdale. He was setting up his practice there, he's a dentist. Basically, I think Mom was afraid if she didn't get really far away from Daddy, she might change her mind and go back to him, for *our* sake. But she didn't really like California, so she came back to New York after a while."

Lyle cleared his throat. "But I thought when I called, a man answered, an older man. That wasn't your father?"

"Uh-uh. He still lives in Scarsdale with Boots and their kids. He's been remarried for ages. . . . I guess that must have been Elliott."

"Elliott?"

"Mom's friend. He lives with us."

"Is he a boarder?"

"A what?"

"I mean, well, where I come from, people rent out rooms if they have a big house. To help pay the bills."

"Oh, I get what you mean. Well, Elliott does split the rent with Mom. I'm not sure if they split it *exactly*, because I don't think he has that much money. He was married, only now, well, he's not divorced exactly, but he's separated. His wife doesn't want to give him a divorce."

"That must be hard on your mother," Lyle said sympathetically.

"Uh-uh! Mom says wild horses wouldn't make her get married again. Of course she said that before she married Philip too. Only this time she claims she really means it."

"Who's Philip?"

"My stepfather. He lives right near here. He teaches physics at Columbia."

Whenever I tell someone the saga of my life, I can tell they're feeling sorry for me. Partly they're thinking: Poor thing, her parents split when she was such a tender age, a mere babe, as it were. But, in fact, I can't really remember much about that time. Elliott would probably say I was repressing it, but, to tell the truth, I can't even remember much about our whole time in California. I was only three when we went there—Eric was one and a half—and five when we came back. Even of the

19

time after we came back to New York the only thing that really stands out in my mind is that it was then Mom started working at this literary agency—before she set up her own with her friend, Henrietta. Before she always used to be at home during the day, and after that she almost never was.

When Mom and Philip broke up, I did take it pretty hard. I was eight when they got married and thirteen when they split, and even though Mom says those five years were the hardest of her life, for me they were kind of nice. I really liked Philip a lot. I was still at the age then when I hoped Mom would stop working and have more babies. I remember I used to beg them practically all the time to have babies. I guess I was kind of a pest.

I tried to explain to Lyle. "Mom says her main problem is that up till now she always married the men she fell in love with. Now she realizes you can love someone but maybe not be suited to live with them. It's not that she *regrets* the other marriages. I mean, even with Philip, she gets really mad when friends of hers say, 'Oh, God, I'm so glad you split with Philip, because I couldn't stand him.' She says, 'After all, I was *married* to him.' I can see what she means."

Lyle was sitting there, looking at me with a serious, kindly expression. "That must have been tough for you," he said finally, "all those changes."

"No, not so much. Anyhow I still see Philip a

lot. He's more like a friend than a stepfather. He taught me to play chess."

Lyle smiled. "Maybe we can play sometime."

I shook my head. "Never! You're probably some kind of Bobby Fischer whiz kid."

"Jody, I'm not good at everything," Lyle said. "I think you're getting the wrong idea."

"What *aren't* you good at?"

He turned red. "Maybe we'd better be getting back," he said. "Renee likes me back at six." He offered to walk me home, but I told him I'd just take the bus down Riverside. Otherwise he would have had to go way out of his way, since his sister lives in the Bronx. I don't know anyone who lives in the Bronx, in fact I've hardly ever been there. To me it seems almost like another state.

2

On the way home I started thinking about Lyle's being an orphan. I never met an orphan before. I don't think people are orphans as much as they used to be, or maybe it's just you don't hear about it. Though I suppose it's different to be one starting at seventeen than starting when you're a baby. The thing with Lyle is that you can tell he doesn't say right out what he feels about things, but you know he does feel them, it's just sort of buried way down somewhere. I would have liked to ask more about his parents, what they were like and how he got along with them, but when he started to talk about it, his voice got sort of tight, like it was painful for him.

The funny part is I could tell he felt about my family the way I did about his, as though Mom's being divorced twice made *me* practically like an orphan. But I suppose he doesn't realize that here in New York everyone's parents are divorced. In my school there's almost no one who has both of the same parents they started out with. It just seems to be extremely rare. So I don't think of our setup as being that odd or unusual. And frankly I'm glad Mom isn't marrying Elliott. Not because I wouldn't want her to get divorced again. But he's just kind of—well, Mom hates me to use the word gross all the time, so I'll say he's just sort of ponderous. He's a psychology professor, and he has all these really outmoded ideas about women, which you'd think would bother Mom, but she kind of glides over it.

If I told Elliott about today and feeling so awful about losing to Lyle at tennis, he'd give me a big spiel about how it was all due to my wanting to be a boy and my not accepting my femininity and all kinds of crap. It's not! I don't *want* to be a boy! I just want to be a really good tennis player. Why can't *I* be five feet eleven and have it something un-equivocally good? If I *were* five eleven but still a girl, I'd have to worry about it, unless I were one of those super-confident people, which I'm not. But if I were five eleven, I'd be a better tennis player too. I still might not be as good as Lyle, but I bet my serve would be better.

"Who won?" Eric said. I'd told him I might play a set or two with Lyle today. Eric is completely unathletic, like Mom, so he can't understand why I care about sports.

"He did," I muttered, going in to shower. I have to share my brother's bathroom because mine doesn't have a shower.

"What was the score?" That's really typical of Eric. I don't think he cares about the score per se. He just has this sneaky desire to see me humiliated.

"Six-two," I said. I simply couldn't say 6-love.

"He must be pretty good," Eric said. He was lying on his bed reading some science-fiction book, which is what he does a lot of the time.

"Yeah, he was pretty good," I said.

The shower in Eric's room is great. It's called a needle shower because you can turn on an extra knob and water comes at you from all directions. It might sound masochistic, but I like to take a shower that's so boiling hot I practically pass out. Then I lie down and recover slowly. I was lying on the other bed in Eric's room, kind of sprawled out with the towel wrapped around me, when Elliott looked in and said, "How hungry are you guys?"

"Starving," we said in unison.

"Can you wait till seven?"

"Do we have a choice?" Eric asked.

"Sure, make yourself a hamburger."

"Okay, we'll wait."

The cooking situation in our house could be improved on. Since Mom works full time, she decided it wasn't fair that she should do all the cooking. So some nights Eric and I cook—we've done it since we were ten or so. When Elliott moved in, he said of course he'd be glad to share in meal preparation and other domestic tasks. But the problem is his specialty is Chinese food—he once took a course in Chinese cooking. At first he was making these giant feasts that wouldn't be ready till around eleven. By then everyone was passing out from starvation. Mom said it was a ploy to make her say she'd take over. She also said that anyone in the family who wanted to eat first could if they were willing to make their own stuff. Basically I think that's a good idea, but I don't always feel like cooking, and hamburgers can get sort of dull. But lately Elliott's been a little prompter on his nights.

After I'd recovered from the shower, I went into the kitchen to get some juice and pretzels. Mom wasn't home yet. She often doesn't get home till after six.

"Who were you playing tennis with?" Elliott asked. He was chopping up some obscure-looking vegetable on this special plastic chopping board that he brought with him when he moved in with us a year ago. He has all these special things like woks, so our kitchen has gotten sort of crowded.

"Lyle Alexander. I met him over the summer."

"At Sloan-Kettering?"

"Yup." I always get the feeling with Elliott that he's storing up all the information I give him and filing it away in a little cabinet in his mind for a paper on neurotic disturbances among seventeen-year-old Jewish girls. Mom says he's just shy. She says I shouldn't mind it or take it personally. Elliott's forty-nine years old, ten years older than Mom. He has frizzy grayish hair and very thick black eyebrows and black eyes; he's a little paunchy around the middle. Philip was five years younger than Mom, so I don't know why she suddenly picked someone so old. I guess there's no accounting for tastes.

"My serve wasn't working that well today," I said, biting into a pretzel. I have to admit there's something interesting about watching Elliott cook. He keeps chopping up one thing, then leaving it, then chopping up some other thing. You see all these little piles all over the place and you think: This is going to be a meal? Then suddenly, maybe eight hours later, just when you're losing consciousness because your blood-sugar level is down to zero, there it is, and it's usually pretty good.

"Oh? Did that throw your game off?"

"Umm." I sat down on a stool. "I think I wanted so much to win, it made me play worse or something."

"That can happen. Competitiveness can be a hard thing to handle."

"Is it hard for you?"

Elliott looked up, startled. "Me personally? Well, I don't . . . I think I *can* be competitive, in some areas anyway. Though I admit I've had some problems with it."

"How?"

"Well, I think men are somehow primed to feel they have to get out there and make it. Naturally their wives encourage them in this."

"They do?" Elliott has this antiwife prejudice, which surfaces now and then.

"Okay, maybe not *all* wives. Having only had one, I can only speak for her. I used to say to her, 'Pam, if you want me to put the whole thing aside and earn less, fine. We'll have to live more simply, but that's okay with me.' But she didn't *really* want it, Jody. That's the contradiction with wives. They *say* they want you to be soft and sweet and liberated, but at the same time, when Tom Jones gets ahead of you, they go plummeting after Tom Jones, who has all the qualities they presumably deplore." He looked discouraged and dumped some leafy green things in the garbage.

I didn't mean to get into a thing about Elliott's wife, who, to hear him tell it, was an arch bitch and, as he says, "thoroughly inconsistent in her values." I guess there's something about being *thor-*

oughly inconsistent. I mean, if you're going to *be* inconsistent, why not go the whole hog?

After dinner Lyle called. "Jody, how do you feel?"

"Stuffed. We just had an eight-course meal."

"No, I mean you looked so downcast when you got on the bus."

"Don't worry about it. Seriously. Elliott would say it's all a kind of wanting to outdo men. . . . It's true, kind of. I bet if I'd lost and you'd been a girl, I wouldn't have cared so much."

"Really?"

"Yeah, I mean, I still would've *cared,* but I wouldn't have felt utterly crushed and humiliated."

"You shouldn't feel that way."

"I know. I'm working on it."

There was a pause.

"The reason I'm calling is I wondered if you might like to go to a movie or something like that this Saturday?"

"Sure."

"What time would be good?"

"Do you want to come for supper?"

"Wouldn't that be a lot of work for your mother?"

He really has incredible manners, this boy. I wonder if that school he went to was some kind of military academy. "Come at seven. Do you like Chinese food?"

"I haven't eaten it that often, but I'd be glad to try."

Hanging up, I suddenly felt a little apprehensive. Why invite him for dinner? If *I* strike him as weird, wait till he sees the whole show in action. On the other hand, I hate trying to give a false impression. I mean, they *are* my family and they do have certain virtues. Maybe it'll be interesting for him to see a real New York family. I may never see him again, but that's another story.

3

"I want Lyle to decide," Mom said. It was her night on as cook, so we were just having lamb chops and string beans and baked potatoes.

"He doesn't even know you," Eric said.

"That's the whole point," said Mom. "He'll give an objective opinion."

"Beth, let the guy eat his lamb chops," Elliott said.

"I just want to give my side of it," Mom said, "since you're all being so damn pigheaded."

Lyle was sitting there, eating quietly and minding his own business, which in our family is a bit rare. "I'd be glad to give an opinion," he said, "only I'm not sure I understand the issue."

31

"Do I strike you as being too old to have a child?" Mom said.

"Beth, now that is a really unfair way to begin," Elliott said.

"Let him answer!" she shouted.

"How old *are* you?" Lyle said.

"Thirty-nine. Okay, so here's the thing. I had these kids"—she waves at me and Eric—"when I was a kid, I was twenty-two, my God, I knew *nothing*. I raised them any old way, Dr. Spock, every kind of old-fashioned junk in the book, and I just think—I'm not saying I'm going to *do* it—but I just think it would be interesting to have a child now, when I've kind of gotten the whole thing together."

Elliott raised one hand in the air and intoned in this deep voice, "A pox on thee, Rifka Rabinowitz."

Mom got really mad. "It has nothing to *do* with Rifka Rabinowitz."

Eric said, "Sure, sure."

Rifka Rabinowitz is this old friend of Mom's who has two teen-age kids. Suddenly, around three years ago, she had a baby, Judd. The trouble is, she now has all these weird theories about bringing children up, like they should nurse forever and that they should sleep in the same bed as the parents from the time they're born. In fact, everyone in the family, even Trudy and Evan, is supposed to sleep in the same room. I forget why, but it sounds like a lousy deal all around to me.

"What will you do with this child?" Elliott said.

"Do? What do you mean, *do?* I'll take him to the office. That's the whole *point!* Before it was this thing of babysitting, a whole rigid system of rules and regulations. Now I'd just bring him, let him sleep in the corner in a box or something."

"Sweetheart, I think your memory about babies is a little foggy."

"Anyhow," Eric said, "what's so bad about us?"

"There's nothing *bad* about you," Mom said, "but you're not really free. You have the same old hang-ups our generation did."

"Every generation is going to have hang-ups," Elliott said. "It's human nature."

"Quiet, pessimist!" Mom said. "Listen, Lyle, you're sitting there quietly but with a very intelligent expression like you're about to sum the whole thing up and shed light on everything."

Actually Lyle was probably sitting there thinking How did I get into this loony bin, but he just said, "I suppose I have certain convictions about population control, which might enter in."

"There!" Elliott said, delighted. "A man after my own heart, a man of reason."

"*You* should talk!" Mom yelled. "You have four!"

"That wasn't me," Elliott said hastily. "It was Pam."

"Oh, come on. It takes two to make a baby," Mom said.

"No kidding, Mom," Eric said. "Hey, listen, I'm supposed to meet Dick at eight. Are we going to sit here all night jabbering away about this?"

Mom and Elliott brought in some melon. "No, I think Lyle's point is valid," Mom said. "That *is* true. Though, well, three is sort of borderline, don't you think? I mean, four is clearly unforgivable in terms of the population thing, but three?"

"Our teacher, Ms. Littman, says any is unforgivable," Eric said.

"Well, that kind of thing is just *dumb*," Mom said, flaring up again. "No one in the world should have any more children? How would *that* solve anything?"

"She just says people shouldn't be forced to," Eric said.

"Who's talking about force? Of course! No one should be *forced*. Listen, if you and Jody don't want any, don't have any. I'm talking about *wanting* them. Lyle, how many children do you plan to have?"

"He doesn't plan to have *any*, because he's not a girl!" Eric said, doubling over as though this were hysterically funny.

"I haven't actually thought about it that much," Lyle said. "One or two sounds like a good number."

"I think you'll make a very good father," Mom said, eyeing him. "I can just tell. You should have them."

"How about me?" Eric said. "Will *I* make a very good father?"

"You!" She grunted. "I don't want to think about it."

"Well, I'm not going to have any," Eric said. "I'm going to have a vasectomy when I'm eighteen. Then you can sleep with anyone you want and you don't have to worry."

"Jesus!" Elliott said.

"That's just what I mean about your generation," Mom said. "It's this know-it-all junk, and basically you know nothing. A vasectomy, for Christ's sake!"

"Mom, he's just teasing you," I said.

Mom is sort of a peculiar mixture of views about sex, some rather liberal and some sort of strange. I happen to know that when Eric turned sixteen last spring, Daddy called Mom and said he had this great idea for a birthday present for him. He wanted to take him to a really good call girl. Well, Mom hit the ceiling and started screaming about how that was the most disgusting, macho idea she'd ever heard and if he so much as dared try anything like that, she'd do this and that and blah, blah, blah. I admit, it does seem like kind of a gross idea, but it's typical of my father. It's also typical of him that, even now, he doesn't know better than to call

35

up and tell Mom something like that on the phone, expecting her to agree. As far as I can see, Eric isn't even especially interested in girls yet. I mean, he doesn't have any weird hang-ups about them, but he just doesn't seem especially interested.

Eric left before coffee, which reduced the decibel level slightly, but not much.

"Lyle, I'm glad you said that about population control," Mom said, "because you're right. It *was* a selfish idea. And anyway, who says the third one would be any different than the first two? I mean, I had my chance, and that's it. On to bigger and better things!"

"Bravo!" Elliott said.

"No, I guess it's just," Mom said, "like, in my job I'm dealing with all these creative people, so maybe the urge to, you know, create something myself, even despite my advanced age, sort of creeps over me from time to time."

"It creeps over all of us," Elliott said.

"But pregnancy isn't the answer, that's obvious," Mom said. "In fact, it's a very reactionary solution. I don't know why that didn't occur to me."

If you give Mom enough time, she usually works her way around to taking the exact opposite stance of whatever she was saying at the beginning of any given conversation. Logic is not exactly her strong point. Come to think of it, I'm not sure it's the strong point of anyone in our family. Eric has a kind of nit-picking mind, but I'm not sure it's all that much more logical.

When Lyle and I got outside, I said, "Listen, they're like that. I'm sorry."

"No, I liked them," he said. "Your family is very unusual. I guess I've just never seen anything like that before."

"What's so unusual about them?" I said quickly. It's weird that, even though I could recite my family's faults forever, when someone else sounds at all critical, I feel very defensive.

"Well, the openness," he said. "Talking about things like that."

"Didn't your parents?"

He shook his head. "Sometimes one of them would take me aside and talk about certain things, but it was always, well, just the two of us and not in that style."

"Were they happy together?" I asked suddenly.

"My parents? Yes, I think they were. They'd fight sometimes, but they . . . well, you always knew they really loved each other."

"That's nice, that they were like that."

He nodded, bemused. "They were good people," he said.

Lyle uses these sort of quaint expressions, like saying his parents were "good people." I wonder what his family would have thought of mine.

After the movie we came back to the apartment.

It was dark and quiet, though the lights were on in the living room, which meant Mom and Elliott were out. When they come home, they usually turn the lights out. Anyway, I think Mom said they were going to some party.

Lyle and I went into my room. I love my room, even though when people see it, they always say it's not fair since Eric's room is much bigger. But I like even the smallness of it. I have a bed with built-in shelves over it and a nice woolly rug on the floor and my records and books. It's way at the end of the house, near the back door, away from Eric's and Mom and Elliott's bedrooms. I like that too. I guess privacy is quite important to me. I'd hate having to share a room with someone, the way some of my friends do.

Lyle sat next to me on the floor, and we listened to some music. I don't have any overhead light in my room, just the desk light and this standing lamp in the corner. It was kind of dark, but not pitch-black. We could still see each other.

All of a sudden Lyle said, "Jody, would you mind if I—" and then we started kissing each other.

It's funny with being horny. Sometimes you just know you're in that kind of mood, and in some ways I don't like that because I've gone out with boys I didn't even like very much and ended up making out with them out of sheer horniness. I guess it only happened once or twice, but I always

38

felt bad afterward. I suppose I'm not too liberated in that sense. But tonight I hadn't felt it especially. Maybe it was being rattled from the dinner and everyone screaming at each other. I don't know. Also, well, I guess I wasn't sure how Lyle felt about me. I sort of thought he looked on me more as a tennis partner, or just an interesting kind of peculiar person, but not so much in a sexual way.

But when we started kissing, it really got involved, right away. He must have kissed a lot of people. Then after we'd kissed for a long time, he slid his hand up under my shirt. I don't wear a bra. It's not a matter of principle. I mean, I can see if you have really *huge* breasts that would swing back and forth and really bother you that a bra would be a good thing. But I'm just about in between. My breasts are one of the good parts of my body. I used to wish they were bigger, but now I'm fairly content with them. In fact, I'm fairly content with my body in general, except that I have a tendency to be chunky—I was sort of a plump child—and my legs are a bit short.

After we had continued in that vein for a while, Lyle reached down and slipped his hand below my waist, under my jeans, down to my underpants. He kept going till he reached my vagina. But then it was funny. He put his hand on it just for, like, one second, and then he took his hand away. "Listen, I'm sorry," he said.

"What about?"

"I didn't . . . I really swear I didn't come here tonight planning on this."

"Sure, well, that's okay."

"I didn't even know you didn't wear a bra," he said. "Otherwise I might not have—"

"It's just, they're sort of uncomfortable," I said. We were both breathing a little too fast.

"I guess I got carried away," he said. "I apologize."

"Why should you apologize?"

"We don't even really know each other that well," he said.

"Lyle, will you quit apologizing? I *mean* it!"

"Do you really not mind?"

"Well, why would I do it if I minded?"

He looked puzzled, like that had never occurred to him. "I just don't want you to think that I don't respect you or anything," he said.

I don't think I'd ever had a conversation like this before. "But, I mean, like, do you think being attracted to someone means you don't respect them?" I said.

"No, I don't exactly think that," he said.

We sat there in silence a few minutes.

"It's probably irrational," Lyle said after a minute, "but I just have the feeling you're mad at me."

"I'm not!"

"Really?"

"Sure. Only I guess I don't really understand why you sort of stopped in midstream suddenly."

"Well, I didn't actually mean to go that far." Suddenly he smiled. "Jody, you're so pretty. And, you know, I did really know you weren't wearing a bra. I was lying before. I could tell."

"That's okay."

"You looked so nice, and I guess the idea came into my head that, well, you might not mind."

"I didn't!"

"Would you still—I mean, I really would like to see you, just to talk and other things. I didn't want you to think this is all I'm interested in."

"I don't think that."

"Okay, well, I believe you," he said finally.

I looked at him. His hair was rumpled and I could tell he'd washed it earlier in the day. It had a nice shampoo smell. "Did you ever sleep with anyone?" I asked suddenly.

He stared at me. Then he said, with an awkward smile, "I—Why don't we talk about that tomorrow?" We had planned to meet at his sister's house for lunch. She and her husband were going up to Bear Mountain for the day.

"Okay," I said.

I walked with him to the door and stood there, leaning on the wall as he waited for the elevator.

When it came, he leaned over and kissed me lightly on the lips. "Sleep tight," he said.

When I went back to bed, all kinds of sinister thoughts began running through my head. When he said, "Let's talk about that tomorrow," it seemed to imply that it was a long story, like maybe he's slept with millions of people so he couldn't tell it all at once. Basically I have several fears, some of which may be contradictory. The first one is he might be involved with some girl back in Ohio. That would explain all that stuff about apologizing for making out. Maybe he promised her he'd be faithful and feels guilty because he wasn't. I know he went to an all-boys high school, and I think there it's more formal in terms of taking girls to dances and going steady and that kind of thing. In my school nobody goes steady anymore, but in Ohio it's probably different.

I have the feeling he might have had quite a lot of sexual experience. People do in small towns, according to some of the books I've read. There just isn't that much else to do. The other thing is that in small towns teen-agers go around in cars most of the time, unlike the city, where we tend to go by subway or bus. And so their idea of a date is to park in some dark field and screw in the back seat of the car.

The more I thought about it, the more I became convinced that it was probably one of these double-standard type of things, that he's slept with all these girls that he didn't respect and then has this other girl he's going with. I can just see her. I have this perfectly clear picture of the girl Lyle is going with. I see her as about five eight, sort of thinnish with long legs. I bet she has light-brown hair, which she parts on the side and fastens with a barrette. I think she must have blue eyes. As I lay there imagining her and beginning to hate her in a quiet kind of way, it occurred to me I was imagining someone who was precisely a female version of Lyle. Anyway, why should I hate her? Basically I should feel *sorry* for her, if he's been sleeping on the side with all these girls he doesn't really even *like*. Mom always goes around saying the double standard is dead and Eric and I are so lucky to be living in a generation when everything is equal, but I wonder. That might not be as true as she thinks.

I wouldn't have figured Lyle for a double-standard type, but clearly you can be deceived in these matters. But what was I supposed to do? Act indignant when he reached below my waist? I could tell he expected that. He was just waiting for me to say whatever girls are supposed to say at times like that. The trouble is, I never could understand that whole philosophy. When I was little, like ten or eleven, I'd read these books about teen-age romances with the parts where the girl would say, "You can touch my right breast, but not my left"

43

or "You can put your hand two inches up there, but not two inches down here" and "We can do that on the third date but not the second." It all seemed like some weirdly elaborate code that I assumed I would suddenly understand when I got to be sixteen. I don't know why I picked sixteen, but I pretty well decided that by then the light would have dawned and I would understand it all.

But the funny thing is, I *still* don't understand it. I suppose I feel that if I like someone enough to do anything with them, even kiss them, I don't see such a difference between that and all the rest. I admit the matter hasn't come up very often, and maybe I'm more the type that doesn't even like to kiss many people, but once you've gotten that far, the matter of degree seems sort of immaterial.

I finally fell asleep at around four in the morning, wishing I'd never asked Lyle about his sexual experience. Why *know* everything all the time? There was this line in a play by Oscar Wilde we read in school last year: "Ignorance is a delicate, exotic fruit. Touch it and the bloom is gone." I should probably take that to heart.

4 〰〰〰〰〰〰〰〰〰〰〰〰〰〰〰〰〰〰〰〰〰〰〰〰〰〰〰〰〰〰〰〰〰〰〰〰

"Eric, if you're not dressed by twelve, there's going to be big trouble."

"Relax, I've got ten minutes," Eric said, reaching for another piece of coffee cake.

On weekends Mom and Eric have a running battle about his getting dressed. Eric says if it's a weekend and he's not planning to go out, why shouldn't he stay in his pajamas all day? He says there's nothing he can do dressed that he can't do in his pajamas. Mom says it's decadent and loathsome to be in pajamas all day and to even come to meals, such as dinner, in pajamas. She says his brain will rot away. He says that's completely illogical, wearing pajamas has nothing to do with his mental processes. Anyway, they usually bat this around until noon or one o'clock, at which point Eric gives in.

I gave a big yawn and shook my head.

"When'd you get in, Jody?" Mom said. "I didn't hear you."

"You weren't home yet. We got back around eleven."

"Why didn't you ask him in? He seemed like such a darling boy."

"I *did* ask him in."

"Yeah, Mom, since when do we have to file reports on our sex lives with you?" Eric said. "I thought privacy was such a big deal around here."

"Who's asking about her sex life? I just didn't see any light on in her room when we got back at midnight, so I assumed they were still out."

"People usually do it in the dark," Eric said.

"Will you shut up?" I said. "Mom, tell him to cut it out."

"Look, I don't want to start the day with a lot of bickering. Jo, I just wanted to say he's a sweetheart and I hoped you had a good time. . . . You"— pointing to Eric—"get in there and get dressed this *second,* and when you have a sex life to talk about, we'll all be glad to listen."

Eric got up and staggered into his room. Usually he lifts weights for about half an hour. He used to be chunky, like me, when he was little and he still has kind of a thing about it, even though in the last couple of years he's suddenly gotten much taller than me and isn't chunky at all anymore.

I took the subway up to Lyle's sister's house. It was way far up, around two hundred and something street. They live in one of those small houses, the kind with about five or six stories, and you had to walk up—there wasn't any elevator. It looked a little shabby: There were papers in the hall, and the walls needed painting. Mom always says Eric and I don't know what economic deprivation means since when she got divorced, Grandma and Grandpa always helped us out and now she's earning a lot or at least fairly a lot from her job. I suppose that's true, but we've never really lived lavishly either. There are some kids in my school who go to Paris every spring vacation or go skiing at Vail for New Year's. We never did really expensive, exotic things like that.

"Hi, Jody." It was a cool day for late August, and Lyle was wearing a white sweater and chinos and his tennis sneakers. He was tan and he suddenly looked almost oppressively good-looking; I got that low, sinking feeling again. Partly I just felt tired and when I feel tired, I tend to get depressed. I knew I was honor bound to hear the whole grisly story of all these girls he had slept with and somehow I didn't feel at all in the mood.

Maybe he could tell that, because he didn't bring

it up right away. He took me into the kitchen and made grilled-cheese and bacon sandwiches. "Is bacon okay? I mean, you don't observe any dietary rules, do you?'

At first I thought he meant was I on a diet, but then I realized he meant about my being Jewish. "Oh, no, we don't do any of that." Actually Mom used to go to Hebrew school when she was little and was even Bas Mitzvahed, but now she says she thinks the whole thing is a lot of junk and eight million wild horses couldn't get her near a synagogue. She says Eric and I can do whatever we want, as long as she doesn't have to listen to it, because she thinks all religions are one form of idiocy or another. Actually, I haven't thought about it that much so I don't know if I agree with her or not.

"Kitty was a little feverish this morning. They almost didn't go," Lyle said, spreading the bacon on a teflon griddle.

"Their cat?"

"Kitty's their baby. Her name's Katherine, but that's what they call her. I'm glad they went, though. Renee's been kind of depressed lately. Wesley thinks she ought to get out more."

"Doesn't she work?"

"She used to. She was a math teacher, but she gave it up when Kitty was born."

"Yeah, well, that's probably the problem," I said. "Then people start going crazy. This woman I baby-sit for, Mrs. Hart, says that happened to her."

"Renee says she wants to devote herself to the baby till she's three or four, till the baby's three or four."

Talk about babies always depresses me, especially talk about women who have them and then start going crazy. I wish I'd meet some more women who just had them and kept on being the way they were before. I mean, they can't *all* start going crazy, but it seems like the only ones I meet or hear about are those kind.

The cheese-and-bacon sandwiches were good; I began feeling better.

"So, I guess you would like me to answer the question you raised last night," Lyle said finally.

"You don't really have to. I mean, don't feel you have to—"

"No, it's—well, it's not that complicated. I haven't slept with anyone."

I set my mug of milk down on the table. "Really?"

Lyle laughed. "Really."

"You really haven't slept with *anyone?*"

"Jody, look, I know things are probably different in New York, but I haven't even, the truth is I haven't gone *out* with girls that much."

I looked at him suspiciously. "Then how come you kiss so well?"

He turned red. "Do I?"

I nodded.

"Well, Louise Bender and I used to—she was this girl who lived in my town. We went out a little and we did kiss, but that was about all."

"How come?"

"How come what?"

"How come all you did was kiss?"

He frowned. "I just thought she wouldn't like it if I did anything else."

"I just can't believe it."

"Why? What did you expect?"

"God, I thought you had slept with *millions* of girls. I guess because you come from a small town. I thought that was all people *do* in small towns practically."

"Where did you get *that* idea?"

"From books and movies and stuff."

"Sorry, not in our town. Listen, before we proceed in this investigation, how about dessert? Do you want some cake? Renee said we could have it."

"Okay." The word "investigation" got me a bit nervous.

"So . . . have *you?*" he said, putting the slice of cake in front of me."

"Have I what?"

"Slept with anyone."

"Well . . . just one person actually."

Lyle looked taken aback. "Who was he?"

"He was in my school. He was a year ahead of me. He'll be in college in the fall. I mean, we broke up last spring."

Lyle had a funny kind of expression on his face. He jabbed at his cake with his fork.

I looked at him, worried. "Do you mind—about my having done it?"

"Well, I have to admit it's going to take me a little while to get used to the idea," Lyle said. "Where I come from, girls usually don't. It's rather rare."

I just nodded. "Okay." I felt kind of depressed again.

Lyle reached out and took my hand. "Listen, Jody, it's okay, *really*. It wouldn't be honest for me to say I wasn't surprised, but I don't . . . I still want to see you. . . . How did your parents feel about it? I mean, your mother? Did she know?"

I made a face. "Well, we never actually discussed it. But one day I found this letter she wrote to one of her friends. It was really gross. She had all this stuff about, 'Jody is having an affair with this *lovely* boy and he is so charming, blah, blah, blah.' "

Lyle was silent a long time.

"I guess I shouldn't have told you," I said finally.

"Why? No, it's good you told me."

"It just seems like you're riddled with all these middle-American prejudices."

"I'm not."

"Really?"

"Sure." He smiled uncertainly.

I suddenly had the feeling I had just blown the whole thing in one fell swoop. What is this mania I have for laying my cards on the table? As though sensing my mood, Lyle stood up. "Let me show you the rest of the apartment, Jody."

"Where's your room?" I asked. I hoped he didn't think I was implying something. After a conversation like that, it seemed like *anything* you said had sort of overtones or a double entendre or whatever.

"I sleep in here," he said, pointing to what looked like the living room. I say that because there was a piano, a couch, and a tilt-back chair.

"That looks like the living room," I said.

"It is."

"Well, how can you sleep in there? Where do you put your stuff?"

"Oh, I don't have much," he said. "I keep my clothes in the bottom of Kitty's bureau."

He showed me the rest of the apartment, and it was true, it really was small. There was what I guess was the master bedroom, but it wasn't like the one Mom and Elliott share, where there's room for a desk and an extra chair and everything. This one just had a double bed, which about took up the whole room. There was a TV in one corner on a bureau, and that was all. The baby's room was even smaller, just a crib with a mobile hanging over the bureau and some kind of changing-table thing.

We went back into the living room and sat down on the couch. As I said, to me privacy is pretty important so I really felt sorry for Lyle. I would hate sleeping in a room without even a door. "What do you do at night when they have friends or have dinner parties and things like that?"

"Oh, they don't entertain much," Lyle said. "In fact, I don't even think they've been out since the baby was born."

"How old is the baby?"

"Five weeks. Renee had just told us she was pregnant when my parents were in the accident. Mother was planning to come stay with them to help out."

"Where would they have put her?"

"I guess here on the couch. No, it's not really so bad. They go to bed early, around ten thirty, so I can stay up and study or read or whatever. The TV's in the bedroom, so sometimes they go in at eight and watch movies; it's almost as though I had the house to myself."

I wasn't convinced. Obviously Lyle was the type who would find a way of making even a situation like that seem not so bad. I'm not sure I'd be that adaptable. I looked around at the rest of the room. On the piano were some photos. One was of a man and woman sitting in a wicker lawn chair. "Are those your parents?"

He nodded. "That was around ten years ago, just after Dad got the job at Kendall."

Lyle looks like his mother. She was not as tall, but she had that same expression, sort of serious and a little puzzled, as though she was trying to fit everything together. His father was tall and thin with a dark moustache, and he was laughing.

"Why don't we go to one hundred and twentieth and try to get a court?" Lyle said suddenly. "Do you feel like it?"

"Sure." Suddenly, for no reason, I felt a lot better. At least now we knew all there was to know in terms of basic things about each other.

"Why don't we work on your serve?" he said.

I thought of those movies where they show a man teaching a girl how to better her golf game. They stand there, he with his arms around her, while she looks up at him adoringly and murmurs, "Oh, Bill, you're so strong. Will I ever be as good as you?" Even the possibility of that type of thing is sure to turn me off. Not that I would act like that, but certain situations kind of bring it out. "Could we just rally instead?" I said.

"Sure." He grinned. "I always like rallying." He put his arm around me. "You know me, the non-competitive type."

"Sure," I said. "I know your type."

5

Every year I go to the U.S. Open with Philip at Forest Hills for the quarter- or semifinals. This year I asked if I could bring Lyle, and Philip said sure, he'd try and scrape up another ticket. I thought Lyle would like it. Of course, we could always watch it on TV, but it's more exciting to actually go there.

First I ought to explain about Philip.

In the beginning I remember thinking he was practically the ugliest person I'd ever seen. He looked almost like a monster to me. He's about six feet four and has very light skin and very light blue eyes, so light he almost looks like an albino, and his hair is that sort of white-blond that you usually see only on little kids. Philip says Mom married him because she likes challenges and he seemed like such a hard nut to crack. It's true that no one, especially any of Mom's friends, ever could understand why she did it. The thing is, Mom is sort of sociable, not that she goes to parties all the time, but she likes people and stuff, and Philip is about the most antisocial person you'd ever meet. Even his job is not so much teaching as just sitting in this little room thinking all day. He says he'd be perfectly content to go half the year without hearing the human voice.

When Mom and Philip had these fights, which they did pretty often, Mom would do her usual ranting and raving bit, even throwing the occasional plate, which is a habit of hers at times of stress, and Philip would do *his* bit, which turned out to be the mirror opposite. He would clam up and not say a word, sometimes for a week or longer. You could say he just did it to irritate Mom—it certainly *did* seem to have that effect—but basically I think that's just what Philip is like. He'd go into these silences. I think the average person, even if they started off like that, would finally break down. I mean, even if it was a matter of principle, at some point you'd just need something and you'd say, "Please pass the salt" or "Does anyone know where the stapler is?" But Philip never would. He'd just go into his study and sit there and think and read or play chess. As I say, he did teach me to play chess, which is in a way how we started getting friendly. Eric, which seemed surprising considering how much he and Mom fight, sort of took Mom's side against Philip. He thought Philip was weird, and whenever Mom and Philip had one of these biggies where Philip would leave for a couple of days, Eric would always say he didn't see why Mom had married him in the first place and he didn't see how being a genius, even if Philip was one, which was what Mom always claimed, was such a big deal.

You could say I liked Philip because he liked me. But that sounds sort of plaintive, as though I was desperate to have *anyone* like me. It wasn't so much that. It was just that particular year Mom had shifted Eric and me from one school, which she decided was too traditional, to Talbot, which was supposedly more free. Actually, she did it for Eric, who is what they call a nonachiever, meaning he doesn't especially like to study. By now, having tried both places, Mom realizes it doesn't make much difference, that it's up to Eric to pull himself together and she's not going to worry about it anymore. But at the time she used to worry, and Rifka Rabinowitz claimed she'd had the identical problem with Evan, who had transferred to Talbot and suddenly started achieving all over the place.

That was all very well, but I had made some friends at the old school, which happened to be in a completely different neighborhood, and suddenly to be pitched into a new one kind of threw me. Eric, whatever you may say about his grades, never has problems like that. I guess he's like Mom in that respect. He just moves into any school or camp and by sundown he has a million best friends. I don't know if it's best friends in the way I'd think of it, but he's calling kids on the phone and they're calling him. The basic difference between Eric and me is that he doesn't worry about the way he is. For instance, he used to be fairly fat and he's never done well at school, he's even lousy at sports, but he just doesn't care. Whereas I have this typical first-child overachieving thing, which means even though I get all A's and grind away and stuff, I still worry a lot about doing well and fitting in.

Anyway, to get back to Philip. There I was kind of at the nadir as far as school went. Marion Givits, who turned out to be my best friend—she just transferred to another school this year, but that's another story—hadn't come yet. She came in fifth grade. And there was Philip, who seemed to like me and who was so weird himself that he seemed like kind of a kindred spirit. We used to have fun just joking around in what I guess was a childish way. There was a line that Philip had cut out of a Dr. Seuss story and taped up in his study. It was from a book called *I Had Trouble in Getting to Solla Sollew,* which is about this little guy who tries to get away from this awful place he lives in called The Valley of Vung to go to this other place he hears about called Solla Sollew, where, they tell him, "You never have troubles, at least very few." Only on the way he *has* all these troubles. He runs into this wild band of tigers called Poozers. The line Philip liked—he claimed it applied to most life situations—was, "Sometimes you are winners, sometimes you are losers. You never can win against so many Poozers." Whenever I'm feeling down and I call Philip, he'll say, "Too many Poozers, huh, Jo?"

Philip lives by himself in this horribly messy apartment near Columbia. It's a real bachelor apartment. Mom says Philip is a bachelor at heart and should never have married anyone, much less her. Philip has all these theories about why Mom married him. First, there's the one I mentioned, the "hard-nut-to-crack" theory. Then there's the mad-genius theory, which is that Mom considers Philip this brilliant but very screwed up person and if only he could get himself straightened out, he'd be another Einstein. It's true, Mom and Elliott have discussions about Philip sometimes in which Mom says she's really worried that Philip will never live up to his potential and that deep down he's horribly self-destructive. She even called him up and said Elliott would recommend a shrink to him if he wanted to go, and Philip muttered something vague about it sounding like an excellent idea, but he never went.

During the tennis matches I sat between Lyle and Philip. Philip, by the way, is more of a watcher of tennis than a player. One reason is he's a chain smoker. He smokes even on the court! While he serves, there's a cigarette hanging out of his mouth. It makes his game kind of erratic.

We watched for a couple of hours, men's singles, then men's doubles, then the women's singles. Philip says he likes watching women play more than men, and usually I do too, only this day there was a long, very dull match between Chrissy Evert and Virginia Wade. They just stood at the baseline whopping it back and forth. It wasn't very interesting, even if you were a female chauvinist. I kept looking at Lyle, wondering what he was thinking. I imagined he was thinking he wished I was like Chrissy Evert. She seemed to me just the kind of uptight pretty girl that Lyle was going to fall in love with and marry, the kind who polishes her nails pale pink and wears little gold hoop earrings, who loses her virginity at the right time and with the right person.

When we went down for hot dogs and beer, Philip said to Lyle, "Have you seen Jody on the courts yet? You better look out, she'll clobber you. She's merciless."

I laughed hollowly.

"She's very good," Lyle said diplomatically. "Do *you* play?"

"Not really. I bat the ball around, but I'm not in her class."

Afterward Philip took us back to his place for supper. He made spaghetti, which is all he ever makes. The only difference is that sometimes he makes meat sauce and sometimes clam. I saw Lyle glancing around the living room. There are only two rooms in Philip's apartment, the living room and the bedroom. There were stacks of books and papers piled knee-deep all over the place as usual, and there was a queer, musty smell; Philip always forgets to open the windows.

"Are you interested in going into research, Lyle?" Philip asked. "Jody said you were at Sloan-Kettering with her over the summer."

That's what I like about Philip. Mom says he's self-absorbed and cuts himself off from people, which may be true in terms of his basic life-style, but still he did think of asking Lyle about himself, which is more than anyone in my family did when I brought him home for dinner.

"I think so," Lyle said. "My father always thought he would go into research, but somehow he got waylaid at Kendall and he always felt like he'd missed out on something."

Philip began talking about when he'd been a graduate student and described a teacher he'd had.

"But Jody's the practical one," he said. "She's going into medicine, did you know that? When Jody's done with her internship, I'm going for a checkup finally. By then I'll be pushing fifty, and at least one of my lungs will have caved in. I figure I'm going to need someone I can trust."

"Did you ever try to give up smoking?" Lyle said.

"Never," Philip said, horrified. "As Jody can tell you, for me life without cigarettes wouldn't be worth living. Frankly even *with* them there are times when I have to admit I wonder. Not that I'm recommending it, if you haven't picked up the filthy habit already." He smiled at us with his crooked smile. By now I don't think Philip is ugly at all, but I realize to a stranger he might still seem pretty weird, maybe even weirder because he's let his hair grow and it's kind of lank and stringy, almost down to his shoulders.

"Hey, listen, Philip, what ever happened with that job?" I asked suddenly. Last spring Philip was offered this very big-deal job at Harvard with all kinds of special benefits where he would hardly have had to teach. Mom got all excited because she said it showed Philip was so brilliant that, despite being self-destructive, people came to him and singled him out. She felt like it justified her having married him.

"I turned it down," he said flatly. "Lyle, do you want wine?"

"Wow, Mom's going to kill you," I said.

Philip cringed. "Uh-oh. You think so, huh?"

"She'll never recover."

Philip sighed. "There I go, disappointing her again. But, you want to know something? I don't have one single regret. It would have done me in, that's all there is to it. That whole we-will-sit-at-the-feet-of-this-presumably-great-man deal. Plus Harvard and all that stuffy intellectual ivory-tower junk. Here they leave me alone. That's all I want. That's worth every damn benefit in the world."

"Should I not tell her?" I asked.

"No, go on, tell her. I'll take my phone off the hook for a couple of weeks." He had his funny, abashed expression. I think he does care what Mom thinks, even though he jokes about it. "Why is it men aren't ambitious anymore?" he said. "What's happened to us?"

"Elliott is," I said. "Or he says he *can* be."

"Well, the famed El Yut is a class unto himself," Philip said. Philip always calls Elliott El Yut. He has this theory that Elliott is really an Arab chieftain posing as a Jewish psychology professor.

"Though he does say he might not keep on being editor of that journal," I said. "He said worldly acclaim doesn't mean as much to him as it once did."

Philip lit another cigarette. "Poor Beth. She's always taking on these potential world beaters who end up throwing in the towel. Look, *I* don't know. It's not bad to be ambitious. How about you, Lyle? Are you going to make some woman happy by discovering a cure for cancer and getting the Nobel Prize?"

"I don't *know*," Lyle said, surprised. "Probably not."

"I have it! You and Jody can be the next Curie team, working side by side."

"If I go into research, who's going to look after your lungs?" I said.

"Good point. Okay, Lyle will win the Nobel Prize and you get the Park Avenue practice, Jo. How does that strike you?"

"Great, he's the genius and I'm the materialist. Thanks a lot."

"Lyle, what're we going to do about this girl? Is she this hypersensitive with you?"

After supper we smoked a little grass that Philip had around; he usually does. I've given up on being the kind of person for whom grass performs any great wonders. Mostly I get sleepy, and once I had this really bad anxiety attack. I never seem to get any wonderful insights into the meaning of it all.

Lyle and I walked home, down Broadway, holding hands.

"I know Philip's kind of strange," I said falteringly, "but—"

"No, I liked him," Lyle said. "He seems very fond of you."

"Yeah, well—" There was a time about two years ago when Mom said she didn't like the idea of my going over to see Philip alone, like she was afraid he was going to seduce me or something. Which is sort of ridiculous because, first of all, Philip says he's scared of women and that marriage to Mom was enough contact with the female sex to take care of the rest of his life. Also, I just know that there's nothing of that sort between us, even under the surface, and it got me really mad that Mom would even bring it up. She said I was too young to appreciate the complexities of these things and that people didn't always understand their own motives in things, especially where sex was concerned.

If you ask me, Mom's whole generation has a lot of really dumb hang-ups about sex. She says all the time how in the fifties, when she was growing up, things were so awful and girls were so repressed and felt so guilty if they even masturbated or anything, and she's always regaling me with these horror stories about girls who admitted they had slept with someone and then were shunned and never had dates and married awful people as soon as they got to college just because their self-image was wrecked forever. All this may be true—since I wasn't around, I can't say one way or the other—

but I think sometimes, like in the idea that Philip has some mad passion for me, it's a little wacky. It's not even that consistent, because when Eric makes cracks about Philip and calls him the mad scientist or El Weirdo, Mom flies off the handle too.

So now Lyle has met all my fathers except my real one. Daddy is a little trickier; I think I'll postpone that for a while if possible.

One thing is true—you certainly can't always predict peoples' reactions. I had no intention of telling Mom about Philip turning down the Harvard job, but at breakfast she kind of brought up the topic by saying, "So, how did you find Philip?" She knew Lyle and I had gone to the matches with him.

"Okay," I said casually, munching my bowl of Product 19. "Well."

"Has he turned down the Harvard thing yet?"

I just stared at her. I knew Philip wouldn't have told her because, like I said, he really is scared of Mom. Anyway, he'd said he hadn't told anyone but me. "Uh . . . yeah, actually he did."

"It figures," she said. "Well, he's probably better off that way."

I practically choked on my cereal. "But I thought you wanted him to take it. You said it was the chance of a lifetime and all that."

"Did I? Yeah, I guess I did," Mom said. "Well, I've done an about-face. Let him do what comes naturally. I think I'm in my mellow phase. I mean, face it, Philip would have been *miserable* at Harvard. He hates adulation. Maybe deep *down* he really wants it, but it's *so* deep it'll never surface. It would've driven him crazy. All that stuff that other men would love, coeds drooling over him—he would have absolutely freaked out."

"I bet he'd be really happy to hear you say that," I said.

"I was a bitch with Philip," Mom said, scooping out her grapefruit. "Not that it wasn't excusable. I don't *blame* myself for one second. I just wanted him to live up to some crazy ideal of what I thought a professor should be." She looked at me intently. "Like, take Elliott. In a year or so he says he's going to give up teaching and write that book he's always been planning to. Now a few years ago I would have gotten into a panic and thought, 'My God, what if he can't get his job back? What if the book is no good?' Now I figure it's something he wants to do and he should do it. Life is taking chances."

"What's this I hear?" Elliott said, walking into the room.

"You're giving up teaching," I said.

"I am?" He looked startled.

"Your book, your book!" Mom said.

Elliott held up his hand. "Now, wait a sec, folks.

Let's not jump the gun. Beth, I said cut *down* on my teaching, not give it up altogether."

"Cut down, give up," Mom said. "The main point is, you've had it with all this mad scrambling for prestige and power and you've finally seen the light. You don't want to have another heart attack and you're taking your life sensibly for a change. I tell you, if I could be twenty with the wisdom of forty!"

"Sweetheart." Elliott sat down at the table. "Now, I mean it's okay to talk like this between us, but it's by no means a settled decision. I don't mind if Jody hears about it, but, promise me, don't go around telling everyone under the sun. Because well, face it, it may not even materialize. Look at the problems I have writing articles. Frankly, the idea of a book scares the hell out of me."

"Wonderful," Mom said. "It should. Why *do* it otherwise? Anyway, who's telling people? Don't get nervous. . . . Jo, are you all set for school? When is it, next Wednesday?"

I nodded.

She jumped up. "Listen, I have to run. Will you tell Eric that he has a dentist appointment at two and if he doesn't show, I'm going to blast his head off?"

"I'll tell him," I said.

6

I guess there's always a letdown feeling to senior year. Everyone says that so I'm not surprised about it. Everyone's looking ahead to college and getting a bit sick of gaping at the same faces that they've been gaping at for the last three years. But for me that's just a minor part of it. It's more Whitney, or the lack of Whitney, I should say. I don't like to think of myself as a status-type person, but the thing is, when a guy whom everyone in the school thinks is a big deal picks you out and pays attention to you, you *do* feel sort of flattered. I'm not saying that I would automatically have liked *anyone* who did that to me, but it was a nice feeling. I met Whitney because he was art editor of the yearbook and I was on it for my junior elective, but even before that, I knew of him. Whitney always did all the posters for school dances and fairs and he'd made the covers for the yearbook ever since I was a freshman. Everyone knew who he was.

When he started going out with me, I think everyone was sort of surprised. Partly it's that the kids in your class, especially the boys, become almost like your family. There's a horsing-around, sometimes friendly relationship, but they don't exactly think of you as a sex object, and you don't exactly think of them as one. So the boys in my class were amazed, almost the way Eric was, like: Why would he date *her?* I really don't think anyone knew we were sleeping together, though. The only person I told was Marion, and she's so shy, she wouldn't have mentioned it to a soul. Whitney wasn't the type to go around telling people either. So I got the admiration of being picked out, but not the snide little jokes about my sex life. That would have done me in completely.

I really only started seeing Whitney outside of school in around March, but all last spring going to school would have this special ambience because I knew he'd be there. I used to wake up really early in the morning and lie in bed, thinking about him. When I'd bike to school through the park, everything looked so fresh and beautiful. I'd feel high enough to sail over the treetops. Luckily when he made his big pitch about our needing to see other people, i.e., break up, there were only about two more weeks of school. Otherwise it would've been really hard to take. I had June in which to sit around licking my wounds. Then there was the Sloan-Kettering job, which was good, not only because it was interesting but because it gave me something to do to take my mind off things. No one there knew about Whitney or about anything to do with my "former life," quote unquote. That was a big relief.

Really, now that I see it objectively—which I think I can, it being four months later—I don't blame Whitney at all. I can see his point that when you go off to college, you want to start afresh. It isn't that I imagined we would go together forever. If you'd asked me, even in the middle of it, I probably would have said that we would break up eventually. But that was still different from its actually happening. Its actually happening was pretty bad.

It wasn't the fact that we slept together that made it bad. Really, the sex part of our relationship wasn't the main thing. Whitney had slept with other girls, and I think he got a little impatient with me after a while. I seem to be sort of a slow starter. I mean, I can make the *decision* to do it, but by temperament it's hard for me to really let myself go. I was getting better near the end, but maybe not enough better so that that alone would have made

71

Whitney think he just couldn't give me up. Anyway, I wouldn't exactly want someone to keep on seeing me just because he liked sleeping with me, though maybe that would be flattering in some ways.

This is all to explain why school seems such a letdown this year. I still bike to school, and basically fall is my favorite time of year, more than spring. I look around and see objectively that it's beautiful with the leaves changing, but I don't feel so elated. Maybe if Lyle went to the same school I did, it would be different. But really I'm terribly glad he doesn't. I wouldn't want to go through the thing again of feeling everyone was watching me and teachers were smiling at us and all that.

This year I have French, English Composition, European History, Trigonometry, and Sex Ed. Sex Ed. seems like it might be interesting. In years past they used to separate the boys and the girls, and it would be one of those deals where a woman teacher would have the girls and would explain about menstruation and birth control and all that and the boys would have a man teacher who would explain things to them. The school decided that was old-fashioned, maybe even sexist, and that boys should know about girls' things and vice versa. Our teacher is Hal Meleo, who also teaches earth science and calculus. He's a short guy with thick curly blond hair and a moustache. In the middle of last year he got married to Sally Lippold, who teaches art and pottery.

At the first class he handed out a long questionnaire to be filled out at home. He said we should be as honest as we could with the answers, but that we shouldn't put our names on the papers, just our sex—*m* or *f*. It was really quite a detailed questionnaire, with questions ranging from how often you masturbated and how you felt about it to whether you'd ever slept with anyone to what you knew about contraception. I would say it more or less ran the gamut. When I saw what it consisted of, I was certainly glad he had told us not to sign our names. Even if he didn't reveal them to the class, I would've felt funny about it. But knowing it would be anonymous, I tried to be honest.

The next week he brought in all the questionnaires. You could see them. He had them piled up on his desk. He said he wasn't going to go over all the answers one by one but that it had given him a pretty accurate idea of where we stood on certain issues and that was helpful to him. "Four nonvirgins out of—how many are you? Twenty-two? I guess that's about average."

"Were they girls or boys?" Steve Kozody said.

"None of your business, kid."

You could tell that everyone in the class was sitting there wondering about who the four were, all but me and three others, who were just wondering about three. The funny thing is that I bet if everyone in the class had to guess who the four were, I wouldn't appear on anyone's list. Which makes me wonder about the other three. I bet everyone would guess Louise Gideon because she tells dirty jokes a lot and uses four-letter words, but the thing is, that really doesn't mean anything. I know that most of the boys in the class think of me as this kid who loves tennis and science, not a classic bespectacled type, but still more in that direction than in any other one. To maintain that image, I sat there very serious and thoughtful. I was really glad Marion, who knows my status, as it were, wasn't there to give me a secret little glance or nudge.

"What surprises me," Mr. Meleo went on, "isn't the *number* of virgins, but that so many of you put down as a reason for it 'lack of opportunity.' What is this? You live in one of the biggest cities in the world. But apart from that, you have each other, right?"

That got a big laugh.

"What's wrong?" He looked surprised.

"We know each other too well," Miriam Leonard said.

"So? To have sex you have to be strangers?" He gave us all a fishy glance. "Listen, kids, do you mean to tell me it's one of these Last Tango in Paris numbers? You can't exchange one single word or the mood would be wrecked? That's sad."

"What's so sad about it?" said this quiet girl named Ginny Potter, who just entered our class in high school.

"Listen, don't get the wrong idea, kids. Don't come away with the idea that I'm advocating you all jump in bed together. Frankly I think there's too much of that already, not too much in that it's bad in and of itself, but too much sex for the wrong reasons. But it puzzled me that for a generation that's supposed to be so realistic about things, there was this kind of pseudoromantic image of: One day I'll see her across a crowded room. I mean, fine. But you can get just so much mileage out of that kind of thing, the mystery thing, and then what?"

No one seemed to know and then what. Mr. Meleo looked down at the papers. "Okay, what else? Oh, yeah. Another little area in which your answers surprised me was contraception. I mean, guys, answers like, 'I think there's this *thing* a girl can put in her. . . .' It seems there's a certain vagueness here about detail, which I'd like to try and clear up. And there still seemed to be a tendency for a lot of you, even you girls, to regard the whole area of contraception as entirely the woman's responsibility. It's not. So that's another thing we'll go into." He smiled. "Frankly, I would say that we seem to have an unusually large number of Bridge Crossers in this class. Anyone here acquainted with the bridge-crossing school of contraception?"

"You do it on a bridge and you don't get pregnant?" Virgil Newman shouted.

Mr. Meleo just gave him a dry glance. "There seems to be—which frankly troubles me—a prevailing philosophy of 'We'll cross that bridge when we come to it,' which, as you ought to know, is simply a time-honored means of passing the buck. Like, 'I don't really expect to be doing it so I won't learn anything, I won't be prepared, I won't take responsibility for my actions.' Bridge crossing isn't smart, kids. Okay! I don't mean to lecture you. As I say, we'll be going back over all this and there'll be plenty of time for questions. Meanwhile, I want to read you a little excerpt I cut out of the *Times* this week. 'Recreational Sex and Procreational Sex.' Roughly translated, we say that means Sex for Fun and Sex for Babies."

Everyone listened. This was certainly going to be different from our usual classes.

After school I kept thinking back on some of what Mr. Meleo said. At least I don't think I'm what you'd call one of the bridge-crossing school. I went on the pill last year when I started sleeping with Whitney and I decided to keep taking it, as long as I'd started.

But I know what Mr. Meleo means. I hate to tell people, even other girls, I'm on the pill. I think it's hard to admit that sex is something you want to do or might do. It's one thing to say you believe in it in the abstract, but to come right out and say I guess I'll probably be sleeping with someone tonight, I might as well be prepared, is hard.

7

On weekends Lyle and I get up early and meet at the courts at 120th. You have to get there by seven thirty if you want to play between eight and nine. It's pretty cool some mornings now that it's mid-October, but by the end of the hour I've usually taken off my sweater and feel warmed up.

I've gotten over feeling humiliated at the knowledge that Lyle is so much better at tennis than me. In fact, now I really enjoy playing with him. We do rally well together. Sometimes the ball will go back and forth forty times before one of us—guess who?—hits it out or into the net. When I watch Lyle play, I feel like I'm watching some beautiful animal loping through the forest. He moves so gracefully and easily, not as though he'd taken a million lessons and was carefully remembering everything he'd been told to do but more as though he'd just strolled on the court and was playing the way other people breathe air. He claims that's not the case, that it's a learned thing. In other sports, such as basketball, he was never good at all. He says till he discovered tennis, he was considered by most of the guys in his class to be kind of clumsy, not especially athletic. That's interesting, but hard to believe.

Afterward we go for breakfast at Chock Full o' Nuts.

"Listen, you can shower at *our* house if you want," I said one Saturday. I'd noticed he had his nontennis clothes in a bag as usual, since he always changes in the locker room.

"Okay." He hesitated just a second before agreeing, as though afraid I might have some devious plan up my sleeve. I didn't. I really just thought that since we'd planned to spend the day together, why separate, go to our respective homes to shower and then meet again, which would take around four hours? It was just a practical suggestion.

We arrived at the apartment around ten. Eric was lying on the living-room couch, watching TV, still in his pajamas, naturally. Mom and Elliott were still asleep, or at least their door was closed. They usually sleep late on Saturday and Sunday mornings, sometimes till noon, even. Maybe that's so they can make love. I heard Mom say to Henrietta once on the phone that having a decent sex life is impossible with teen-age kids because they're always up and there's no real privacy. She even had a lock installed on the bedroom door. That's because, she said, Eric was always barging in. Elliott said that was a common Oedipal tendency, that Eric deep down was *hoping* to interrupt them making love. Eric said that was just dumb, he had better things to do on Saturday morning than watch two middle-aged people climbing all over each other.

Anyway, on this particular morning their door was closed. "You go first. Try the needle," I told Lyle, showing him the shower and how it worked.

"What's that?"

"It makes the water come at you from all these knobs, see? It's a great feeling once you get used to it."

Slowly I went back into the living room. I have to admit that I couldn't stop wondering what Lyle looked like without any clothes on. I kept imagining him standing there, turning on the shower. It's not that I'm a sex maniac. I mean, since I have a brother, the mere sight of a male body in the nude doesn't make me keel over in a dead faint, but it's different with someone you don't know. There's more mystery to it.

In general everyone in our family is pretty casual

81

about wearing clothes or not wearing them. In fact, the other night Mom and Elliott had a big fight on the topic. Eric and I were sitting in the living room when Mom came in with just a half slip on, nothing on top. She was holding up two dresses. "Which one do you like best?" she said. We said the blue one, but then I could hear her and Elliott arguing about it in the bedroom. Elliott said he thought it was provocative and sexually stimulating to Eric to, as he put it, "parade around in the nude." Mom said, "Oh, come *on*, he's seen me naked since he was a baby." "He's not a baby any longer, in case you hadn't noticed," Elliott said. Mom said, "Don't be so uptight. He's my kid. Let me wreck him my own way. You claim Pam wrecked them by being too rigid, right? Anyway, I'm almost forty. What's so sexually stimulating about a naked thirty-nine-year-old lady?" Elliott said, "Beth, come on, you're in great shape and you know it. Don't pull that kind of thing." "Well, don't give me all that Oedipal garbage," she said.

She did end up wearing the blue dress, incidentally.

One theory of Mom's is that you should never fight behind closed doors, which means that I get to hear a lot of fights which, frankly, are not that interesting. If people fight behind closed doors, you think: Wow, if I could only hear what they're saying. But if you actually hear it, it's sort of dull.

"When're *you* going to shower?" Eric said.

"When he gets done."

"How come you're not taking one together?"

I glared at him. "Eric, will you keep your voice down?"

"Why?"

"He comes from Ohio, remember. So please, while he's here, don't make lewd remarks."

"Me, make lewd remarks?" Eric said innocently. "Anyhow, what's so special about Ohio? Don't they have any fun there?"

Just then the phone rang. It was Marion. She was in for the weekend from this posh boarding school her mother decided she ought to go to for her senior year so she would get into some snazzy Ivy League college. "Listen, Marion, I do want to talk to you," I said, "but the thing is, now isn't such a great time." The extension I'd answered was in Eric's room, and I could hear the water in the shower being turned off. I was afraid Lyle would think I'd been waiting there on purpose, hoping to catch a glimpse of him naked.

"How's school been?" she said. "I guess you must really miss Whitney a lot."

"Yeah, well, I'm kind of over that," I said.

"Did you meet someone new?"

"Sort of." I heard the shower door opening.

"Who is he? Is he from school?"

"Marion, could I call you back? He's—well, he's

here now and he's about to come out of the shower."

Marion let out a hoot. "Jody!"

"We were just playing tennis, it's nothing like that." Just as I'd hung up, Lyle came out of the bathroom with a towel wrapped around his waist.

"Uh . . . I just came in a second ago to answer the phone," I said, trying not to stare.

"I'll be ready in a minute, Jo," he said. He grabbed his clothes and ducked back into the bathroom.

He did look kind of nice in the quick glance I got, allowing for the part covered by the towel. Still, I really have to cool it. I've been reading all these articles about how aggressive women can make men impotent and stuff like that. Not that we've even reached that stage. In fact, we're still around the stage we were that first night of above-the-waist, kissing, etc. We may never progress beyond that if I'm not careful.

Lyle watched TV with Eric and me till around noon, when Mom and Elliott staggered out of the bedroom. They say you can tell by looking at someone if they've just been making love. I wonder if that's really true. To me Mom always looks the same in the morning, sort of rumpled with her hair standing on end. She certainly doesn't have any special glow or anything.

"Jody, Marion called last night," Mom said. "Did you see the message?"

"Yeah, I spoke to her."

"How's she liking Miss Whatever It's Called?"

"We didn't have a chance to talk that much. I'm going to call her back."

Mom gave a big yawn. "I suppose you two have been up since the crack of dawn. I hate to even *think* about it."

"It's beautiful at seven in the morning," I said. "You should try it some time."

She shuddered. "Perish the thought."

"So, who is he?" Marion asked. She'd come over after supper. Lyle was baby-sitting for his sister and her husband.

"I met him over the summer. I really like him a lot."

"God, you're always meeting guys!"

Marion is small and white-skinned with blondish-orange hair and big blue eyes. She's very shy. Whatever I do she thinks is the greatest. I think if I robbed a bank or killed someone, Marion would find some way of thinking it was a great thing to do. When I went with Whitney, all she could think of was what a big honor it was, how he had picked me out of countless thousands because I was so talented and pretty, etc., etc. With Lyle, even though she'd never met him, I could tell she would make it into a big deal too if I gave her half a chance.

"He's sort of shy," I said, frowning, remembering how he ducked back into the bathroom.

"Have you been out a lot?"

"Well, we play tennis. We haven't been out in the evening so much."

"Are you going to sleep with him?"

"I don't know. It sounds crazy, but I don't know if he wants to."

"How come?"

"Well, it's strange, but he's a virgin. I'm sort of afraid I shouldn't have told him about Whitney. I think maybe I scared him off."

"So, why'd you tell him? Boy, you're a dope!"

"What was I supposed to do? Lie?"

"Sure."

"Marion, come on. Would you really lie about something like that?"

"Of course! Not that the matter's likely to come up for about a hundred more years."

"Why would you?"

She hesitated. "Because now he might not respect you."

"That's so old-fashioned! Boys aren't like that anymore."

"Wanna bet?"

"Well, Lyle isn't. He says it doesn't bother him at all that I'm not a virgin."

"So, why'd you say you were afraid you'd scared him off?"

I grimaced. "Okay, it's true if I'd known he hadn't ever done it, maybe I wouldn't have brought it up. So soon anyway."

"What made you think he'd done it?"

"Well, when we were making out, he just seemed to know what he was doing."

"Did he actually say he doesn't want to do it *ever?*"

"No, but he . . . well, he just doesn't seem **ex**actly eager."

"Maybe he's gay."

"Oh, no! Never."

"Well, you ought to know." She looked dubious.

"It's not so much that I'm going crazy *not* doing it, it's more—"

"You want to know he thinks you're attractive?"

"Not even *that* so much. Oh, I don't know what it is!"

"Well, Jo, at my school it's completely different. I told some girls I had this friend who'd slept with someone and they all looked horrified."

"Really?"

"Yeah, though it *may* be kind of a coverup. I mean, they may just say that but really . . . I don't know."

"How's the social life?"

"Nothing. Mom would kill me, but I didn't even

go to the mixer, or whatever they call it. It's so grisly, these boys you don't even know kind of looking you over. You'd hate it!"

I really felt sorry for Marion. She doesn't care at all what college she goes to. She says she isn't even sure she wants to go to college. But her mother's got this bee in her bonnet about how she has to go to Wellesley because that's where all the women in her family have gone for the last million years.

She really has a tough deal.

8

"I don't mind. Really."

"Are you sure? I'm sorry, Jody. My sister says she told me. I guess I wasn't listening."

"What time are they going out?"

"Around eight thirty. She said why don't you come for dessert? She'd like to meet you."

Lyle and I had been planning to go to a movie, but evidently his sister was counting on him baby-sitting, so I said I'd go up and keep him company.

Renee was tall and slightly thinnish with brown hair, darker than Lyle's, pinned up in back. She looked nervous and had one of those quick, soft voices where you had to listen carefully to hear everything she said. Her husband was quite handsome, though not in the way I like. He was sort of chunky with square features and thick black hair. I had the feeling they were looking me over, almost expecting to find things they didn't like, but, as Mom is always saying, I have a tendency to be hypersensitive, so it might have been my imagination.

"I see in the paper that Moshe Dayan is losing his popularity," Wesley said as we had our dessert.

He was looking right at me, but my mouth was full, so I just muttered, "Oh?"

"I suppose the leadership situation there will be something to watch in the next few months."

"Yeah, I guess so."

Then he went into this big thing about Israel and how he'd heard it was such an interesting country and this friend of his had visited it and the people were so energetic and full of life. It took me awhile to catch on to the fact that he was saying all this because he'd heard I was Jewish and he wanted to make me feel at ease. It's sort of ironical, considering how everyone in our family is supposedly a raving atheist. But I didn't exactly feel I could say, "Look, folks, cool the Jewish thing," because basically they were just trying to be polite. I mean, you could call it inverse prejudice, trying to bend over backward that way, but I thought it was more a kind of awkwardness. At the same time I kept wondering what Lyle had said to them. Had he said, "I met this girl and she's Jewish," as though that was the most important thing about me?

"Have you ever been to Israel, Jody?" Renee poured me some more coffee.

"No, I never have. The thing is, my mother is sort of an atheist. I mean, she's not that much into Jewish things, so I never, we never really—"

"Oh." Her eyes widened.

"I guess I shouldn't say atheist so much," I said quickly. "It's more she went to Hebrew school when she was little and so she wants us to find our own thing. Like, if it happens to be Judaism, fine, but if it's some other thing or even no thing, that would be okay too."

"Dad was like that," Renee said. "He never interfered with Mother, but he wasn't as orthodoxly Catholic as she was."

"I guess I've never met an actual Catholic," I said.

They all stared at me.

"I mean, maybe I did, I just didn't know they *were* one," I said hastily. "In our school it's more, well, mostly Jewish, I guess." I wondered if they were religious. Sometimes you have the feeling that no matter what you say, it's going to be the wrong thing; I was beginning to have that feeling.

"Lyle tells us that you're a native New Yorker," Renee said.

"Well, we've lived here since I was six."

"It's a fascinating city, no doubt about that," she said. "But I'm still not sure if it's a place to bring up kids."

"You mean, muggers and pollution and that sort of thing?"

"Well, that, but also . . . Did Lyle mention to you I was a teacher? I'm not doing it right now, but I taught for a few years before Kitty was born and, you know, it's not that I'm that naive, but, my goodness, the number of broken homes! You wouldn't *believe* it. It came to the point where if I met one set of parents who were living under the same roof, I'd practically fall off my chair."

"It's a little like that in our school," I said.

"These women!" she said. "They say they want to be liberated, fine, I have no quarrel with that, but why do they have kids then? Those kids have had so many fathers, they don't know *any* sense of stability. It's dreadful, really."

I took a big gulp of coffee. "I guess it can be pretty bad."

"I said to this one woman one day, maybe this wasn't very tactful of me, but there she was pregnant for the *second* time, no husband, this lover who appears and disappears . . . 'Why bring this child on earth?' She went off into a tirade about her freedom and how she could do whatever she wanted. But what about the *children?* That's what I want to know."

"Renee really cares a lot about children," Wesley said.

"Tell me, Jody, Lyle said your father's a psychologist. That must be interesting."

"My father? No, he's a- um- dentist."

"Really? Where did I get the psychologist idea? I guess it's just every other person you meet in New York seems to be going to a psychiatrist and I—"

"Rennie, I think we better get going," Wesley said.

"Oh, right!" She jumped up. "Jody, I'm so glad you could come. As you see, we're a little cramped for space, but I hope you come often. I feel guilty using Lyle as a baby-sitter, but since I quit work, our economic situation is kind of—"

"Rennie, seriously," Wesley said.

"Coming!"

As they were going out, Renee said, "Should I call during the intermission?"

"What for?" Wesley said. "Lyle knows what to do."

"Okay. Lyle, I changed my mind about letting her sleep through. Why don't you wake her at ten, the same as usual? I just think the cereal thing isn't going over too well."

"Okay," Lyle said, smiling. "Don't worry. I think I can handle it."

"Jody will help you," she said, giving me a really nice smile, which made me feel better. I didn't want to say that I'd never done much with babies so I wasn't sure how big a help I could be.

We watched TV in the bedroom for a while and then we went into the living room and started making out on the couch. In the back of my mind was the thought that maybe tonight was going to be the night. I mean, we had the house to ourselves and they'd said they wouldn't be back till midnight. We were lying down, facing each other. Lyle said, "This is my bed."

"I know."

"I bet you didn't expect to be in bed with me this early in the evening."

"Well, I had hopes. Why don't we open it up?"

"We better not."

"Why not?"

"Well, it would look funny if they came back and we—"

"We have loads of time. It's only nine twenty."

"True." But he sounded reluctant.

"It would just be more comfortable."

"Okay." I stood back while Lyle opened the couch up into a bed. It made quite a large bed, but there weren't any sheets on it. "I guess I'll put the sheets on," he said. He got some out of the closet in the hall.

Then we looked at each other.

"We could take our clothes off," I said. "I mean,

we might as well." Maybe I shouldn't have said it right out like that, but I felt nervous.

He looked worried. Then he said, "All right. Why don't we?"

I pulled my shirt and jeans and underpants off and tossed them in the corner. Lyle was getting undressed sort of slowly. He lay down facing me. He put one hand on my hip, but his eyes were looking me up and down. "You're so beautiful, Jody."

I know I'm probably the first girl he's ever seen naked, but still, that kind of remark always makes you feel good. It's funny that you can't say the same thing to a boy. "Thank you," I said. My heart was beating very fast.

He put his arms around me, and we lay there like that a minute, our whole bodies touching. One thing I couldn't help noticing was that even though he'd had an erection before, when we were making out with our clothes on, he didn't have it anymore. In fact, his body was trembling slightly all over.

"Listen, we don't have to do it," I said.

"I'm sorry," he said. "I know you want to."

"No, really, I don't care. Why don't we just lie here?" Our faces were so close, I could see his eyes looking right into mine.

"Jody." He broke off and then sat up and said, "There's a reason. Maybe we should talk about it."

"Okay."

"The only thing is, it's almost ten. Would you mind if I fed Kitty and *then* we talked about it?"

"Uh-uh. I mean, I wouldn't mind."

"Maybe we ought to get dressed again," he said.

"Okay."

After we got dressed, we went into the baby's room. She was lying there on her back, wearing a green stretch suit. As soon as she saw Lyle, she broke out into this huge grin. It was really something. I know it sounds dumb to say you can be jealous of a baby, but I really was. Lyle was so tender with her, so intimate. He took her wet diaper off and wiped her vagina with baby oil, and all the time she lay there looking up at him and beaming.

"There, how does that feel? Better?" he said. He lifted her up. "I usually feed her in the living room," he said.

He got the bottle from the kitchen and sat down in the chair to give it to her. I sat on the floor, cross-legged, watching him.

"You seem to know a lot about babies," I said finally.

"There's nothing to it," he said. "Is there, Kitty?" He took the bottle away. "I better try and burp her. Sometimes she throws up if you don't." He walked back and forth with Kitty leaning against his shoulder. She still had that dreamy, contented expression. If anyone looked the way people are supposed to look after they make love, it was that baby.

"Why don't *you* give her the other half?" Lyle said.

"Should I? I don't know how to hold her."

"Just do it the way I did. It's easy."

"She doesn't know me, though." I took the baby, who didn't seem to mind. She snapped onto the bottle and began drinking the other half.

Lyle smiled at me.

"She's in love with you, you know," I said. "You're robbing the cradle."

"You're really doing fine, Jody," he said. "You seem to have a way with babies."

"I don't! I'm scared to death of them."

"You're holding her just right."

I started having this fantasy that we were a teenage couple that had "had" to get married and had dropped out of school to live in a small apartment. This was our baby. Interwoven with that was the way Lyle had looked when he lay down next to me on the couch and his eyes had gone over my body for the first time.

After we put Kitty back, we went back to the living room. We lay down again on the bed, this time with our clothes on.

"Is it that you just don't want to do it?" I said. "Because we don't have to. It doesn't matter."

He frowned. "Well, the thing is, I'm just not sure I'm in love with you."

I felt relieved. "That's okay. I'm not sure I'm in love with you."

"That's what I mean."

"I don't care if you love me or not."

"You should."

"Why?"

"That's your birthright, Jody, to be loved."

"It is?"

"Sure. And I think maybe it will happen with us. We just have to get to know each other better."

"But that might wreck it," I said. "Then I won't have any mystery."

He laughed.

"Anyhow, maybe this whole love thing is sort of—I mean, Mom says we've all been so influenced by this romantic stuff in movies and books that we expect sparks to fly and all that whereas love might be different. It might be something where you don't even know it's happened."

He had a worried expression again. "Listen, the love part isn't the main thing. It's a little hard for me to talk about."

I wanted to hold him and make him feel better. "Well, don't, Lyle, seriously."

"No, I want to. I want you to know. Really, what it is is the thing with my parents. I just feel like this year is going to be pretty tough for me. I've just got to get a scholarship and work hard, and yet to start all over with teachers who don't know me . . . and underneath, I suppose, I'm afraid of going to pieces."

"Really? You mean, cracking up?"

"I know that sounds melodramatic. But what I'm really afraid of is if we start having an affair and it doesn't go well, it might kind of throw me, and I just can't afford that right now."

"But maybe if it did go well, it would make you feel better."

"That's possible. I've thought of that too." He smiled. "They say that everything up to intercourse is more fun for the girl and everything after that is more fun for the boy."

"They do?"

"That's what the guys at my school used to say."

"So . . . have some fun!"

He didn't crack a smile. "Will you mind, Jody? Will this make it too difficult for you?"

"Well, we can do other things. I mean, even if you're against intercourse, there are, like, other options."

"Jody, I'm not *against* intercourse. I have the feeling it's probably pretty great, but . . . I guess it boils down to, can you be patient with me?"

I nodded. "I think so. Would you like me to take off my clothes again?"

"Maybe *I* could take your clothes off."

"Okay." We lay down, and Lyle pulled my shirt off over my head and then after a while he eased down my jeans and then my underpants. He let himself stroke my body all over, but tentatively. Then he took his clothes off again.

"Should I . . . can I touch you?" I said.

"Okay."

I felt a little funny touching him below the waist. He had an erection again, and I wasn't sure if he'd mind if I touched his penis. He might think that was forward or aggressive.

"That feels good," he said softly.

As we lay there caressing each other, I began imagining that he was inside me. His penis was right against my leg, and I thought how funny it was that that one extra step or extra inches had such psychological meaning, even for a boy. Then all of a sudden I came.

"Are you all right?" Lyle said. I guess I cried out or moved.

"Yes, I came. Is that okay? I couldn't help it. You felt so nice."

"You feel pretty nice too."

"Would you like me to do it to you?"

"Sure."

I touched him, but very gently. When he came, he rolled over on his stomach and sighed. "Jody." He kissed my hand.

"Did I do it all right?"

"I think maybe I am in love with you."

"That's just sex."

"No. I don't mean because of what we just did. But . . . you're so kind. You're such a kind person."

"No, I'm not. I like touching you."

"Do you? I guess I never could understand that, how a girl could like it. Penises are so funny looking."

"Well, vaginas aren't that great either."

He sat up. "I guess we should fold the bed back up. They'll probably come home soon."

When Renee and Wesley came home an hour later, Lyle and I were playing chess. Needless to say, he was extremely good; I was hoping for a draw, at best.

"How was Kitty?" Renee said.

"No problems," Lyle said.

"She's really cute," I said.

"Jody gave her half the bottle," Lyle said.

"Well, Jody, you must come here often and keep Lyle company. I'm sure it made it much pleasanter for him."

We looked at each other and I tried not to smile. "I will. It was pleasant for me too," I said politely.

9

Sometimes I think Rifka Rabinowitz is a bad influence on Mom. She came for lunch today and right away started in on this thing about Trudy and Evan, her two older children whom she had before she saw the light about child rearing. Evan dropped out of college and was living at home with his girl friend for six months last year. Now he's back in college and so is the girl. "I should have my head examined," Rifka was saying. "It was the worst possible thing for Trudy, seeing her brother, whom she adores—you *know* how she's always adored him—with Kisha. The house *reeked* of sex! She rushed out to find someone herself, and now this year she comes to me and says, 'Mom, why did you let me?' They want rules! That's all there is to it. We've deprived them by all this liberal shit about sex. It's fine, it's great, it's marvelous. Now it turns out the affair she had was a *disaster!* An absolute and utter disaster! She wasn't ready. Why should she have been?"

"But I thought you said she was going with a nice boy now," Mom said.

"Now is a different story. Sure, he's darling, though I could have killed her the other day. She says to me, 'Mom, do you have one every time?' Here she is, eighteen, and if she doesn't have an orgasm *every time*, she feels cheated. Jesus, it took me ten *years* to even come close. These kids! They want orgasms on a silver platter! I could have belted her!"

I went into the kitchen to get a snack. "Look at you, Jody!" Rifka said. "You look terrific!"

"Thanks." As I went out with my apple, I heard her say to Mom sotto voce, which with Rifka means you can hear it three rooms away, "What's with that boy she went with last year?"

"Oh, that's all kaput," Mom said.

"You handled that really well, Beth. God, with Trudy, I was ready to hit the ceiling."

"Jody's old enough to take care of herself. She has very good judgment," Mom said.

"Come on! They're babies! Let's face it. I don't care if they're having orgasms every *second*, they're

104

babies! In a lot of ways we were much tougher than they are at this age."

I went into Eric's room. "Is she still here?"

"Yeah."

"Hey, did I tell you Philip called? You're supposed to call him back before noon."

"Thanks for telling me."

"It's only eleven forty."

Philip wanted to know if I felt like going to a photography show with him. I was glad he called. I felt like I wanted to talk to someone about Lyle. I thought getting a masculine viewpoint might be helpful. Daddy is impossible, and Elliott would undoubtedly get into a big spiel about castration anxiety. Eric is such a wise-ass, apart from being a virgin, so Philip seemed like my best bet. I feel like I can trust Philip. He's so quiet most of the time that I know he wouldn't tell anyone, but apart from that, he's the kind of person you know would respect privacy. Even when I was nine and something happened that I didn't want anyone to know about, I'd tell Philip, and I don't remember one single time when he betrayed me.

Philip said he had to go downtown early in the day and could I meet him at this gallery in Soho around two. I said I could. I know the place he means because we've gone there before; Philip knows the guy who runs it. Actually, it's a gallery that sells photos. Philip collects photos, mostly of old buildings and things like that. It's funny—if I collected photos, I think I'd want ones with people in them, but Philip says they detract from the abstract line or something like that.

I went down by subway. It was a chilly November day, and I wore my sheepskin coat. I've had it a few years now, and it seems each year when Mom makes me get it cleaned, it gets a shade lighter in color and shabbier looking, but I still love it. It's the warmest thing I ever owned.

Sitting on the subway, I began thinking about this thing that happened two weeks ago at school that sort of threw me. It was in English-comp. class. Our teacher, Ms. Sirota, said we should write a story about what we'd done on Saturday night, the one just past. She claimed that we were all writing stuff like science fiction and that none of us was taking the time to really examine the life and people around us, which could be much more interesting. Well, it happened that was the Saturday I'd been baby-sitting with Lyle, so I wrote a story about that. Usually Ms. Sirota is not that crazy about my stories. Marion, who used to baby-sit for her—she's divorced and has a five-year-old son—was kind of her prize pupil, and she read Marion's compositions aloud in practically every class. But on mine she mostly writes "Lacks detail" or something. Because of that I was really surprised when she said she wanted to read the best "What I Did

Last Saturday Night" paper aloud and it turned out to be mine.

No one knew it was mine because she never tells who wrote anything. But after she'd read it, she asked for comments from the class. It was that part that really bothered me. First, most of the boys couldn't believe that there was a boy who wouldn't sleep with a girl who was willing to sleep with him. In fact, they found that idea so hysterically funny that they kept making remarks like, "She must be a real loser" or "a real dog." Then the girls started in and they all latched onto that one line about Lyle having said it was my birthright to be loved by someone. They all said they couldn't understand a girl "stooping so low" as to be willing to sleep with someone she knew didn't even love her. "She must be desperate or really hard up" were the variations on that theme. Ms. Sirota just listened to all this and then, at the end, which is when she gives her own opinion, she said she thought everyone had missed the point, that they were all looking for romance or some ideal version of true love, and the touching thing about this story was its sense of reality. You could tell nobody was at all convinced.

When I got home, I started worrying if what everyone had said was true. I don't think I'm a "dog" or a "loser." I may not be a candidate for Miss America, but I'd say I get my share of comments from construction men and in general, I think, I err more on the side of good looks than bad. As for being willing to sleep with someone who doesn't love me, well, maybe that is bad. I guess deep down I'm afraid if I wait for someone to fall madly in love with me, I might have to wait the rest of my life. I guess on that score I am somewhat insecure. Mom says that peer-group pressure is an insidious thing, and you have to find or make your own standards, but still. To top it all off, I met Ms. Sirota that evening. Each year two seniors are chosen to be on the board of trustees, and I was one of the ones chosen. After the meeting Ms. Sirota, who's on the board too, came over. She asked about Marion and if I'd seen her and how she was doing and if she liked her new school. "Tell her I miss her," she said, "and so does Tommy." Then she added, "I think the class was a little hard on you, Jody. Don't take it to heart. That was really a very poignant little tale."

Obviously she'd said it to make me feel better, but "poignant little tale" didn't sound that different from the comments the class had made.

Philip was already at the gallery, walking around, his hands clasped behind his back, looking at the show. The owner and his girl friend were sitting in this little room at the back.

"Have you met my daughter?" Philip said after

we'd gone around looking at the photos. "Jody, this is Hal Malzman and Marya—"

"Berger," she said.

They were kind of staring at me. It's funny that Philip always introduces me to people as his daughter. I can tell they think it's strange; if Philip were my real father, he'd had to have had me when he was practically my age. So you can tell they're thinking he must be lying and are wondering why. Maybe I just think that, but I had that feeling.

At the same time I sort of like it. I don't see my real father that much, and if I had to choose someone for a father, Philip is the person I'd choose. As we walked out, he looked at me. "A dress, Jo?" he said. "Since when do you wear dresses?"

Actually that dress, which is kind of a long purple T-shirt, is one of the few dresses I own. I like it because you can just pull it on and that's all there is to it. "I do sometimes," I said.

"It's very becoming," he said, sort of formally.

We walked around Soho awhile and then stopped to have a drink. It was getting dark. Philip ordered a Jack Daniels and asked if I wanted one too.

I kept trying to think how to bring the conversation around to Lyle without it seeming like I'd had that on my mind all the time.

"Jo, what's going on in that mysterious head of

yours?" Philip said. "I seem to see little wheels churning around and around."

I laughed. Philip can be pretty observant. "Well, it's kind of a personal question that I wanted to ask you. Is that okay?"

He took my hand and squeezed it, then took it away. "What other kind do you ever ask me?"

"How old were you when you first slept with someone?"

Philip brushed back his hair and looked at me with a kind of sheepish expression. "I'm afraid you'll be shocked."

"Eleven?"

"Try the other end of the spectrum."

"Thirty?"

"Closer. Twenty-two."

It was a little hard to imagine. "You mean you went all the way through college without sleeping with anyone?"

"Right."

"How did you manage that?"

"It was hard, believe me."

"Was it really?"

Philip smiled, sort of sadly. "Oh, Jody, I wish it had been. It was easy."

"Didn't you ever go out on dates?"

"I had what you'd call crushes, you know, wouldn't-it-be-great-if-she-liked-me, that kind of thing." He ordered another drink. Mom says that until Philip has two drinks, he's so shy he can't put a single sentence together. I don't know about that, but certainly with two drinks he doesn't seem at all drunk. Maybe he just is a little less withdrawn and awkward. I decided maybe I was going about the whole thing too indirectly.

I licked my lips nervously. "What if some girl had just said, 'Here I am, sleep with me.' How would you have felt?"

"You mean, an attractive one?"

"Umm."

He smiled. "I probably would have been scared out of my wits, frankly."

I sighed. "I was afraid of that."

"Who are we talking about? Lyle?"

"Yeah."

"*Are* you scaring him out of his wits?"

I frowned. "I don't *want* to, I really like him. Maybe I shouldn't have told him about Whitney."

"Because now he knows you're not a virgin?"

"Oh, not that so much. But I think he's built up this big thing of—"

"—he won't be as good?"

"Sort of."

"Did you make it sound that way?"

"No! What do you think I am, a dope?"

Philip was looking at me with a kindly expression. "Don't worry, Jo. He likes you."

"How do you know?"

"The way he looked at you. Just give him time."

"I'll give him plenty of time!"

"No, I mean, don't make him feel like you're impatient or critical. He obviously sees you as this experienced woman of the world."

"It's so dumb!"

"Well, compared to him, you are. So don't scare him."

I sighed. "I guess I just can't believe men ever feel insecure. Look at him! He's gorgeous!"

"He'd probably faint if he heard you say that. Jo, where do you get these crazy theories? Men are never insecure?"

"Well, I don't see why they should be. They have everything."

"Do *I* strike you as that secure?"

"You're different. I know you too well. I don't think of you that way. I think of you as a person."

"We're all people."

I stared at him. "I guess you're right."

"Just go easy on him, that's all."

"What do you mean? I'm not going to rape him!"

"That's not what I'm worried about."

"What *are* you worried about?"

"Look, maybe I'm identifying with him too much. He kind of reminds me of myself at that age. I suppose I'm afraid he'll fall disastrously in love with you and you'll—"

"Philip!"

"No, I mean it." He finished his drink. "All you macho young girls today can be pretty terrifying. When I was young, girls used to be fat or wear braces or whatever. Now you all seem to rise full blown, ravishing, sexually adept—"

I really felt angry. "Philip, cut it out, will you? I mean it! Sexually adept? I've never even had an orgasm!" He was beginning to sound like Rifka Rabinowitz. Actually, it's not strictly true that I've *never* had an orgasm. What I meant was I'd never had one during intercourse. That does bother me, but actually Whitney and I only did it around a dozen times, and I was always sort of nervous. I haven't given up hope of ever having one.

Philip looked embarrassed. "Okay, I'm sorry." He took my hand again. "You'll have one, Jo, don't worry."

"I'm *not* worried. I'm just saying you claim I don't allow for the insecurities of men. Well, *you* don't allow for the insecurities of women!"

"Fair enough."

After that we dropped the topic. It really is ironical, though, Philip thinking the whole problem is that Lyle is going to fall disastrously in love with me. I certainly do have a bunch of conflicting theories on the subject, from Marion thinking Lyle will never respect me to the class thinking I'm some kind of loser who's desperate for a guy to Philip, who sees me as this ravishing, sexually adept teeny bopper.

The truth lies somewhere in between, I guess.

10

Mom has decided to have her tubes tied. She claims the pill is unsafe for women over forty (which she'll be in a couple of months) and the diaphragm is messy and the loop isn't reliable. So that about takes care of all the possibilities except condoms, which I guess grown-ups never use, and celibacy, which I guess she isn't ready for.

"Look, even if you and Eric were killed tomorrow, I'm not sure I'd have the heart to start again," she said. "It's an era of my life and it's over."

"Who says we're going to be killed tomorrow?" Eric said.

"I'm not saying you *are*," Mom said, "I just

meant that there is a time and place for everything, and you have to go on to the next stage."

She's going to have the operation in January, and then two weeks later she and Elliott are going away for a week to some island in the Caribbean to relax. At first she wasn't sure if it would be okay to leave Eric and me here alone. In the past when she's gone away, we've stayed with her friend Henrietta or her younger brother, our uncle, Howard. But this time we insisted that we were perfectly able to take care of ourselves and that it was treating us like babies to dump us on some relative. Finally she agreed.

The week after the operation I came home and found Mom standing stark-naked in front of the mirror in her bedroom, looking at herself. The door wasn't closed, but no one was home but me.

"Jo, come in here one sec," Mom said.

I came in and sprawled out on the bed.

"I want you to be brutally honest," she said. "Do you think I can still make it in a bikini?"

"Sure," I said. I've learned from past experience that when Mom says she wants you to be brutally honest, that's not exactly the truth. But, in fact, she looked pretty good, maybe a little hippy, but basically okay. Mom has a good figure; in fact, she's more busty than me. She once showed me this story that some guy who was in love with her in college had published where he said she was built "like a brick shit house," which I gather was an expression people used in that era. Anyway, if anything, she tends toward too much rather than too little, if you know what I mean.

She looked at me. "You know, I wasn't going to bring this up, Jo, but I think we're heading into a potentially dangerous time, you and me."

"We are?"

"Yeah. I mean, I have to be frank. You're looking fantastic these days, and there are times when I can't stand it. There are times when I feel like killing you. I just don't want you to take it personally."

"Okay," I said. "I'll try not to."

Mom started getting dressed again. "See, the trouble is, if I'd had kids when I was in my late twenties, like Henrietta did, you'd just be ten or so now, and we wouldn't be facing this for another ten years. But it's sort of hard. I guess I'm just not ready, at thirty-nine, to pass on the torch to the new generation and all that."

"Why do you have to?"

"I don't! That's the point. But there are days when I wake up and think: It's not fair! I wish I could borrow your body for the weekend."

"Doesn't Elliott like the way you look?"

"Sure, that's the dumb thing, he really does. No, it's all me, it's all my own thing. Rifka says it's a premenopausal state, you know, being filled with self-doubt. It's not just the physical thing. I guess I envy you for being young now and being able to do all these things!"

"What sort of things?"

"The whole sexual thing, it's so open now. You don't have to live through that hideous, repressed thing we did. You just find someone, you do it. When I was in college and started having sexual feelings, you wouldn't *believe* how guilty and scared I felt! No one your age would even believe it! I was too ashamed to talk about it to anyone. I thought I was some sort of freak, just for having feelings that were the most normal, natural thing in the world. So I went leaping into marriage with the first guy I slept with, and, well, you know the rest."

"Maybe if Daddy hadn't pressured you so much, you wouldn't have."

"No! He didn't pressure me. I know after we split up I kept saying how he'd roped me into it and all that, but that's not true. I roped *myself* in. I thought if I didn't marry quick, I'd turn into some kind of whore and sleep with everyone in sight." She stared at me intently. "I bet you can't even understand what I'm talking about."

"No, I think I see what you mean," I said.

Mom bent over and started brushing her hair. She has long, thick black hair with some gray in it. It's straight and reaches nearly to her waist. My hair is so curly I can never let it grow long because it just grows out, not down. For years I used to

118

wish I'd wake up and find I had long, straight hair like Mom's. "What the hell was I talking about?" she said, still bent over, slightly red in the face.

"Getting married?"

"Getting married?" She looked startled. "No, the thing about sex. What I mean is, part of my thing, my current crisis, if you will, is living in the house with a gorgeous seventeen-year-old. I don't care what *anyone* says, American men still have this thing about women over forty being out of it, and I'll be forty in four months."

"I thought Elliott didn't care. I thought you said he thought your worrying about it was masochistic."

"Jo, aren't you listening to me? I said it's an *inner* thing. It's all inner, okay? But the other part, which I was *getting* to, is that it seems like it's happened so fast! One second ago there you were this chunky little thing, and one minute later you're sprouting breasts and swaggering around with your behind in the air. So it just takes some getting used to." She sighed. "I suppose I have that classic feeling of, 'What ever happened to my little girl?' "

I should say I am now almost three inches taller than Mom, though I gather that isn't all she meant. Still, I can understand how she feels about me because I feel the same way about Eric. For years, till we were teen-agers, in fact, Eric was shorter than me. Then suddenly when he hit fourteen, he began growing around four inches a year, and now, well, he's not a giant, but he's five nine or ten at least. I can't get used to the fact of having to look up to Eric when I talk to him, just like sometimes I don't recognize his voice when he answers the phone and this deep basso voice comes out.

We heard the front door open. A minute later Elliott came in. He looked kind of greenish and slumped over.

"What's wrong?" Mom said. "Jesus, you look awful."

Elliott collapsed on the bed, his arm over his eyes. "What a day."

"Beth," he said in this very soft voice, "would you do me a tremendous favor? Could you get me a glass of cold water, two Empirin and a Librium?" As Mom scurried out of the room, he said, without opening his eyes, "Hi, Jody! I'm sorry I didn't greet you. I was just kind of—"

"That's okay," I said quickly. I went into the kitchen, where Mom was getting ice water from the refrigerator. She had a worried expression on her face.

"Jo," she said, but sort of abstracted, as though she wasn't really into it, "all I meant was if I start screaming at you about something, remember that even though I'm probably seventy-five percent in the right, maybe even eighty, there's some little part that is the thing I was talking about, the jealousy thing."

I'm glad Mom told me that because right after supper, when I went out to see Lyle and she saw me in my sheepskin coat, she began yelling about how if I wore that old rag one more time, she was going to burn it and would I, for Christ's sake, go down to Bloomingdale's and get a decent coat?

11

I think I've been good about Lyle. You could say: How does goodness enter into it? What I mean is, I don't ever say anything about our sleeping together. I haven't, like, been proselytizing in favor of it or anything. Which doesn't mean that I've put it out of my mind exactly. In fact, you could say it's sort of sneaky because I have to admit that deep down I keep hoping that we will end up doing it one day. Mostly, we do our usual routines, and I get my satisfaction and he gets his.

I sometimes wonder if I'm not making too big a thing out of actually doing it. The other day I began thinking: What if society had worked it the other way around so that intercourse was what you did first and you ended up, say, kissing someone on the lips, so that kissing would be considered the final thing and intercourse just the first step? Then I bet people would build up all sorts of taboos about kissing.

One thing is true: Having done it, even just the dozen times or so with Whitney, it's hard to go back to an earlier stage of development, as it were. It's sort of like what they say about the mountain was there so I felt I had to climb it. And doing it is there so you want to do it. I should, I guess, say fucking. "Doing it" is kind of a euphemism, as is "making love," and obviously "having sex" or "having intercourse" sounds a bit clinical. My problem with the word "fuck" isn't that it's an ugly word, which is what Marion claims. It's more that it's used in so many other contexts, all of them involving being really mad at someone. "I feel so fucking mad I could scream" or "Get your fucking feet off the table." So, to me anyway, it has that element of sex being a hostile act, and I don't like that.

I think I understand now more than I did why men rape women. I don't mean the kind of thing where the man doesn't even know the woman, but more those in-between kind of situations where the woman is putting up some resistance and the man thinks: Maybe once we do it, she'll really like it. Like if I could just do it with Lyle *once,* I feel maybe he would see the light and realize his inhibitions and stuff weren't necessary.

I don't feel anymore that telling him about Whitney or about my not being a virgin made that much difference. First of all, I still feel I couldn't lie about something like that. But, also, going with Whitney did give me a kind of self-confidence, even if we did break up and even if our sexual relationship wasn't the most glorious the world has ever known. To put it most simply, I guess it just made me think in a very specific sense: I'm a girl whom someone nice, someone I like, would want to sleep with. Now Lyle might say I shouldn't have to have that proved to me. I should just feel it or be born feeling it. But the fact is, I wasn't. Mom may see me as this blooming seventeen-year-old with breasts and a sexy behind, but when I look in the mirror, what I still notice are mainly the things I don't like or that could be improved on. If I hadn't slept with Whitney, and Lyle had seemed as reluctant as he is about sleeping with me, I probably would have taken it personally and thought: There, I'm not attractive, no one will want me. Whereas now I can see that really it's his problem, having to do with this thing he mentioned about his parents and maybe his general background. But I have the self-confidence not to mind so much.

* * *

Mom and Elliott left on their trip Friday evening. On Saturday Lyle and I were planning to go to a folk-music concert. I used to play the guitar and even took lessons for a couple of years at school. I stopped the lessons, but I still play sometimes, mostly alone in my room.

Eric was in his room packing his pajamas. "I'm sleeping at Steve's," he said, "so the coast is clear."

"I thought you were baby-sitting tonight."

"I'm going from there to Steve's house. Just thought I'd keep you posted."

"Thanks a lot."

Last summer Eric was a mother's helper. He got the job through *The New York Times,* just like it says in those ads in the subway. It took him quite awhile to get it, though. Some women thought they shouldn't hire him because he might molest their five-year-old daughters, and others thought that because he was a boy, he couldn't possibly know anything about little babies, and one woman said that her house was in a deserted part of Long Island and her husband was away a lot and she was afraid the neighbors would "talk." The job he finally got was with a woman named Mrs. Pitts, whose husband was around and who had two little boys, Michael and Sean, who got so crazy about Eric that now they'll only have him for a baby-sitter.

When he took the job, everyone kept ribbing him

about how Mrs. Pitts was going to be like Mrs. Robinson in *The Graduate,* a sexy type in her thirties who would drag him off to the dunes and seduce him, but I gather it wasn't quite like that. She and Mr. Pitts were perfectly happy, and the only social life to speak of was talking to a girl who worked as a mother's helper at a house nearby.

The concert was good. Afterward we went out for pizza and beer. I got a little drunk, which I sometimes do from even one glass of beer. Mom says that's not possible, I just must be very suggestible. Anyway, it put me in a benign, dreamy mood. I sat, chin cupped in my hand, staring at Lyle, more listening to his voice than taking in what he was actually saying. It's funny. Sometimes I have this fantasy that Lyle is my older brother. When I was little, I always wanted an older brother. Eric was always kind of a brat, and I had this image of an older brother who'd be kind and friendly and show me how to do things.

By now I feel, even apart from sex (which, within its limitations, has been very good), we have a kind of rapport. What I mean is, I don't have to pretend I'm in a good mood if I'm not. If I wake up with a pimple on my nose, I don't think: Oh, my God, now I can't see him. With Whitney I always felt I was onstage, like he was judging me and maybe about to find me wanting. Whereas with Lyle, despite the fact that our backgrounds are so different, I think he accepts me as I am. Maybe that's just what I want to think, but I believe it's true.

We didn't get back to the apartment till almost two. Lyle looked around the living room. I saw him look down the hall. Eric's door was open. "He's sleeping at a friend's house," I said.

Lyle knew about Mom and Elliott being away. He glanced at me.

I cleared my throat. "You wouldn't, like, want to stay over?" I said. "Would you? I mean, nobody's here."

He looked at me and smiled.

"We don't have to do anything we haven't done before. I just thought it would be nice to have breakfast together."

That wasn't a complete lie. I do think it would be nice to have breakfast together.

Lyle was standing there, looking thoughtfully at the wall. "Okay," he said. "Where are we going to sleep?"

"I guess in Mom and Elliott's bed. Mine is so small, we'd kind of be on top of each other all night." I swear I hadn't meant any sexual innuendo, though I know what Elliott would say to that, but as soon as the words were out of my mouth, I blushed, partly because of the expression on Lyle's face. "What I mean is, they do have a king-size bed."

We went into Mom's bedroom. "See, it's really

128

gigantic," I said. "We don't even have to touch each other if we don't want."

"Should we put a sword between us?"

We got into our pajamas. I lent him a pair of Eric's that fit pretty well. I guess I should have a sexy nightgown, but I don't because I never spent all night with anyone, and for just regular sleeping, pajamas always seem more comfortable. But I got a clean pair, some yellow ones with a bird embroidered on the collar. I felt a little bit self-conscious, which might have been being in Mom and Elliott's bedroom or maybe just the idea of sleeping in the same bed with Lyle all night. Anyway, I didn't feel especially sexy, more sort of nervous.

We lay in the dark, holding hands. We talked for a long time, about all sorts of things that had nothing to do with where we were or why we were there. Then Lyle leaned over and kissed me lightly on the lips. "Sleep tight, Jo," he said.

I turned on my side and tried to go to sleep, but I couldn't. I felt so disappointed. It wasn't that I'd expected we would have intercourse necessarily, but the thought of his lying there, about three inches away, not even taking me in his arms or anything made me feel awful. I thought of masturbating, but that seemed worse, to do that with Lyle lying right there.

"Jody, are you crying?"

I tried to make my voice sound normal.

"No. . . . I think I just might be—getting a cold." And then, as though to completely belie this, I burst into loud howls, slumped over onto the pillow.

"What is it, Jo darling? Tell me."

He'd never called me darling before; I felt my heart flip over. "I just want you to make love to me!" I wailed.

"I want to, I've been wanting to all evening."

I gulped. "You have?"

"I felt so guilty because I didn't even listen or anything at the concert. All I could think of was that."

"How come?"

"Well, I guess I sort of suspected this might come up . . . when you told me your mother and Elliott were going away. I even brought along some—the man at the store said these were the best kind." He got out of bed and showed me some Trojans that he'd evidently been carrying in his back pocket.

"You didn't have to," I said, still bewildered. "I'm on the pill."

He dropped the bag at the side of the bed and climbed back in next to me. We took off our pajamas. "It was a worthwhile investment, anyhow," he said.

"Maybe Eric would like them."

"Does he have a girl friend?"

"Not yet. But he could, like, put them away. But Lyle, I guess what I can't understand is how come you changed your mind. I mean, I thought you were so dead set against it."

He was holding me and stroking the hair at the back of my neck. "Jo, I never didn't want to, I've wanted to—well, ever since—you remember that day we went to the Arsenal together?"

"The day you got your tennis permit?"

He nodded. "You probably don't remember, but you were wearing this top with a Mickey Mouse face on it that left your whole back bare—"

"My halter?"

"I don't know what it was called, but, well, it revealed a fair amount of you, more than I'd seen under that lab coat, anyway. That night I had a dream about you, which was, well, pretty explicit. I remember the next time we met, I felt embarrassed to even look you in the eye. You seemed like this fresh, healthy young girl who loved sports. I couldn't believe you ever thought about things like that."

"Oh, wow!" I sighed. "But how about after that?"

"Well, what I said was true. I did have all those doubts, and I guess I wasn't sure what you wanted of me. I kept feeling you looked on me as some kind of hick, you know, the guy with hay seed in his ears who wanders into the big city. I suppose I was afraid, apart from everything else, that you'd make fun of me."

"Lyle, will you tell me the absolute and honest truth?"

"Sure."

"Are you just saying all this to make me feel better or do you really want to do it?"

"I really want to. Can't you tell?"

I guess he meant from his erection, but he's had those before.

"I was afraid you might have given up on me by now," he said softly, moving over me.

"I never gave up," I admitted.

We must have talked about it too much, or maybe it was just both of us being so nervous, but the actual act wasn't that much. That is, Lyle took his penis and pushed it into me, but he came so fast I didn't even have time to try and come myself. In some ways it reminded me of those books they give you in grade school about sex education where they usually have a line, "The father puts his penis in the mother's vagina." That was more or less precisely what happened.

But the crazy thing is that afterward, when we were lying side-by-side, I felt so happy I was afraid I might start to cry all over again, though in a different way from before. It's certainly ironical, because whenever I used to read about some guy feeling a sense of "triumph" after he'd deflowered a virgin, I would think how macho and awful that sounded. I don't think it was just triumph I was feeling. It was also that I felt Lyle trusted me. I'd never thought of it that way before, but it is a kind of trust to put part of your body into someone.

"You're so sweet, Jo," Lyle said, kissing me.

I smiled at him. "So, was it all that it's cracked up to be?"

"Better."

"Really?"

"Well, things are always better in real life than when you just imagine them, don't you think?"

"I thought it was supposed to be the other way around."

"Not for me, not in this case."

"Lyle, listen, what if I love you?" I said. "Is that okay?" I didn't mean to say it. It just kind of slipped out.

"It's okay. I love you too, Jody. And I'm not just saying it."

I sighed and kissed his shoulder. "Hey, look, it's morning."

"We better get some sleep," Lyle said.

It *was* nice having breakfast together in the morning just like I'd thought. I mean, obviously it was nicer because of what had happened the night before, but it was nice anyway. Usually Sunday-morning breakfasts are sort of chaotic at our house with everyone wandering in and out, yelling they can't find something. Whereas this morning Lyle made scrambled eggs, and I heated up the rest of the Sara Lee coffee cake, and there was just this very peaceful, contented feeling. I don't intend to get married for years, maybe ever, but it was the way you wish being married could be, without people yelling and ending up saying they can't stand each other.

While we were having breakfast, Philip called and asked if I felt like going for a walk around the reservoir with him. I know Mom probably told him about her going away just in case "something came up."

"The thing is," I said, feeling awkward. "Lyle sort of happens to be here. Would it be okay if he came too?"

"He sort of happens to be there?" Philip said ironically, slightly stressing the happens. "Fine, bring him. The more the merrier."

I know it's dumb, but it seems like every other sentence that emerges from my mouth has the word "come" in it, and I can't help thinking of the sexual meaning as well as the regular one. It reminds me of how once I wrote this story for Ms. Sirota's class, and the first line was "Max came first." I had just meant he "arrived" first, but she wrote something in the margin like "You're really starting in with a

134

bang, Jody." I don't know if she used the word "bang," but it was something like that.

Eric still wasn't home by two when Lyle and I went to meet Philip. I wasn't that sorry. Since Mom wasn't around to say anything, I decided to wear my old sheepskin. I did finally go to Bloomingdale's and got a coat she approved of, one she said would be good for college. It's brown plush and it's nice, but I just have a very deep and tender attachment to my sheepskin. I promised Mom I wouldn't wear it except on casual occasions if she promised that she wouldn't throw it out or burn it. Not that going for a walk with Lyle the morning after we'd become lovers seems casual, but still.

The year after Mom and Philip got divorced, Philip used to meet me every Saturday. We'd walk around the reservoir together. I guess he knew how bad I felt about his not living with us anymore, and so he would always take that walk with me, just like he was my real father. This particular day it was pretty cold, but the sun was out. There were muddy places where the snow was melting. My nose kept running, which it tends to do in cold weather.

"I suppose one doesn't have to worry about muggers that much," Lyle said. "There are so many joggers."

It was true, about every minute a couple or some little old lady would come zipping past us. Some of them seem to like to jog on the bridle path, where there aren't many horses, but the others prefer the reservoir. You really have to duck to get out of their way. I think they get mad if they have to break their pace.

"Of course, the joggers could be muggers," I said thoughtfully.

"You mean, they could alternately jog and mug?" Philip said. "Hey, that sounds like a pub, doesn't it? The Mugger's Jog . . . or the Jogger's Mug. I'm not sure which I like best."

We went around to the East Side entrance at Eighty-ninth and Fifth and then decided to find a place where we could get something hot to drink. One other thing Mom keeps telling me to get is some really warm boots. I should. The tops of my toes were freezing!

Philip took us to this place he knew on Third Avenue, a kind of pub, I guess. He ordered a Jack Daniels, like he always does. Lyle and I said we'd have cider. Then Lyle excused himself to go to the men's room.

Philip was looking at me, smiling.

"What's so funny?"

"Nothing. I'm just glad to see you two finally made it together."

I blushed. "How can you tell?" I was sure that was an old wives' tale, like being able to tell a girl who isn't a virgin by the way she walks or sits. I think it's that if she crosses her legs, she's a virgin, but if she doesn't she's not.

"You'll clobber me for saying this," Philip said, "but you look incredibly radiant, Jo."

"I do?"

"Yeah, really."

"How about Lyle? Does he look radiant too?"

"Lyle exudes an air of being quietly pleased with himself and the world, which with a man is the same thing."

I sighed. "Listen, it took me five months. It was a long hard struggle."

"I'll bet it was. Uphill every inch of the way, huh?"

"You'd better believe it."

He shook his head. "Stop it. You're making me feel old."

"Why? You don't *look* old."

"It's my birthday today. I'm thirty-five. Which means I've lived out half my allotted span or, given my general physical shape, maybe more like two thirds."

I felt awful about having forgotten Philip's birthday. "I'm sorry," I said. "I've never forgotten before."

"That's okay. You had other things on your mind."

"No, it's *not* okay. It's terrible. But thirty-five

137

isn't *so* old," I added to make him feel better. "Mom's almost forty."

"It's an inner thing."

"That's what Mom says."

"Somehow, seeing the two of you together, young love and so forth—"

"Philip, would you mind—"

"It's not just that. It's also seeing you so— grown-up. Can I say grown-up? Will that make you mad?"

"You mean, like, not being able to believe I'm not a little girl anymore?" I said, remembering what Mom had said that day.

He looked bemused. "I remember the day Beth brought me home that first time. Eric came clambering out of the kitchen, talking a mile a minute. At first I thought she had just one child. Then I saw this plump little creature kind of eyeing me silently from the doorway. Not saying a word, just staring. I must have been nervous anyway, but I remember thinking, '*She's* the one I've got to win over.' And then you came over and said in this quiet voice, 'Would you like to see my turtle?' and I felt like I'd won."

I guess I probably was a plump little creature, though it's never too great to be reminded of that. "It was awful with that turtle," I said. "Remember what happened to him?"

"Uh-uh. What?"

I shuddered. "I left him on the radiator, I mean his bowl on the radiator, and he kind of . . . melted."

"Poor fellow."

At that point Lyle came back. I looked at him to see if he did look quietly pleased with himself the way Philip said, but it was hard to tell. "What were you talking about?" he said, sitting down next to me.

"Turtles," said Philip, "and growing old."

"They live a long time, don't they?" Lyle said. "I think their life cycle is one of the longest."

"*If* you don't leave them on a radiator," Philip said.

Lyle looked at him, startled.

Lyle and I walked back alone, just the two of us. Philip said he had some work to do. Actually, we only walked to Eighty-sixth and Madison. Then we took the crosstown. It was getting dark and cold.

"I wish Philip had a girl friend," I said suddenly. What made me think of it was that, even though I don't remember the time Philip mentioned, when he came home with Mom the first time, I do remember that when he and Mom used to go out together, I felt really left out. I didn't understand why they couldn't take me along. Now, to have it reversed, with me having someone and Philip not, seemed odd. Not that I felt so grown-up, like he said, but it was a peculiar feeling.

"Philip was saying—" Lyle said. Then he stopped. "Well, maybe I shouldn't tell you this."

"Go on, tell me. What?" I was a little afraid that when I'd gone to the ladies' room, Philip had started reminiscing again about what a plump little creature I was or about some other dumb thing I'd done, like the turtle incident.

"Well, he said I shouldn't be fooled by your cocky exterior. He said, 'Underneath she's really very vulnerable.'"

"Oh, Jesus!" That was even worse. It sounded like some description from a Barbra Streisand movie.

"Isn't it true?"

"Which part—being cocky or being vulnerable?"

"Either."

I felt embarrassed. "I don't know." Lyle leaned over and kissed me.

We sat side-by-side on the bus, not talking. I kept wondering if all the people who got on the bus, seeing us, had an instant flash of knowledge and thought: They're lovers. Or was it just because Philip knew me so well that he could tell?

Lyle had to go home after supper. Eric came back just after Lyle left. I was glad about that. By then I was in my room, doing some schoolwork. I asked him how the baby-sitting went, and he said okay.

12

The rest of the week wasn't that idyllic. Nothing went wrong, it was just that we both had school and Lyle didn't feel he could stay out overnight. To tell the truth, I would have felt funny having him stay with Eric in the house, even with a lock on the bedroom door. On Wednesday night Mom called to ask how we were doing. Eric and I got on different extensions. He went into his room, and I went into the kitchen.

"Are things okay, kids? I don't remember, Jo, did I tell you the window cleaner was coming Tuesday?"

"Yeah, you did. I paid him out of the kitty, like you said."

"Has Eric been okay? Is he helping out with the house?"

"Mais oui," Eric said in his telephone voice, which always sounds deeper than his regular voice. "We have zee contract of zee domestic laboors."

"Okay, okay. How is it at night? Are you getting any sleep?"

"Plenty," Eric said.

"How did the baby-sitting go, Eric?"

"Same as always."

"Did you mind being in the house alone at night, Jo? I really think it's safe. Did you remember to double-lock both doors?"

"Uh-huh." I was scared to death she would ask something about Lyle, but she didn't. "Are you having fun, Mom?"

"It's wonderful. We're both eating like pigs, lying in the sun, even skin diving. Okay, well, listen, I just wanted to make sure everything was all right. Remember, I can always call Howard or Henrietta and ask them to—"

"No!" we both shouted in unison.

"See you Saturday, kids."

On Friday afternoon, Eric had his drum lesson. He usually doesn't return until six. Lyle came over after school, at around four, and we went straight into Mom and Elliott's bedroom again. This time it was a lot better. I still didn't come, but I don't think that was Lyle's fault. He really tried to go

142

slow and did everything right. As I suspected, he's probably going to be an old pro after about three times. I don't think he knew I didn't come. I mean, I'd never stoop so low as to pretend or let out groans to indicate I had when I hadn't, but he didn't ask me. He said, "How was it for you, Jo?" and I said, "It was good," which was true.

The reason I hated to tell him I didn't come is that I once read a story that was all about this man trying to make a woman come. They were working on it for hours, and it was about the most depressing thing I ever read. If anyone started that with me, I don't think I could take it.

The only awkward part of our sleeping together that afternoon was when we came out of the bedroom. We'd fallen asleep afterward. When we woke up, it was after six. We opened the bedroom door, and there was Eric with his friend, Steve, sitting on the floor in his room, playing cards. Eric's room looks right into Mom's room, so there was no way we could duck or sneak down the hall so they wouldn't see us.

"Hi, Jody," Steven said. Then he looked at Eric, and they kind of smirked.

"Um . . . we were taking a nap," I said quickly.

I don't know why I said that. I should have said nothing, but I really felt embarrassed. Steve is a kid Eric has been friends with since I was ten. Seeing him and Eric look at each other that way really threw me. After Lyle went home, I made dinner for both of them. Eric kept crooning things like, "Love, oh love, oh careless love," and then the two of them would start rolling with laughter. At first I tried to ignore it, but it was really getting to me. Finally I yelled, "If you don't shut the hell up, I'm going to belt you one, Eric, I mean it!"

The trouble is that threat was a lot more effective when we were eight and nine and I was a couple of inches taller than him. It's true I was second in my class in karate and Eric is not in such good shape, but still it didn't seem to exactly strike terror into his heart.

Instead he began cowering, pretending to be terrified. "Oh, no, my God, she's going to get me. Help, protect me, Steve!" Then they both started in.

"What'll we do?" Steven said. "She's coming closer! Quick, behind the couch!"

I stood there, arms akimbo, looking at both of them. I shook my head. "It's your turn with the dishes, dope. So get cracking."

Eric bowed obsequiously. "Yes, massa, anything you say, massa."

Saturday morning I went into Mom's bedroom to try and decide what to do about the sheets. There were some stains on them. I couldn't decide if it was likely she would notice. I didn't know if she'd just changed them before she went away. If they

were old ones, the stains could be from her and Elliott, though I didn't think so. You'd think the obvious solution would be to just change the sheets. The
problem there, though, was that Mom keeps buying
all these different sheets. Some have a jungle pattern, some have flowers, some, like the ones on the
bed already, are just a solid blue. So it was practically impossible to find another set that would be
identical to the ones already on the bed. And it was
too late to wash them.

Would she even remember which ones she'd put
on? If she did, would she care? I guess in the back
of my mind was the realization that I didn't want
Mom to know Lyle and I had been in her bed while
she was gone. I wasn't sure that she'd mind exactly,
though with Mom it's sometimes hard to tell. Certainly in the great broad spectrum of mothers,
you'd have to classify her as liberal, but she can be
sort of inconsistent. Like, sometimes some tiny
thing will throw her that you could never predict.
For instance, she's always saying that following
fashion is dumb and women should just wear whatever they feel comfortable in, but then with something like my sheepskin, she'll say, "How can you
wear that ugly old thing?"

But it's not just that. The other thing is that,
even if Mom wouldn't mind our having used her
bed, I don't really want her to know. I don't mind
her knowing in the abstract that I sleep with people

145

or even suspecting that I'm making it with Lyle. But I don't feel like having it spelled out, as it were. Not that she'd make cracks, like Eric. She might not even say anything. In most ways she is fairly good about respecting my privacy. But the thought that she knew would bother me.

Eric looked in and saw me sitting there on the bed.

"Hi," he said. He looked remorseful. I could tell he was feeling sorry for last night. I guess if you've lived with someone all your life, you can just look at them and tell something like that.

"I was just wondering about these sheets," I said. "There are these, like, stains on them. Do you think Mom will mind?"

"I don't *think* so," Eric said. "Why don't you rub some of that stuff she does our sweaters with on it, you know, with water? That might work."

"Hey, that's a great idea." I smiled at him.

"Listen, Jo, I'm sorry Steve and I were ribbing you last night. We didn't mean to hurt your feelings."

"Oh, that's okay," I said.

"Lyle seems like a nice guy."

I nodded. "He is."

Eric smiled. "I bet you won't believe this, but Steve was saying that he hopes the first girl he makes it with is exactly like you."

I stared. "Like *me?*"

146

"Yeah. I mean, he's kind of crazy, you have to allow for that. He kept saying how sexy you were! I told him that was a complete coverup and if he lived with you, he'd probably change his mind in about three seconds, but he was pretty adamant."

I smiled. "Thanks a lot."

"He wanted to know if you wear a bra. He said he didn't think you did. I thought you do, don't you?"

"I used to, but I don't anymore."

"Yeah, well, he claimed he could tell. There's this girl in my class who doesn't wear one, but she has more, it's easier to tell with her."

"I get the picture."

Eric was looking unusually embarrassed for him, "What's it like?"

"Huh?"

"Fucking."

"Oh, right, fucking. It's nice, it's . . . enjoyable."

"Are you doing it just because he forced you to?"

"Not exactly."

"Steve said he read that girls won't do it unless you give them some kind of line about how you're madly in love with them and you'll die or something if they won't do it with you. His older brother did that with some girl and it worked right away. I just ask because, well, maybe some day I might—"

"Eric! Jesus! That's the most male-chauvinist

thing I ever heard! You just say what you really feel."

"But what if that doesn't work? I mean, what if you just want to do it, but you're not in love?"

"You always tell the truth," I said severely.

"You do?" He looked dismayed.

"Girls like to do it too, you know."

"Do they really? I thought they just kind of go along with it."

"Of course they enjoy it!"

He didn't look at all convinced. "Just tell the truth, huh?" he said as he left the room.

"Right."

Boys really have strange notions. Anyway, the idea about using Woolite on the sheets sounded like a good one. I tried it and it seemed to work quite well. If you looked really closely, there were still stains, but they were pretty faint. I turned the sheet around so they were more toward the back of the bed.

13

"Think of him like Miss America," Mom said. She was sitting cross-legged on the living-room floor, sewing a button on a blouse.

"Think of *Daddy* like Miss America?"

"What I mean is, don't blame him. It's not his fault. He's been programed into this Jewish boy, first son, money, money, money shit since he was born. My son the doctor, my son the dentist. Same difference. He didn't have a chance of getting out alive."

That sounded a little spurious to me. I mean, you can excuse anyone by saying they were programed into this or programed into that. By that theory Hitler was programed into hating Jews and men are programed into dumping on women. "So he was programed into it," I said. "He could have programed himself *out* of it, couldn't he?"

"*If* he'd been another person, sure. But, Jo, listen to me. There are some people, and Sidney is one of them, who just don't examine things. They're not introspective. So you just have to accept him as he is."

"Why do I? Why do I have to even see him?"

"Because he loves you in his own benighted way."

"Sure. That's why he's so eager to see me, he only calls once a year."

"Hon, look, you're almost eighteen. It's really up to you. If you want to sever the connection altogether, do it. Okay? If you ask me, it would be a little bit cruel and unnecessary, but if you have to do it, do it. It seems to me it would be a lot more mature to accept him for what he is and give up trying or expecting him to change."

I sighed. "Sure."

For some reason Mom, even though she was once married to Daddy, is much more detached about him than I am. Sure, she's had plenty of times of calling him an unfeeling bastard and that kind of thing, but lately she's mainly promoted the theory she'd just mentioned, that he's more to be pitied than censured and all that kind of junk. Even Eric has always been much better about Daddy than I have. For instance, Daddy used to take Eric to sports events, football games, and the like. The big one was the Harvard-Yale game, since Daddy went to Harvard, but there were plenty of others—soccer, ice hockey, you name it. Maybe it was partly because Eric is his only son—he has two daughters with Boots—and his idea of what you do with a son is to take him to sports events. But Eric, without any seemingly great inner struggle, finally went to him and said something to the effect of: Dad, I just don't dig sports, so let's do something else when we get together. Daddy was maybe a little surprised, maybe disappointed too, but he never took him to another game.

Mom says it's only once a year so why make such a fuss? Actually, it's partly the once-a-year thing that bothers me. Why do it at *all* if it's only going to be once a year? I mean, if you only care enough about someone to see them once a year, then what kind of relationship is that? It's always on our birthdays. When I was little, it was some big-deal puppet show or ballet extravaganza. Two years ago, when I was sixteen, he wanted to give me a sweet-sixteen party at the local country club, to which I would invite all my friends. I just can't figure Daddy out. Like his idea of taking Eric to a call girl. It's one thing to have an idea like that rush madly through your head in one insane moment of folly, but to actually act on it! To actually call up and say, "Listen, I just got this terrific idea . . ."

What I should try to do, as Mom says, is just figure: This is what he's like. Why be hurt by it? Why feel, in some weird and incomprehensible way, devastated every time I return from one of these annual weekends? I suppose deep down what bothers me is the feeling that whatever I do, whatever I become, whomever I marry or don't marry, Daddy will always think of me as some kind of weirdo, some kind of freak. So what? as Mom would say. That's *his* problem. And really I agree, but it seems like each time I want it to be different and want us to break through and attain some magical rapport that will make up for all the years of garbage. Fat chance.

This year, for my eighteenth birthday, Daddy called two weeks before, as he always does, and suggested I come out for the weekend. "The girls are dying to see you," he said.

Why say that? They're not *dying* to see me. Why *should* they be? "Beth says you're going with a guy," Daddy went on. "Would you like to bring him? We have the den fixed up as an extra guest room now."

"I'm not sure," I said tensely.

"Well, we'd love to meet him, honey. It's up to you."

To take Lyle along and have him meet Daddy

152

would, for me, be an act of trust that would go beyond practically anything I can think of. There's not a sexual act on earth that would come anywhere close. None of my friends have ever met Daddy, not even Marion. In fact, till I was fourteen, I used to lie to most people and say Philip was my father. I went back and forth in my mind for quite awhile about whether I should bring Lyle. I ended up deciding I would. Maybe his presence would give me courage or moral support.

On the way up on the train I started getting my usual stomach cramps. I'd taken a couple of swigs of Pepto Bismol before we left, but, despite that, I kept rushing to the ladies' room every three seconds.

"Why is your father's last name Krebs and your last name is Epstein?" Lyle asked as I'd slumped back into my seat for the sixth time. We'd both cut school for the day, since it was Friday.

"Well, I guess after the divorce Mom figured why not go back to her maiden name, which is Epstein. And when she married Philip, not that she knew they'd end up getting divorced too, but she figured why change all over again? I'm glad. Jesus, if I had to have Daddy's name, that would really do me in. Oh, listen," I said suddenly. "Mom and Elliott are married."

"They are? Since when?"

"No, I don't mean really. I just mean pretend

they are for this trip, because Boots and Daddy think they are."

"How come?"

I bit my lip. "Well, it's really because when Mom and Philip were living together for a short while, Daddy didn't—it might not have been *just* Daddy, Mom thinks it was Boots too—but, anyway, they thought it wasn't a proper atmosphere in which to raise kids and they were threatening to take us away, Eric and me, and have us come live with them. Mom says they wouldn't have ever really *done* it, but, still, they kept on about it till she and Philip got married."

"Is that *why* she and Philip got married?"

"I don't think so. I think they were planning to anyway. It's just, well, Mom thinks people should live together before they get married for a year at least, to see if they're going to get along or not."

"You think your father would still mind, even now that you and Eric are almost grown up?"

"You just can't tell with him. Probably not, but she says: Why get into a hassle? Do you mind? Lying, I mean."

"Do I have to actually lie?"

"They won't make you swear under oath. Oh, it may not even come up! Don't worry."

"I'll go along with it, Jody." I was standing up again. He looked at me. "What's wrong? Do you need to go *again*?"

154

I sighed. "Isn't this dumb? I feel like there must be nothing left *in* me."

"This is really an ordeal for you."

"No! Or it shouldn't be, if it is."

"Come sit next to me. Let me comfort you."

I leaned against him. He put his arm around me. "It'll be okay," he said, holding me close. "Don't worry."

Feeling him against me, so solid and warm, did make me feel better. "They'll probably give us separate bedrooms."

He smiled. "We can visit each other, can't we?"

Boots and Daddy have lived in this particular house for about two years. First they had a small house with a little yard, not that fancy. Then they bought the present one. It has a huge swimming pool out in back. I gather the latest fantasy is to move into still another one with a swimming pool *and* a tennis court. They looked into building a tennis court on their property, but the land isn't right or something.

You'd say I should be the last person to not understand about wanting your own tennis court, if you can afford it. But the thing is, Daddy's interest in tennis seems to me not a real love of the game. He's interested in it just because suddenly everyone is interested in it. If everyone he knew had their own plane, he'd buy one of those. It's that whole statusy, upwardly-mobile trip, which Mom would claim he's been programed into and therefore isn't responsible for. Their house is sort of a prime example of that. There's a twenty-five-inch color TV in practically every room! Usually they're all going at once with some sports event or other. The kids have their own to watch whatever they watch. There's even one downstairs in the den, so you don't have to walk five feet and miss even one touchdown.

As the train was pulling in, Lyle said, "Which one is your father?"

"He's the one in the leather jacket."

"I thought he'd be taller."

"Only in my imagination."

14

Daddy isn't bad looking. His hair is brown and thick and always looks carefully "styled," which no doubt it is, and he's what you'd call a sharp dresser, which probably accounts for my own penchant for boys who look a little sloppy and wear jackets that don't match their pants. He sat with us in the breakfast nook while Boots gave instructions to the maid about lunch.

"I hope it's all right if we just have something light," she said, "since tonight we'll be eating at the club."

He sat down across from me, and we waited till Josephine, the black woman who lives with them, brought in our sandwiches. I can't even tell anymore if everything at Daddy's house bothers me just because of my feeling about him. I mean, obviously lots of middle-class people have maids. Certainly plenty of my friends' families do. It happens we don't because Mom, in the Marxist tradition of our family, doesn't believe in it and says it's each person for himself. What that means is that our apartment can get pretty sloppy at times. I heard Elliott begging her the other day to relent on her convictions and get someone to come in and clean, but she said the only thing she was willing to do was have some service once a month to do the heavy things like the floors.

It just seems weird to sit there and have someone bring you in sandwiches! I mean, if it was a huge, elaborate meal, it would be different. Daddy and Boots's two daughters, Nicky and Eliza, weren't around, but when they are, they'll shout in, "Hey, Josephine, get me a glass of milk!" I always feel like yelling, "Get off your butt and get it yourself." Whenever Josephine is out of earshot, Boots is always saying how impossible servants are these days, how they want all these "extras." I don't know. As I say, I'm probably hypersensitive just because of its being Daddy's house, but I think some of my reaction is genuine too.

"How's your tennis, Jody?" Boots said. "Did I tell you I finally learned to play? I play with some women friends every Wednesday now."

"That's nice," I said, biting into my chicken sandwich. "Do you like it?"

She nodded. "We're going to a tennis camp in Maine this summer, even the girls."

"Lyle is a terrific player," I couldn't help saying.

"A slight exaggeration," Lyle said quickly.

"I didn't know that," Daddy said, looking interested. When he's not talking, his face gets this impatient, bored look, as though he wishes he were a million miles away. "You never told me that, Jo." As though we talked so often on the phone that I'd told him everything else about Lyle *but* that.

"Yeah, he's the best player of anyone I know," I said. Which is true.

"Damn, I wish I'd known that." Daddy took a long drink of beer from a plastic glass with a tiger painted on it. "I say that because, you know, Gilbert and I have our Friday-afternoon game at four. If I'd known, I could have gotten a fourth, and we could have had ourselves some doubles. Did you bring your racket, Lyle?"

Lyle shook his head.

"Well, that wouldn't matter, I could lend you one. Do you use wood or steel?"

"Wood," Lyle said.

"Yeah, I prefer wood myself, but sometimes, it just depends, if I'm on, the steel can be pretty effective too. Have you ever tried a steel racket?"

"A couple of times," said Lyle.

"You could try mine, if you like. Listen, you're wearing sneakers, aren't you?" He peered down at Lyle's feet. "Okay, so what's the problem? I'll call Gilbert, and he'll round up a fourth for us. How about it?"

"Well." Lyle looked hesitant. "Sure, I guess I could."

"Terrific! Now we'll see if you're as good as Jody says." His eyes were already gleaming with a kind of competitive zeal.

I swallowed. "Daddy, I'd like to be the fourth."

He looked bewildered. "What do you mean, honey?"

"I mean, why don't Lyle and I play against you and Gilbert?" I know Daddy hates mixed doubles. He either plays singles till he turns red in the face and practically passes out or he plays men's doubles. It has nothing to do with Boots not playing that well. He just doesn't like to play with women. And I knew just how the unorthodox combination of three men and one girl would strike him.

"I thought you might like to watch us," he said. "Root for the home team." He grinned.

"No, I think I'd rather play," I said, hoping my voice wasn't shaking.

"Well . . ." He frowned. "You know, we don't really *have* to play. You kids probably want to just take a walk around and do your own thing. Why don't Gilbert and I play a couple of sets and then come back here, the way we usually do?"

"Lyle and I *would* like to play," I said. I looked at Lyle, and he looked at me. In his eyes I saw a mixture of pity and bewilderment. What he saw in mine I don't know.

"I haven't played indoors much," Lyle said, turning from my intense gaze. "Is this indoor tennis?"

"It's a bubble. The club just built it last year. Just regular courts. No, I know what you mean, I hate playing on a wooden surface myself. It throws my game off completely."

Finally it was agreed that we would play at four.

"I love your dress, Jody," Boots said as we got up from the table. "Where did you get it?"

"Bloomingdale's." I felt somehow exhausted from the confrontation with Daddy about the tennis thing. Yet there I was, wearing a dress, a new one, in fact. It was deliberate. From the time I was fourteen through sixteen, I would come to Daddy and Boots's wearing the most wretched item of clothing I had. Similarly I made a point of using the foulest language possible, much more than I would have at home. But this year I began thinking that was sort of dumb, going out of my way to try to get a rise out of Daddy and Boots. I decided to try to play the game by their rules, as it were, to bring just dresses or very neat pants suits. But the trouble is, even though I think that is a good policy, it seems I can't be in their house five minutes without saying, in effect: Who sez? Who made the rules this way? Who sez women can't play doubles with men? I suppose the part of me that wants to please runs head on with the part that wants to antagonize. You can guess which part pulls into the lead fairly early on.

Later in the afternoon Nicky and Eliza came home from school. Eliza is ten. She's a really evil child. I suppose evil sounds too melodramatic. She's not actually a Bad Seed or anything, but she's always had a kind of calculating air about her, like she was sizing people up and figuring what she could get out of them. She's pretty with black straight hair, kind of skinny. When she was little, Boots used to dress her in dresses that just grazed her buttocks and she'd go swirling around the house like some miniature Barbi doll. Today she was in bell bottoms and a white shirt with a Super Shark iron-on pressed into it.

Nicky, who's eight, always reminds me of myself as a child. She's not obese exactly, but definitely plump and her expression always seems to say: If you possibly can, please like me, but I know you probably won't. When I see her reach for an extra brownie and wolf it down guiltily when she thinks her mother isn't watching, I feel a horrible pang of identification. She doesn't know how to handle Eliza's teasing at all. She stands there like a lump, terrified, which, of course, goads Eliza on even more. Both Boots and Daddy dote on Eliza, who, I gather, is kind of a whiz at school as well. Frankly, I doubt she's intrinsically that bright, but she's probably learned how to manipulate all her teachers by now. Nicky, I gather from their conversations about her, does well only sporadically and in some subjects. She doesn't "apply herself."

"Hi, Jody," Eliza said. "Did your boyfriend come too?"

"Yeah. He's outside taking a walk."

"Is he going to take the guest room or are you?"

"I think I am. He's going to sleep in the den."

"Aren't you going to sleep together?"

"Uh-uh."

"How come?"

"Why should we?"

She smiled mischievously. "Don't you like to fuck?"

Boots, needless to say, was out of the room during this exchange. "Sure, I love it. But never on weekends."

She looked at me, puzzled, not sure if I was kidding her or not.

Then she peeked through the large glass window at Lyle, who was talking outside with Daddy.

"He's handsome!" she shrieked.

"Yeah, I think so."

"Are you going steady?"

"Well, not exactly."

"*I* am."

"Oh? Who's the lucky guy?"

"He's this boy in my class . . . Roger Calhoun. Wanna see his picture?"

"Okay."

She raced upstairs. Nicky was standing to one side.

"Hi," I said.

"Hi," she whispered. She always whispers.

"Are you going steady too?"

She shook her head and smiled hopelessly at such a foolish question.

"I still have that drawing you made for me, Nicky," I said. "Remember? The one of the girl on the horse."

She nodded.

"Are you still drawing?"

"Sometimes."

"I'd like to see some of your stuff."

"Okay," she said, raising her voice just a notch. I'm always complaining about being a teen-ager, but every time I see Nicky and remember what it was like to be a child, I change my mind.

There was a slight crisis about what we should wear for tennis. You have to wear white at the club, and Lyle and I didn't have anything white. We ended up borrowing some things from Boots and Daddy. Boots is thinner than me, but I managed to squeeze into her tennis dress, which was one of those fancy ones with a big red apple over one breast.

"Can I have a bite?" Lyle said, squeezing it. I was changing upstairs.

"Help yourself." But I felt more tense than jokingly ribald. I sat down to put on my sneakers. "Lyle?"

"Umm?"

"I know you don't believe in this, but could you play as though your life depended on it? Like be utterly merciless."

"Even if it's crystal clear we're going to win?"

"Even if it's crystal clear."

"Why, Jo?"

"Don't why-Jo me now, Lyle. Just do it. I'll do anything you say afterward."

"Anything?"

"Anything. You name it. We can go through *The Joy of Sex* backward, page by page."

My stomach cramps were coming back again. I prayed that they wouldn't start during the game.

We got there a little early. "Gilbert's girl friend might come and watch," Daddy said. "Did I mention he was divorced?" Daddy and Gilbert were in college together.

"No," I said, "since when?"

"His wife—I think you met her, Jo—was kind of a bitch. A pretty girl, not fantastic, but—she just left him! They'd been married fourteen years. Not even for another guy! Just 'freedom,' well, you know *that* old spiel. But the joke's on her because Gilbert found this marvelous girl in about two weeks. Wait'll you see her. She's a doll."

She was a doll, literally as well as figuratively—a great figure, platinum-blond hair tied back in a pony tail, blue eyes. She was dressed for tennis, but just sat on the side of the court while we played. While we were waiting for the court, Daddy and Gilbert began talking about their work. They're both dentists and they both do very well financially. It was a peculiar kind of conversation, sort of boasting about what movie stars they had among their patients. And yet at the same time they kept insisting that all their patients were bores and that the best thing is to anesthetize them as quickly as possible so you don't have to talk to them.

I glanced at Lyle, wondering what he was thinking.

We played three sets. We won all three: 7–5, 6–4, 6–3. Daddy and Gilbert, once they saw how good Lyle was, tried to hit all the shots to me, but I was proud of myself. I really held my own, even at net, which is where I usually go to pieces. I didn't overhit. I just tried to play consistently, knowing Lyle would back me up. Once we won the first set, which was pretty close, Daddy began trying to cheat. He always does. He claimed shots

166

were out that were clearly in. Once, when Lyle served an ace, Daddy said, "I hate to say this, Lyle, but I'm afraid that was a wee bit out." I think even Gilbert was a little embarrassed after a while. Then Daddy began going into this thing about his tennis elbow, which he hadn't mentioned when we started. When we took a break after the second set, he said he'd gone for cortisone treatments and they seemed to help, but now it was coming back again.

"Those guys don't know what the hell they're doing," Gilbert said. "Joe Moroz was going from one of them to the other, and all he did was lose his shirt."

Gilbert's girl friend, Nancy, had a kind of far-away expression. It was hard to tell if she'd been following the game or what.

In the third set, when Daddy tried to cheat on another shot Lyle made that was clearly in by about a foot, I finally said, "Daddy, that shot was perfectly good."

"Jo, I know you want to win, but I'm sorry, honey, it was out. Not by much. I'd say about two inches. Wouldn't you say so, Gilbert?"

"I didn't see it that well," Gilbert said.

"It was *in*," I said. "For God's sake, why do you do that?"

"Why do I do *what*?" he said quickly.

"Why do you cheat?"

"What do you mean? What does this have to do

with cheating? Maybe I was wrong. I'm not saying I'm infallible. *I* saw it as out. Do you want to play it over?"

My heart was thumping because I'd just done what I'd sworn not to do, but it must have been the sixth point in two sets he had cheated on. I knew we'd win anyway, but it just infuriated me.

We played the point over, and they won it. "I guess it was out," Daddy couldn't resist saying with a grin.

"Why?"

"Well, that's how you can tell. Whoever wins the replay."

After the match Daddy got very genial. He began praising Lyle's game all over the place. "That's some backhand you have there, Leo."

"His name is Lyle," I said quietly.

"You must have taken a lot of lessons, huh? Did you go to one of these tennis camps ever? Boots and the kids and I are going to try one this summer."

"You told us," I said. God, was I in a bitchy mood!

"No, I never did, my mother taught me," Lyle said.

"Your mother?"

Thank you, Lyle, for having had a mother who taught you to play tennis. I'd love you anyway, I'd sleep with you anyway, but thank you.

"She played in college," Lyle said.

"Does she still play?"

Lyle hesitated for one second. "No, not anymore," he said.

"Say, were you watching his backhand, honey?" Daddy said to me. I knew he was embarrassed, now that we'd won, about the cheating.

"He's terrific," I said.

"You ought to let him give you a few lessons."

I felt devastated. Why a crack like that, about my needing lessons, when I'd been playing my absolute best, had made at least as many points as Lyle? Yet I knew Daddy would never say anything good about my game. We could have won 6–0 all three sets and he just wouldn't have said anything. I knew if he even remembered this day, he'd think that they'd only lost because he and Gilbert were such gentlemen they couldn't really play their best with a woman in the game.

15

Lyle and I went upstairs to shower.

"So, we won," he said gently.

I sighed. I was trembling, my hands were like ice. "Thanks. You were wonderful."

"We'd have won anyway, Jo. They weren't very good."

"I know."

"Just explain to me why it was so crucial that we annihilate them."

"Because I hate him!" I said, my voice quavering. "I hate that whole vile macho thing of male tennis and Gilbert and that dumb girl. I hate it!"

"But they're pathetic. What's there to hate? They're people whose lives are nothing."

"Nothing? He earns over a hundred thousand a year!"

"So what?"

"Okay."

"I just think it's sad because you make yourself so vulnerable by caring."

"No, you're right." I felt a little calmer, listening to Lyle's even, objective assessment.

"Look at how he cheats," Lyle said.

"I know! He *always* does. Always! Did you see Gilbert's face when he called that serve of yours out?" I had yanked all my clothes off, but, although I was sweaty from the game, I felt chilled, if you can be chilled and sweaty at the same time. I sat cross-legged on the floor, my arms wrapped around me, shivering. "It's just—here's this father who supposedly loves tennis, right? And here he is *lucky* enough to have a daughter who happens to excel at the game, who may not be a professional tennis player, but who is damn good for her age."

"Agreed."

"So, why doesn't that give him pleasure? Why doesn't that make him happy? Why doesn't he say, 'Gee, Jody, it's your birthday, you only come up here once a year, by all *means* play with us. Nothing would make me happier. Nothing would make me prouder.' Why doesn't he say that?"

"I gather that's a rhetorical question."

"Only if you don't know the answer."

"Maybe he doesn't like to play with you because you're *too* good. Jesus, Jo, you could beat him hollow at singles! Maybe he's like you—he wants to win."

"But I could've played on his side! Listen, if Eric were one *tenth* as good as me, Daddy would be out of his *head* with joy. He's even offered to buy him the best tennis racket in existence, free lessons, anything. But with me, it's just indifference, contempt. 'How's it going, Jo? Still at it?' "

"Jo, he's a bastard. Okay?"

I sat in silence, gazing at the wall. "You know the fantasy I have? One day Boots is going to come to him and say, 'Sidney, you can take your hundred thousand and you know what you can do with it.' And then she's going to go off and become the first woman on the Supreme Court."

Lyle laughed, "Your mother didn't do too badly and it didn't seem to change him. He'll find another Boots."

"Yeah, I guess. You don't think he'll ever have one terrible moment of confronting his whole rotten life and letting out a piercing scream?"

"I doubt it."

"Darn."

Lyle was lying naked on the bed, gazing at me thoughtfully. "Putting tennis aside, though, how about the fact that he made you?"

"He *made* me?"

"He gave you life."

I contemplated that. "Sure, okay, he gave me life. Only even there—I mean, if it was a thing of one night thinking: I guess I have nothing better to do tonight. I think I'll create a dark-haired tennis-playing neurotic Jewish daughter to let loose in the world. Then, okay. But it *wasn't* that! It was just one lousy roll in the hay. Mom said he was *rotten* in bed—you know: slam, bang, thank you, ma'am. I bet she didn't even have an orgasm! She probably lay there thinking: *This* is what it's all about?"

"So, why did she marry him?"

"Well, she *claims* she was just beginning to discover her own sexuality, and it scared her. She says, 'I wanted to be domesticated.' I guess she was afraid if she got to like sex too much, she'd go wild or something. So maybe his being rotten in bed was *good*, even. I mean, you can't go wild over something that isn't even fun."

"Jo, you'll kill me for saying this, but I feel sorry for your father."

"Why? Save your pity. He doesn't even know what he *is*! If he did, for one *second*—okay."

"That's part of what's pitiable about him."

Suddenly I said, "Lyle, how can I talk to you when you're lying there with an erection?"

"Jo, you have to admit it's a little distracting for *me* to sit here trying to listen to you when you don't have a stitch of clothes on."

174

I laughed maniacally. Talk about mood changes! And the fact was that, for whatever crazy combination of circumstances or feelings, I felt incredibly turned on. I felt like I wanted Lyle to make love to me more than I ever had before. I felt almost ashamed to feel it so strongly. "So, now you get your reward," I said, getting up.

"For what?"

"For beating Daddy and Gilbert."

"How could we *not* have beat them unless we'd played with our eyes closed?"

"Nonetheless . . . now, look, clearly you didn't spend your adolescent years jerking off into the centerfold of *Playboy,* but you must have some special little thing—"

"Why don't we take a shower together?"

I let out a yelp. "My God! Even your fantasies are clean-cut! Lyle, remember, this is your big chance. One day you'll look back on this and say: 'If only I'd said what I *really* wanted.' "

"That's what I really want."

"Okay."

We went into the bathroom and locked the door. Actually I had felt a little uneasy sitting in the guest room with both of us naked and no lock on the door. Sure enough, just as we were about to go into the shower, little feet came padding up outside the bathroom door. I heard Eliza's piercing voice yell, "Jody! Do you know where Lyle is?"

"Lyle? Who's he?"

"Your boyfriend!"

"I think he went for a walk or something."

"Well, Daddy wants to know if he has a tie. Because you have to wear a tie at the club."

"Oh, he brought dozens of ties. Does it have to be white?"

"I don't know. Should I ask him?"

"No, we'll negotiate later."

"Are you coming down soon?"

"Very soon."

Ah, privacy. But peculiarly that didn't distract me a bit from my keyed-up, incredibly horny mood, if anything, the opposite. Lyle really did seem to enjoy the shower. He let me wash him, but mostly he seemed to like washing me. I don't think I've ever gotten so clean before.

When we got out, we wrapped up in this huge blue bath sheet and dried each other off. One thing I've never understood in books is why people make love on the bathroom floor. I mean, I can see it in moments of desperation, with no viable alternative, as was the case now, but to actually *select* a bathroom floor out of various other possibilities always seemed a little strange. I must say, though, that this particular bathroom was very well equipped. Not only was the shower the kind with a glass door where you got all steamy, like in a sauna, but the towels were those thick, blotting kind that you see in magazine ads. Better still, the whole floor was covered with some kind of bath-mat-type stuff, soft and shaggy so it was a little like lying on a grassy turf.

I began kissing Lyle all over. It's funny, but with Lyle, maybe because he always seems so pleased and touched at anything I do for him sexually, I really enjoy doing it even more. I lay there with my face between his legs and tried to do all the things he might have really wanted me to do, but was too shy or inhibited to mention.

Oral sex always makes me think of Grandma. One time we were visiting her in Florida, where she and Grandpa used to go in the winter. She'd read some article in *Newsweek* on a current sex survey where they cited statistics—I forget what they were—on how many American women enjoyed oral sex. Grandma said to Mom, "*You* know all about these things, Elizabeth. What *is* this thing they call oral sex?" I forgot what Mom answered, but later Eric and I used to have a joke that Grandma really knew all about oral sex, that she was one of its foremost practitioners, but that in Yiddish it was called something completely different, so she just hadn't recognized the word.

"Is it okay if we don't go all the way this way?"

"Hmm?"

"I know it's some kind of inhibition, only I—"

"Jo, come here."

"Was that nice? Did you like it?"

He had this dreamy kind of expression. "No, it was lousy. Are you comfortable?" He reached into the bathtub and took out a plastic pillow that was stuck at one end of the tub. "Here, all the comforts of home."

I don't know what it was, doing it in the bathroom, having beaten Daddy and Gilbert at tennis, having just showered together, the way Lyle looked as he entered me, but all of a sudden, right in the middle, I came. I was really surprised. I opened my eyes and said, "Oh!" very loudly. But Lyle was sort of into his thing, muttering something like, "Jo . . . sweetheart," so I don't think he even noticed.

Afterward we lay on our backs, staring up at the ceiling. The whole bathroom, including the ceiling, had blue and yellow elephants dancing in one long endless line.

"That was incredible," Lyle said finally.

"It *was* pretty good, wasn't it?" Then I couldn't restrain myself. I sat up and gleefully shouted, "I came!"

"Huh?" Lyle turned to look at me, puzzled. "What do you mean?"

"I came! I had an orgasm!"

"Don't you always?"

"Never, I never have in my whole life."

178

He looked flabbergasted. "What do you mean, Jo? You *never* had one? How is that possible?"

"What's not possible about it?"

"Well, how come, in the past, when we were just getting to know each other, you were so eager for us to make love?"

"What does *that* have to do with it?"

"Anyway, I thought you—didn't you used to come when we just caressed each other, when I used to lie on top of you even with our clothes on?"

"Yeah, *then* I did. That was what was weird. It seemed like I could do it practically any way *but* during intercourse. Maybe I was just too nervous or something."

"Why didn't you tell me? We could've worked on it. Maybe there was something I could've been doing that I wasn't."

"No, it didn't have anything to do with you. You were doing everything right. And I thought that would make it worse, having you say, 'Is that better, is that worse?' "

"Jo, you're an enigma."

"I am?" I felt really pleased, because everyone is always telling me how straightforward I am.

"What was different this time? We have to figure it out so you always come."

"Oh, I don't care! Look, it happened once, that's enough."

"That's enough for the rest of your life?"

179

"Oh, it would be good to always come," I admitted, "only I'm not sure *what* was different." The trouble was I was afraid maybe it had been just this weird combination of circumstances and I would never be able to come again unless we made love on the guest-bathroom floor after beating Daddy and Gilbert at tennis.

"I think maybe this time you lowered your legs more," Lyle said. You could tell it appealed to his scientific mind, trying to analyze the whole thing.

"I thought I kept them *up* more."

"More in the beginning, but toward the end you lowered them, I think. Also, well, it ought to be the other way around, but I think I did it a little faster than usual."

I shook my head. "Listen, Lyle, it's sweet of you, but I don't want to get too self-conscious about it. I'm afraid then it'll never happen again."

"Oh, no. I think it's like my serve in tennis. One day—I even remember this day—I did something different with the way I tossed up the ball, and ever since then my serve has been a million times better. So even if you don't know what it is, maybe your body did some little thing and it'll remember next time."

"You think so, huh?"

"Absolutely. But I guess what I still don't understand, or I feel sort of badly about is how you could have enjoyed all those other times. I was blithely going along, assuming you were coming all over the place."

"I still enjoyed it."

"I suppose it's hard for a man to understand that, so much of it is a matter of—"

"Lyle, you know, that kind of remark is not good to make to someone like me."

"What kind of remark?"

"About how sex is always so great for men because they never have to think about coming. That really depresses me."

He kissed me. "Jo . . . I didn't mean it that way."

"There're lots of nice things about sex besides coming!" I said.

"No, I can see that. Listen, maybe we ought to—I have the feeling Eliza will be tramping up here in a minute to see what we're up to."

"You think she knows you're here?"

"I have the feeling. She seems to be a sharp-eyed little kid."

"Yeah, she's adorable. Well, she's only my half sister, so I don't have to feel responsible."

Lyle had to get back into his stinky tennis clothes because his regular clothes were downstairs. He went down to put them on, and when he came up again, I was already in the white dress I'd brought along. "See? All white. Think they'll let me in?"

He was in a suit, a light blue one that I'd never seen.

"We look like we're going to the junior prom," I said.

"Jo . . . I love you."

"Don't love me because you gave me my first climax."

"I won't. That has nothing to do with it. That's utterly immaterial. I love you for all the bewildering complexity of your personality . . . and maybe just a little for a couple of other things."

"Like the fact that I play net so well?"

"Exactly."

We were standing there, beaming at each other when Boots peeked in. "Well, don't you look beautiful, Jody! My goodness! Sid says your tennis game turned out very well."

"Yeah, we enjoyed it a lot," I said. "We really did."

16 〰〰〰〰〰〰〰〰〰〰〰〰〰〰〰〰〰〰〰〰〰〰

"This is the breakfast nook," Boots said. "It's really a kind of den, but the real den is downstairs."

She was showing some couple around the house. They had evidently seen the ad Boots and Daddy had placed in the local paper. Lyle and I, having finished breakfast about a half hour earlier, were sitting around reading the paper.

"This is my daughter, Jody," Boots said, smiling brightly. "And this is her friend, Lyle."

"Hi, Lyle, hi, Jody," said the husband.

We smiled simultaneously. I was a little startled at Boots introducing me as her daughter, but I guess any other explanation would have been too elaborate.

"Is the pool a lot of trouble?" the wife said. "I mean, keeping it clean and so on?"

"Oh, no, not a bit. My husband will explain all of that to you as soon as he comes back."

Eliza came out of her room to inspect the visitors. "Are you going to buy our house?" she said.

The wife smiled politely. "We haven't decided yet."

"It's great," Eliza said. "It's a great house. Wanna see my room?"

They didn't have much choice. She dragged them in. "I have my own TV," she yelled. "Nicky doesn't because she's only eight. She has to watch on mine if she wants to. Usually I let her."

"Dear, I think the Moores would like to see the downstairs now," Boots said.

"Did you see the pool?" Eliza said. "Isn't it terrific? We're going to move to a house with a *bigger* pool! *And* a tennis court."

The voices became dimmer as Boots led the couple outside to examine the downstairs den and the pool. I looked at Lyle. "Hi."

"Hi."

The dinner at the club the night before hadn't been as bad as I feared. Maybe it was because I was in a benign mood from our encounter on the bathroom floor. In any case, I let it all kind of drift past me and through me; there were no horrendous moments.

184

Daddy walked in. "Hi kids."

We looked at him. He went over and took a can of beer out of the refrigerator. "Want one, Lyle?"

"No, thanks."

"Is Boots still with that couple?"

"I think she's showing them the pool."

For a moment I thought he was going to join her, but he sat down opposite us, clearly trying to be friendly. "So, where are you applying to college, Lyle? I went to Harvard, I guess Jody told you that."

Sure, the first words out of my mouth were, "I have a father and he went to Harvard." "No, I didn't know that," Lyle said. "Well, my father went to Yale, so I've applied there. And Princeton, Haverford."

"Well, those are good places too," Daddy conceded.

"I suppose I'll go to the place that offers me the biggest scholarship," Lyle said.

"Oh? Money problems?" Daddy looked interested. "Yeah, I guess we all have those, what with the market falling out. But I'll tell you, I have Gilbert to thank that I didn't totally lose my shirt. Gilbert may not *look* like he'd be that sharp, but he is. *Believe* me. He said, 'Sid, get out while the getting is good,' and it's damn lucky I did." He took a swig of beer. "Yale isn't bad," he said again, thoughtfully. "Your team hasn't been doing so well lately. Eric and I like to go up for the Harvard-Yale game every year, you know. I'm hoping he might get in. Of course, his grades aren't too great, but if he can pull himself together . . . And, naturally, having a father that went there can't hurt."

"*And* a mother," I muttered.

"What? Oh, yeah, well, Radcliffe is a little different, but that can't hurt either. Every little bit helps, as they say."

"Jody's applied to Radcliffe," Lyle said. I knew he was seeing all this through my eyes and maybe understanding too keenly how I felt about it all.

"Did you, honey?" He stood up. "Well, guess I better join Boots. She always screws up the explanation of the pool. You've got to present it just right or they start getting nervous about the upkeep. If you think selling a house on today's market is easy, let me tell you. We've run that ad for three months!"

After Daddy had left, Lyle got up and kissed me.

"I didn't say anything," I said.

"What's Boots's real name?"

"Miriam. Any other questions?"

The couple left shortly before noon. Daddy looked a little disgusted.

"*I* thought they seemed interested," Boots said.

"Naw, they won't bite. I could tell. Jesus, the time these people take! They take all morning, tramping through your house and then it's always this bit about let us think it over."

"She really liked it," Boots insisted. "She *loved* my powder room."

"Okay, she loved your powder room. *He's* the one who's buying it, remember that."

"I thought they were buying it together," Boots said in her mild, unemotional voice.

"They're buying it together, but *he's* the one who earns the money, and I can assure you *he* doesn't give a shit about the powder room!"

"In a way," Boots confessed, "I hate to leave this house. It took us nearly two years to get it all fixed up, and now to start all over . . ."

"Honey, relax. We don't even have any offers."

The phone rang, and Boots went to answer it. When she came back, she looked a little flustered. "Sid, could you come here one second?" she said.

She returned about five minutes later. "Jody, um, this is a little embarrassing, but my college roommate, Sheila, just called, and the thing is, she and her husband are passing through tonight and wanted to take us out to dinner."

"Yes?"

"I just wondered if you and Lyle would find it that interesting. Would you mind terribly if you just got a bite to eat in town? There are some *really* good places, and I could lend you my car."

Basically I was almost relieved. "That sounds fine, we'd be glad to."

Eliza came out of her room. "Well, I'm all packed," she said cheerfully.

"Are you leaving home?" I said.

"I have a sleep-over date. Actually, it's a slumber party."

"What's the difference?"

"Well, a sleep-over date is just *one* person. A slumber party is where you invite several people." She looked over at Nicky who was sitting in a corner, drawing. "I bet you'll get Mrs. Weisgall again. Ugh!"

"Eliza, stop that this minute!" Boots said. "Mrs. Weisgall is a very nice person."

"She is not. She doesn't even know how to *play* anything! She just sits there. Boy, I'm glad I'm missing her." She looked at me again. "I have sleep-over dates pretty often. Sometimes *my* friends come *here*. *She* doesn't have that many," she said in a loud whisper.

"Maybe she doesn't want them," I suggested.

"No, it's just nobody invites her. Well, she can't help it, I guess. Do you want to see what I'm bringing? I bring my own sleeping bag. It's a Snoopy one. My pajamas match. I have an electric toothbrush too. Wanna see it?"

"Okay." I sat while Eliza opened up her overnight bag and dumped the contents on the floor.

"Mrs. Krebs," Lyle said. "I was wondering if you'd mind if Jody and I took Nicky out to eat with us. Then you wouldn't have to bother about a baby-sitter."

"Oh, goodness," Boots said. "You don't have to do *that*."

"We'd like to. Maybe she'd like to see a movie with us."

Boots looked at Nicky. "That seems like so much trouble," she said.

"No, we want to," Lyle and I said together.

"Would *you* like to, Nicky?" Boots said.

"Yes," Nicky breathed almost inaudibly.

"Well, I suppose I *could* call Mrs. Weisgall and tell her. You're *sure* it's not too much trouble?"

Eliza looked indignant. "That's not *fair!*" she said. "I wouldn't have planned a sleep-over if I knew I could've gone out to eat *and* a movie."

"Dear, please, let's not complicate things. You're due at Susan's in an hour."

"Boy, she gets all the breaks around here," Eliza grumbled. "Just because she's little!"

"That was really nice of you," I later said to Lyle as we got ready to go out.

"She seemed to be sitting there so mournfully."

"She always does. Jesus, I don't think I could stand it, having children," I said suddenly.

"Why?"

"Well, to go through all that a second time, all

that pain. Maybe with a boy I could take it, but with a girl I think it would be too much."

We ate at a hamburger place and then took Nicky to a Woody Allen movie. She didn't talk much, even during the dinner, just chewed her way resolutely through her french fries. At the end of the meal she said to Lyle, "Are you named after that crocodile?"

"What crocodile?"

"The one in that book. The one called *Lyle, Lyle, Crocodile?*"

He shook his head.

"I just thought you might've been," she said. Then she looked up and smiled. "This was a really good meal. Thank you."

"Thank you for coming with us," Lyle said.

In the movie Nicky sat between us, munching through the contents of a giant bag of popcorn. I'm not sure she understood all of the movie, but she sat solemnly staring at the screen with her big brown eyes, mesmerized. Lyle put his arm around her seat and touched my shoulder just lightly.

When we got out, it was past nine.

"I guess I shouldn't mention this," Nicky said, "but I should have been in bed an hour ago."

"We won't tell," Lyle said.

The minute we got home, she raced into her room, got into her pajamas and into bed.

"I feel hungry again," Lyle confessed. "Let's see what they have in the refrigerator."

He decided on a slice of apple pie and a glass of milk. I sat at the table, watching him. I didn't feel hungry. I just had some juice. It reminded me of a scene from one of those 1940s movies, the healthy blond boy in the spotless white kitchen eating his pie with honest enjoyment. "You realize," I said, "that you've wrecked this child's life."

"In what way?"

"Thirty years from now, four divorces later, she's going to be lying on some analyst's couch, moaning: 'Once, doctor, once when I was eight, I met this perfect man. He was handsome, he was kind, he bought me buttered popcorn.'"

"I think Eliza is more likely to be the one who'll end up on an analyst's couch."

"One *wants* to think that."

"Nicky'll be okay. She'll look up at some guy with those big brown eyes and he'll get lost."

"You're so romantic. Is that going to be her salvation?"

"Not her salvation, maybe." He had finished his pie and milk. "So?" he said.

I regarded him gravely. "I'm afraid there's only one option left to us."

"Namely?"

"To go upstairs and screw ourselves into a state of insensibility."

"Well, if that's the *only* option."

Just as we got into bed, Lyle said, "I think the problem is we may not have been having enough foreplay."

"What do you mean. We've had *plenty* of foreplay."

"You do things to me, but you never let me do much to you."

I sighed. "This is what I was afraid of," I said.

"What is?"

"That if I told you I don't always come, we'd get into a big analysis and that would take all the fun out of it."

"Don't worry about that."

"I do. I can't help it."

"Would you rather just do it and forget all that? That's fine with me."

"Kind of . . . is that okay?"

"Sure." But right in the middle he said, "Why don't you try lowering your legs just a little, Jo."

"Lyle! You promised!"

"No, I just meant—I thought it might . . . am I going too fast?"

I couldn't help laughing. "You're doing fine."

"Are you at all close?"

"Lyle, *please!*"

After he had his climax, he looked down at me. "So?"

"Uh-uh."

"Why don't I stay in you for a little longer?"

"But that won't be any fun for you. It'll be a drag."

"No, it won't."

Maybe because the pressure was off, because I'd already failed, as it were, I came about two minutes later. Lyle was really pleased. "I told you, Jo."

"*I* know. It's all in the way you toss the ball, right?"

It was a little peculiar, having things reversed so totally. Here I'd spent five months convincing him sex was a good thing and now I was the one who was being reassured and told to relax and enjoy it. I wasn't sure how I felt about that. It seemed to put me in Lyle's power in some way. Even though I knew he wasn't the kind who would misuse that power, it made me uneasy.

"Thank you for coming," I said after a minute. "I mean, thank you for coming with me here to Daddy and Boots's. I really appreciate it."

"I wish you could have met *my* parents. I feel like, well, I *have* learned something about you from meeting your father, something you might not have been able to describe, and, well, maybe you'd have learned something about me from meeting mine."

"I've met Renee and Wesley."

"It's not the same. I think you'd have liked them, Jo."

193

"Wouldn't they have thought I was kind of weird?"

"No. Mother might have been taken aback at first, but when she saw what a good person you were, you'd have won her over."

"Lyle, I'm not a 'good person.' Don't say that."

"You are. You're a very good, kindhearted person."

Mom always says that men can't help having illusions about women and that you'd go crazy trying to make them give them up. So if Lyle really and truly wants to think of me as a "good" person, I suppose it doesn't hurt to let him. It's not that I think I'm a *bad* person, even, it's more that I wouldn't have thought, say, if I were describing myself to someone who'd never met me, to list "goodness" as one of my major attributes.

After Lyle went downstairs to sleep in the guest room, I began thinking how I really was glad I had brought him to Daddy's. Not so much to point the finger and say: Look! See why I'm the way I am? Elliott claims that some people are what he calls "grievance collectors." They'd rather spend their whole life saying: "What a wreck I am, but I can't help it because my father or mother was such a beast" than try to really change. I don't want to be that kind of person. But at the same time having someone, outside my own family, someone objective but still caring, see the thing, maybe even see

194

me acting crazily about it, was helpful. It was like seeing it from a slight distance.

I guess I should thank Daddy and Boots for the best eighteenth birthday present of all—finally having an orgasm—but I think maybe Lyle should get more of the credit for that.

17

The second week of April I was sick for most of the week. Lyle says he thinks Linus Pauling's thing about vitamin C is a canard and that when you get a cold, there isn't much you can do but go to bed and sleep. I disagree. Maybe it is psychological, but I do find that taking several giant vitamin C capsules seems to make a difference.

I hadn't been sick for that long—several days— in more than two years. It was a little odd at first, since everyone was out, Eric at school and Mom and Elliott working. It's pretty rare for me to have the house absolutely to myself that way. Unfortunately I slept most of the first day and almost all of the second, so I couldn't take much advantage of it.

The third day, when I was debating if I should go in for half a day of school, the letters came from Cornell and Swarthmore. I got into both of them! Cornell I had applied to more as security, but I was pretty nervous about Swarthmore. Mr. Imbrie, my science teacher, went to Swarthmore—he was the one who got me the job at Sloan-Kettering over the summer. When I was applying to colleges this past fall, he said that he thought Swarthmore would be a good place for me, that their biochemistry department was really excellent and that the general atmosphere was sort of low keyed, something like Talbot.

When Mom got home, I told her, but she didn't react much. She just said, "Oh, terrific, Jo. Did you hear from Radcliffe yet?"

Of course sometimes Mom comes home and is still kind of absorbed in her work. It's like you tell her something but you know that even though she hears you, she's not really paying full attention. Sometimes, about a week later, she'll suddenly react, as though it's finally had time to sift down. That was how I took her reaction anyway, so I didn't mind that much. The next day I found out the real reason.

I get home late Thursdays, almost at supper time. It's also the night Elliott leads this group-therapy thing from eight to eleven, so he often doesn't come home for dinner. It's usually just me,

Mom, and Eric. The second I opened the door, Mom came bounding out of the kitchen, a huge sheepish smile on her face. "Jo, don't kill me," were her first words.

"Why should I?"

She pulled this letter out from behind her back. "This came today. I'm sorry, hon. I couldn't help myself. I opened it." I could see from the stationery it was the letter from Radcliffe. Just as I was reaching for it, she let out this shriek and said, "You got in! You got in!" and she began hugging me and acting like we'd just inherited a million dollars.

I think I mentioned Mom went to Radcliffe. In fact, when I had my interview there in the fall, she went up with me and showed me around, and we looked at the dorm she used to stay in. But it was all kind of civilized and calm. Mom has never been one of those people who carries on about college days and how they were so great. If anything, I'd gotten somewhat the opposite impression. Anyway, I was a little amazed at her going so hog-wild about my getting in.

Frankly, I didn't think I would. My school, Talbot, isn't like the prep school Daddy went to where they automatically shovel such and such many people into Yale or Harvard or whatever. I'd say most of the kids in Talbot end up more at places like Antioch or Brandeis or the University of Wisconsin. Maybe a dozen or so have made it into Radcliffe over the past decade, but they're few and far between. Even Mrs. Weber, the college advisor, told me that even though my grades were good and my college boards were good, she still didn't think I should count on Radcliffe as a very likely possibility. Plus, there's the thing they always say about there being nine million bright New York Jewish girls, so you have that to worry about as well.

"Listen, I called Daddy, Jo. I hope you don't mind. He was so excited! He wanted to zoom right into the city and take you out to dinner tonight. I told him you'd just been sick and he said how about the weekend? What do you think? Would Saturday be good? Let's let him drag us all to some fancy-shmancy place if he feels like it. What the heck."

I was standing there, looking at the letter, which was phrased as such letters always are. "Uh . . . let me think about it," I said. I felt kind of zonked from my cold, as well as from the extremity of her reaction. I went into my room, fell on my bed, and sacked out for nearly an hour.

At supper Mom kept babbling on to Eric about my getting into Radcliffe and it seemed every three seconds the phone would ring and she would leap up to spread the news over the entire Upper West Side and its environs. Finally, when she was in the kitchen putting the dishes in the dishwasher and

Eric had disappeared into his room, I screwed up my courage and said, "Mom?"

"Yeah?" She was trying to wedge a large orange soup plate in beside a big tin pot, without too much success.

"The thing is . . . about this thing with Radcliffe, I guess I should have made it clear that Swarthmore was my first choice. That's where I think I'll go."

Mom straightened up and stared at me. "What? What are you talking about?"

I took a deep breath. "Well, it's just Mr. Imbrie says their science department is really good and I think—"

"Mr. Imbrie! Who the hell is Mr. Imbrie?"

"Mom, come on. You've met him dozens of times. He got me the job at Sloan-Kettering. He's that sort of short man with a—"

"Jody, I don't *believe* this! Who the hell cares what Mr. *Imbrie* thinks! Radcliffe doesn't have a good science department?"

"It's not that they *don't*, it's just—"

"They have the best department in the country!" she yelled.

Big expert, my mother, who wouldn't know a test tube from a Bunsen burner. "Well, I'm going to Swarthmore," I said, "and if you stopped and listened for one second to what *I* want to do, you would have known that six months ago."

"You're going to stand there and tell me that you're turning down the finest educational institution in the country to go to *Swarthmore?*"

Jesus, you'd think I was going to some really crummy, hick place off in the backwoods of Louisiana. "Yeah, that's what I'm saying," I said.

"Okay, well go call your father and tell him that! Go call him!"

That was a wonderful ironical touch, as though she's ever given a damn what Daddy thinks about anything. "Okay, I will," I said, starting to reach for the phone.

She grabbed my hand away. "No! Listen, Jo, this is some crazy kind of—think it over, will you? Promise me you won't write any of them for a week."

"You're supposed to let them know right away."

"Take a week. That's all I ask. Just so you have time to really sit down and think it over."

"I *have* thought it over," I said, which was true. "I've thought it over a lot. I mean, I can wait a week if you want, but it won't change anything."

She stood there with a really angry expression on her face. "God, I thought you got over all this rebellious shit years ago!"

I stomped into my room and shut the door without another word. That there is inconsistency in the world I grant. That there is hypocrisy I grant too. But here is this mother who for *years* has been ranting and raving about how important it is to follow your own lights, not to give in to convention, to group pressure. The main thing, so this mother said, is to wend your lonely and sometimes difficult way, doing what strikes you as the right thing at the time, even if no one agrees with you. This same mother, with one tiny shred of paper grasped in her clammy little hand, completely and utterly abandons everything she believes in! One thing I will never be when I grow up is a mother. I wish you could have children and somehow not be a mother, because it's clear there is something about being one that addles your brain.

I did call Daddy later in the evening. Of course, he was excited too, but I was somewhat less surprised by that. "I'm so proud of you, honey," was his theme song. "You made it."

What did I make? Make what? But I decided not to even get into anything with him about my probably not going there. I let him rant on about how he was going to take me up there this spring and show me this and do this and do that. I guess this should have been the high point of my life. Here was Daddy finally coming right out and saying, "Jody, I'm proud of you." Those were the words I presumably had been waiting all these eons to hear, but somehow, in this context, they didn't seem all that important or meaningful.

Lyle got into all the places he applied to, but

Haverford is the only one that offered him a more or less full scholarship, so he's going there. "We'll be right near each other," he said. He knew I was planning to go to Swarthmore.

"Yeah, that'll be great," I said. I felt too limp to get excited, even about that.

It wasn't till I hung up that I thought how glad I was that I really and truly had made the decision to go to Swarthmore way before I knew where Lyle was going. Because at least my conscience would be completely clear when Mom, as I knew she would, said discreetly, at dinner the next night, "Where's Lyle going?"

"Haverford. He got a full scholarship." I couldn't help being proud.

"That'll be convenient," she said dryly.

"For whom?"

"Well, you'll be right next to each other. I guess that was part of the grand plan."

"No, it was *not* part of the grand plan," I said. "I didn't even find out till yesterday where he was going. He's only going there because they offered him the best deal. If Princeton or Yale had, he'd have gone there."

But it didn't really matter. I could tell Mom had made up her mind that going to Swarthmore was my big act of rebellion, done solely and exclusively to hurt her feelings or get her goat. If I'd brought Mr. Imbrie and Mrs. Weber and a hundred witnesses in to argue with her, it wouldn't have done a bit of good.

Elliott was nice about it. One evening when Mom had just gone into the bedroom, he looked up at me—he was reading in the leather chair—and said with a little smile, "*I* went to City College."

"You were smart," I said, smiling back.

"I was poor." He lowered his voice. "Don't worry, Jo. She'll calm down."

I thought that was really sweet of him. Meanwhile I tried to get Philip on the phone, but according to his answering service, he was away on some kind of trip. If anyone would understand, I thought, it would be Philip. I kept thinking back on how when I'd told Mom Philip had turned down the job at Harvard, she'd said something like, "Great, it's his decision" and how she was now in her "mellow phase." I guess that only applies to ex-husbands, not to daughters.

At the end of one week I went to Mom and told her I'd thought it over and had decided, for all the reasons that were, in fact, my real reasons, that I'd be happier at Swarthmore. I spoke in this sort of toneless quick voice, as though I were reciting a poem.

She stood and listened, arms folded across her chest. At the end she said, "Okay, Jo."

There are lots of things a person can mean by something as simple as "Okay." Mom could have meant, "Okay, Jo. I realize that, since you've attained the age of eighteen, I can no longer treat you like a child, because you aren't one any longer. I realize you are smart enough and mature enough to make intelligent decisions on your own, and I'm willing to abide by those decisions." She could also have meant, "Okay, Jo. You're going to be the same rebellious little brat you've been ever since you saw the light of day, and if you want to wreck your life and throw away all your opportunities, it's your funeral." I would say Mom's "Okay" fell somewhere between those two extremes, maybe farther from the first than I'd have liked, but at least not totally at the other.

That Thursday, Elliott's night away, Rifka Rabinowitz came over for dinner. Since my room is near the kitchen and my door was open, it wasn't exactly eavesdropping to listen to the conversation between her and Mom, which took place when they were having drinks. I know Mom knew I was in there because she passed by on the way to the pantry hall to get something and saw me sitting on the floor. But when she and Rifka get going, a hoard of cameras from CBS could circle around them and they'd probably keep right on going, oblivious.

Rifka started saying, "Let me get this straight. You have this daughter. She's not on drugs, she's not pregnant, she's not into some meshugana religious thing. Your big problem is that she wants to go to Swarthmore and not Radcliffe? Listen, just don't ask me for sympathy, okay, Beth? I mean, we've been friends for years, but there are, like, limits."

"Okay, okay," Mom said. "Maybe I was just being nostalgic."

"About what? You *hated* the place."

"I did? What do you mean?"

"You were *miserable!* You want me to go home and get all those letters you wrote me your freshman year about how you wanted to transfer to City College so you could be with that guy—what's his name—that funny little guy, Artie something?"

"Artie Landeck!" Mom exclaimed. "Would you believe I'd completely forgotten that whole thing?"

"Tell that to your Freudian friend."

"But anyway, that was just the first year or so. After that it got better, I *think*." She sounded a little less certain.

"Sure," Rifka said. "Then you met Super Sensational Sidney, and that made up for it all."

There was a slight silence. Mom evidently decided to let that one pass. Then she said, "This is awful, but you know what was also in the back of my mind? Do you remember Gloria Del Joio?"

"Should I?"

"She was that beautiful—or not so much beautiful as that fantastically *poised* girl who lived in the dorm with me. You met her when you came up to visit that time."

"The one with red hair?"

"Right. Well, I happen to know she has a daughter Jody's age because I ran into her one day, and I guess I kept thinking: Maybe *her* daughter would be in some kind of awful trouble, maybe, like you said, pregnant, on drugs, into some religious thing—"

"Maybe all three if you're really lucky," Rifka said.

"And then one day she would open her alumni bulletin and read: Elizabeth Epstein's daughter graduated summa cum laude."

"So, Elizabeth Epstein's daughter will graduate summa cum laude from Swarthmore."

"But Gloria Del Joio won't know about it because she won't read about it in the alumni bulletin."

Rifka said, "Beth, I'm going to do you a favor and forget this entire conversation. It never happened, okay? Hey, what *is* this stuff I've been drinking? I've been so entranced by your horrible story, I didn't even notice. I *thought* I asked for sherry."

"This is *like* sherry," Mom said. "It's something Elliott likes called Punt e Mes."

"So, how's it going with him? Has he got you shrunk down to size yet?"

I wasn't that interested in hearing them discuss

Elliott and then probably pass on to Rifka's husband, Karl, so I got up and quietly closed my door. The latch on my door always sticks and you have to kind of pry it out with a bent paper clip, which I usually keep a supply of in my desk drawer.

Basically I felt I owed a debt of thanks to Rifka, unusual as that seemed, for trying to make Mom take the whole thing in a less tragic light. As for my graduating summa cum laude, that remains to be seen. At the moment I think I'll just settle for getting through the next four years.

18

I did something stupid.

I don't know if it makes it worse that it was something I had thought might happen. I know in murder cases if it's premeditated, the judge considers that worse because it means the person actually sat down and planned the whole thing. If he was just carried away or momentarily insane, I believe that makes the sentence lighter. Not that I've committed a crime in the sense that I'm likely to be put in jail. But the same judgment may apply, in a moral sense.

Ms. Sirota used to say she felt I had too analytical a mind. On my papers she would say, "Describe first, then analyze." I guess that is a good policy when it comes to creative writing, but I think it has some drawbacks. I mean, there are some days when you really do go around noticing all the little details she loves so much. Your senses are keyed up, as it were. Other times you just don't. But I'll try my best anyway to remember how it went.

On May 14th each year our school has this event called Alumni Day. It goes on all day. Not all the alumni come back. I'd say the ones that do the most are the ones who graduated the year before or maybe two or three years before. After that they seem to kind of lose interest. I can understand coming back. I mean, there you are, finally in college, maybe feeling sort of lost in the crowd and you go back to this place that is so small that everyone knows you, all the teachers remember you and everyone crowds around asking you how it's been. It could be kind of an ego trip, if you were in the mood for that kind of thing.

The point of it, for the juniors anyway, is for the alumni to tell everyone how they think that particular college is and whether they think they were well prepared for their courses and stuff like that. So maybe people who are trying to decide between two places might be helped in making up their mind.

I had the feeling Whitney might be one of the ones to come back. As I said, he was kind of a big deal at Talbot and, well, he's the type who would want to go around greeting people and that kind of thing, not out of vanity but because he's rather gregarious in that way.

So when I got to school that morning, I wasn't really surprised to see him standing in the front hall, surrounded by admiring kids. He looked good. He was wearing a dark blue turtleneck and blue corduroy slacks. Whitney dresses pretty well, not overly sharply, but his clothes fit him and he has a good body, which I have to admit I couldn't help noticing once again. I hadn't made up my mind if I should go over and say hello when he saw me and waved. Then he left the group of kids and came over.

"Hi, Jo. You're looking pretty good."

"So are you."

We grinned at each other, somewhat awkwardly. I guess there are two things that can happen if you see someone you used to love or like after a year or so has gone by. Either they strike you as not half as good or nice or interesting as you remembered or they still seem just as attractive. I suppose the first possibility is both good and bad. Bad in that you think: How could I have had such bad taste? Good in that it's kind of a relief to find that the power someone had over you, which of course wasn't just that they were so great but that you reacted to them in a certain way, is gone. I would say my reaction to Whitney was more the second one. I didn't feel in love with him, not in the least, but it wasn't at all hard for me to remember why I had been. Maybe seeing him in the school setting added to that. It made it seem like not that much time had passed. If I'd just run into him on the street, it might've been different.

During the day we kept meeting and exchanging a few words about this or that. Finally at one point in the afternoon he asked if I felt like going to the Museum of Modern Art with him after school to see a show. Whitney, by the way, is at Harvard. That *isn't* why I turned down the Radcliffe thing. I don't feel in any sense that it was even a mild factor in my decision. Actually, he had wanted to go to an art school in California, but his mother hit the ceiling. When it comes to things like that, important things, he always listens to her. He says he feels she really did have to work hard to send him to private school, and he doesn't get any kind of kick out of flouting her, as Mom claims I do with her.

I like going to museums with Whitney. He notices things I never would, not just the paintings, but the way people look, the shapes of things. He has a very visual mind, unlike me. Whenever I wore a new dress or a new anything, Whitney would notice it. For boys that's sort of unusual. Combinations of colors really get him. Like I had this string of amber beads that I used to wear with a dark red sweater, and he would always admire it. I don't think Lyle would notice something I wore, unless it was conventionally "pretty"; even then it might not strike him. I think he's more like me in that respect.

Strolling through the museum talking was nice. I gathered Whitney had a pretty good year. He said he found some of the courses much easier than he'd expected, compared to Talbot. I told him I was going to Swarthmore. I didn't mention having gotten into Radcliffe, because I didn't feel like going through that whole saga all over again.

So . . . to make a long story short, we ended up—after dinner at this Chinese restaurant—at his apartment. Whitney lives with his mother and two older brothers, but his mother is a night nurse and is never there after eight. His brothers seem to keep irregular hours also. At least the few times I was there—they live at 106th Street and West End Avenue—they were rarely around.

At that point, going there on the subway, it was more or less understood that we were going to sleep together. Certainly I wouldn't have gone otherwise; I knew that was what he had in mind. I wish I could think of some really *convincing* reason for sleeping with Whitney. Like if I had been, for whatever reason, enormously horny or hadn't slept with Lyle for a week or something, or even if I'd just been carried away by passion. But I wasn't. That's what I mean by the premeditated thing. True, I wouldn't have done it if I hadn't felt attracted to him, but it wasn't an overwhelming urge that I just couldn't control.

Really, I know why I did it, and I'm not too proud of my reasons. I did it because I knew I'd been looking about a hundred times better this year than I did last year when I'd gone with Whitney. I'd lost about ten pounds, and my figure had kind of settled into the right places. More than that, this particular morning, looking at myself in the mirror, I knew it was one of my good days. Taken all in all, for me, I felt at my peak. I wanted to show Whitney all of me, show him how I'd improved. And, sad to say, I wanted to show him I could now come when we made love, that I was on my way to being a liberated woman, all that junk.

Whitney is good in bed. He always was, but this time I felt I was too, and that did add a certain something. Still, when it was over, I felt basically ashamed, like it had been a dumb, unnecessary thing to do. Whitney said, "You're in good shape, Jo. You seem to have changed a little over the year." He didn't ask if I was going with anyone. Whitney never would. He's kind of cool that way. And I didn't ask him either. Not that I'm basically cool, but there didn't seem any point, given the circumstances.

When we parted, it was an amiable, see-you-around kind of parting. If Whitney called and wanted to see me again, I might see him, but I know I wouldn't sleep with him. It really was just to prove something to myself that I did it. Doing it another time wouldn't add to that.

I felt guilty though, mainly in relation to Lyle. Whether he knew or not, it didn't seem like a wise thing to have done, especially in view of his declared opinion that I'm such a "good" person. Lyle's definition of "goodness" may be somewhat personal and idiosyncratic, but I doubt it would encompass screwing a former boyfriend. I may be wrong, but I doubt it.

The following night, which was a Saturday, I'd agreed to go up to Lyle's sister's apartment and baby-sit with him. I'd become kind of fond of the place, even of the fold-out couch on which we had passed so many pleasant hours both before and after Lyle sacrificed his virginity to me. It was almost a ritual by now—feeding Kitty, then making love in the hours before midnight. Midnight was when Wesley and Renee usually came home. They were predictable enough in their comings and goings so we could be predictable in ours, as it were.

Just before I was ready to set out, Lyle called. "Jo, listen, I just wanted to mention . . . if Renee seems a little upset, don't let it bother you. She's pregnant and, well, it was somewhat unexpected."

"Why is that such a disaster?"

"Well, Kitty's not even a year. She really believes

kids should be three or four years apart so they get enough attention from their mother."

It still didn't strike me as such a disaster, but to each his own—or her own, I guess I should say.

Whenever I baby-sit with Lyle, I arrive early and have coffee and dessert with him, Wesley, and Renee. That's become part of the ritual too. I've never completely gotten over the feeling that they are judging me. I feel it more with Renee than with Wesley. It may just be that since Lyle's mother isn't around, she feels that as older sister she has to step into that role and make sure no one will do any harm to her baby brother. I suspect she knows we're sleeping together.

I was glad Lyle had told me about Renee's "condition" because she was even more jittery than usual over dessert. At one point she went into the kitchen, and there was a loud crash. She'd just dropped a coffee cup on the floor and immediately burst into tears.

We all went in to try to be of some help. Lyle got a broom and began sweeping up the pieces of the cup. Wesley patted her on the shoulder. I stood by, not doing much, trying to look sympathetic.

"Jody, I guess Lyle has told you my . . . news. Not that that's an excuse for this kind of behavior."

"Rennie, go sit down," Wesley said. "Lyle and I can clean up the dishes."

Renee and I went in and sat down at the dining-room table, facing each other. There was a long silence.

"Have you, uh, thought of an abortion?" I said finally.

She stared at me like I'd just asked if she had thought of jumping off the George Washington Bridge. "I'm married," she said.

"Lots of married people get them," I said. "I think I read that it's mostly married women who—"

"Well, I don't believe in that," she said softly.

"How come?" I was really curious.

"*How come?*" Her voice was trembling. "In what way is that different from murder?"

"I guess I never understood in what way it was *like* murder."

It's interesting how, in about three seconds, a conversation can escalate from being a fairly mild, detached, abstract discussion to a high-charged, intense confrontation. Renee was glaring at me across the table, as though I was responsible not only for her present plight but for all the world's ills as well. I suppose it bugged me partly because I always sense in her a slightly self-righteous, I-know-what-the-Truth-is-and-will-deliver-it-to-others attitude. And behind that a feeling of: Who is this Jewish atheist kid who has seduced my poor innocent baby brother? And behind that my own feeling of guilt about Whitney, which flickered back and forth, like some neon light on the blink, disturbing my sense of focus.

More tentatively I said, "I guess it's just that my brother and I are sixteen months apart, and my mother always said how much work it was, for her, I mean."

"And I suppose she now wishes she had scraped your brother down a drain somewhere?"

I admit there are times when I kind of wish Eric could be scraped down the drain, but that's another story. "I don't think she feels that exactly."

At this point Wesley and Lyle joined us. Renee looked at them and then back at me. "I'm sorry," she said breathlessly. "You'll have to excuse me, but these kinds of attitudes—I just can't—" And she rushed from the room, leaving the three of us together.

About one minute later Wesley ran in after her, to comfort her, I guess. That left Lyle and me. I looked at him and smiled wryly. What I meant by the smile was something like: She certainly does seem a little high-strung, now that you mention it. I expected he'd smile back, but instead he just looked at me with a grim, tight-mouthed expression, his eyes completely cold.

That really did me in. It was bad enough having his sister turn on me, but to have Lyle join in was even worse. Anyway, was it *my* fault that Renee had gotten herself pregnant or that she was so freaked out at the mere mention of the word *abortion?*

We went into the living room. Lyle picked up a book, I picked up a magazine, and we waited. I wondered if they were going to go out after all. Then, after about fifteen minutes, Renee and Wesley emerged from the bedroom. Renee's eyes were red. She had her own version of Lyle's tight-around-the-mouth expression. They edged out the door, mumbling something about they'd be home not too late.

After they'd been gone a minute or two, I looked up at Lyle, hoping his expression might have changed for the better. It hadn't. In fact, the first words out of his mouth were, "You know, Jo, for someone who prides herself on her sensitivity, you can be pretty damn insensitive!"

I didn't much like the way that sounded. I mean, I don't think I'm someone who *prides* herself on her sensitivity. I don't think I'm *insensitive* exactly, but that made me sound like the Princess and the Pea or something. "Look, what did I do?" I said. "Could you tell me? I sat there maybe three minutes and asked in a perfectly calm way if she'd considered an abortion. Why is that so bloody insensitive?"

"Because I called you up especially to let you know how nervous she was about the whole topic. Why bring it up at all?"

"What *should* I have brought up? The weather?"

"Sure! Anything! I'm out of the room three seconds and you've got to leap on your women's-lib soapbox and launch into a big lecture on the advantages of abortion to someone you know is Catholic."

"I didn't know she was a *religious* Catholic."

"I told you they go to church every Sunday."

"But that could be just for form or anything! Anyhow, lots of *Catholics* have abortions. I know I've read that somewhere. Lyle, listen, I wanted to be helpful. I really, truly did. It seems like it misfired, but you have to admit your sister is a little—"

"It just wasn't *smart,* Jo. Renee has this image of you already as—"

"She does? What kind of image?" I was curious, but uneasy.

"All right, you won't like this, but she does, I think, know we have sex, and that strikes her as perhaps—"

"*She* never does it, huh? How'd she get pregnant? Did the Holy Ghost swoop down for a Midnight Special?"

"She considers the fact that she's married makes a difference."

"Lyle, look, I'm not judging *her* behavior, which happens to strike me as slightly weird, no matter *what* religious group she belongs to. What I would like to know is, who gave *her* the right to judge *me?*"

Lyle's expression softened. "No one." He sighed.

"Look, let's forget it. What's done is done. Let's sit on the couch."

"Sitting on the couch" usually is a prelude to our making love, but frankly, I wasn't in the world's sexiest mood. I've heard that certain people love to fight just for the fun of making up, but maybe I feel too hurt and roiled up after a fight, especially one like this, to instantly convert that emotion into some libidinous form. At the same time I wanted to make things right between us again, so I moved over and leaned against him and let him take me in his arms.

It's interesting that Mr. Meleo gave us this big lecture in Sex Ed. a few weeks ago about The Right To Say No. He claimed that women and girls, especially today, feel they somehow have to agree to sex, now that they can no longer claim they're afraid of getting pregnant, and that's bad. He said no one, even if they're married, should agree to sex if they don't feel like it. I thought that was a good point, and probably this was an excellent moment to put it into practice. Only I didn't.

Partly it was that it seemed funny, after having given Lyle this big pitch for all those months about how he'd love intercourse if he tried it, to have *me* be the one to say: Sorry, I'm not in the mood. Before, it seemed like I was *always* in the mood, maybe out of the challenge aspect of the thing, maybe because after several hours of making out

223

you usually *are* in the mood. But now I didn't
feel that much like leaping right into doing it, especially with Renee's image of me as this "loose
woman" in the back of my mind. I would have
liked to feel loose, but instead I felt as tight as a
coiled spring.

Another factor in my not having the courage to
say no was having slept with Whitney the day before. I didn't want Lyle to suspect that I'd already
"had mine," as it were, and therefore didn't need to
do it again. For all these reasons, all lousy, about
half an hour later we were on the couch locked into
the traditional position, doing our thing.

Only right in the middle Lyle said, "Jo, I get the
feeling your heart isn't in this somehow."

Lyle has become more sensitive to things like
that. Before, he couldn't even tell if I came or not.
Now, though I'd been trying to react with more enthusiasm than I really felt, obviously some reluctance had manifested itself. "Well, it's not, really," I
said slowly. "But why don't you go on anyway? I
don't mind."

"No, that doesn't sound too appealing," he said.
He withdrew.

We lay side-by-side. I felt horribly guilty at having committed the cardinal sin of having gotten him
aroused and not going through with it, even if that
had been his decision. His penis looked sort of

plaintive lying there, as though wondering: What happened? What did I do wrong?

"It's okay," Lyle said, stroking my back. "You don't have to always be in the mood."

"Maybe later in the evening," I said hopefully.

"Sure . . ." He was looking at me with his serious long-lashed green eyes. "Was it just tonight and the thing with Renee that rattled you?"

I shook my head.

"Are you still worried about turning down Radcliffe?"

"Well, I guess I still feel Mom hasn't exactly accepted my decision. She says she has, but deep down she hasn't."

"It's crazy," Lyle said. "I really wouldn't have expected that of your mother. Anyhow, Swarthmore's got just as good a reputation."

"I know! It's weird! Whitney says the courses at Harvard aren't even that great! He says the ones at Talbot were much harder." About midway through the sentence I heard what I was saying, but my voice continued going, somewhat out of inertia. I hoped Lyle might not have noticed.

He had, however. "When did you see Whitney?" he said.

"There was this Alumni Day at school. He came back for it."

There was what could only be described as a tense silence.

"You slept with him, right?" Lyle said.

Should I have lied? I definitely would never have brought it up on my own, never. Elliott might say my even mentioning Whitney was a Freudian slip, that some part of me felt guilty and wanted Lyle to know. I don't know. In any case, with Lyle looking right at me, I somehow couldn't lie. "Yeah, I did," I said softly.

The expression on his face scared me. It was a version of the one before, but much more angry looking. "Damn it, Jo! Why do you *do* things like that?"

"I don't do 'things' like that," I burst out defensively. "I just did it this once."

"Is that what our relationship means to you? You see some old boyfriend and three seconds later you're in the sack with him?"

"Lyle, I admit it was stupid, okay?"

"No, it's *not* okay. What happened? Were you so carried away by passion you couldn't resist his entreaties?"

I shook my head. "I suppose it was to prove something."

"What?"

"I don't know. Look, maybe it was a hostile thing to do—to you. Only I think it was more to show him, well, how I'd changed, something like that. I'm not saying that justifies it."

Lyle shook his head. "Well, sorry. I guess I'm

not a liberated, swinging New Yorker yet, but it strikes me as pretty damn inexcusable." I hung my head while he went on, "You just feel like doing it, so you do it. That's all there is to it."

"Lyle, I said it *wasn't* that!" Suddenly I felt angry, tired of justifying everything I did and everything I said. "Your whole moralistic family makes me sick!" I yelled. "Who set you up as these great judges of everyone?"

He was regarding me with a detached expression. "Do you want me to take you home?"

"I want to go home. You don't have to *take* me home." I put my clothes on. Lyle got dressed too.

"I'm taking you home," he announced.

"You are *not* taking me home! I can go home perfectly well by myself."

"Will you take a cab?"

"No! I'll take the subway the way I always do."

"You're not taking the subway alone at eleven at night, Jo. It's dangerous."

"Lyle, I had been coping with the New York transportation system way before you ever *saw* a subway and I can manage perfectly well by myself."

"I won't let you."

"You won't—"

"I'm coming with you."

"You can't. You can't leave Kitty all by herself."

"I'll take her, then." And he marched into the

227

bedroom, scooped up the sleeping baby, and set off with me.

Kitty really is amazingly good-natured. She woke up, but all during the subway ride, while Lyle and I sat there, glaring ahead at the ads, she began cooing and giving these big grins, as though being awakened in the middle of the night was the most exciting, interesting thing that could happen to her. We must have been an odd group, two angry-looking teen-agers and one egregiously happy baby.

When we reached the door, I said dryly, "I think I can make it upstairs in the elevator by myself."

Lyle gave me a long hard glance and wheeled away into the night.

19

The next two weeks were bad. Maybe it was that since all the tension of where I'd get into college was over and classes no longer seemed that interesting, I didn't have anything to occupy my mind with, to take it off of Lyle. But I couldn't help thinking about him most of the day and most of the night. Mom and Elliott were really nice to me. One night they took me out to dinner, and Elliott, especially, went out of his way to try to cheer me up, telling funny jokes and some not so funny ones. But they didn't cross-examine me about what had happened.

One evening, alone in my room, I started to cry. I closed my door really tightly so no one would hear me, but I guess my eyes were red when I came out for dinner. Peering into my room after supper, Mom said, sort of hesitantly, "Jo?"

"Umm."

"You don't feel like talking about it, do you?"

I sighed. "I don't know." I ended up giving her a brief account of what had happened.

She sat on the floor, looking at me with her dark eyes. When I finished, she said, "Oh, Jo, what a dopey, cruel thing to do. Why did you tell him?"

"I should have lied?"

"Why not? Lyle is such a sensitive, vulnerable person. He must have felt devastated."

That, of course, made me feel terrific, that right away she was sympathizing with *him*. "How about how *I* feel?"

"Honey, you've got to learn a couple of things, one of which is that the truth *per se* has no value whatever. I mean, none. You think of people's feelings! That's what counts."

"Why couldn't he understand why I'd done it? Not just *that* I'd done it."

"Because people aren't that rational when it comes to things like that. With men you have to make all kinds of allowances."

"You do?"

"Sure, they're terribly vain or insecure or whatever you want to call it."

"I thought you said it wasn't fair that women spend all their time coddling men's egos."

Mom smiled. "True." She looked at me. "Have you thought of calling him up to apologize?"

"Apologize! For what?"

"Or maybe just writing him a letter would . . . you know, sometimes one bursts out with things in the heat of the moment that can be pretty cruel. But in a letter—"

"Let him write *me* a letter."

"Okay, maybe he will. Jo, you're so damn stubborn. You've just got to learn to give a little."

I sighed. "Okay. Let's drop it, okay?"

I was sort of sorry I'd even discussed it with her.

I guess I was so immersed in self-pity or whatever about the thing with Lyle that it didn't even strike me, a week after Mom and I had our conversation, that *she* was in a real bitch of a mood. What did strike me by around Friday was that Elliott hadn't been home for dinner since Sunday.

Friday, at supper, Eric said, "Hey, Mom, where's Elliott? How come he's not here?"

Mom was in the kitchen. "He just isn't!" she snapped.

Eric and I looked at each other.

"He's moving out his stuff tomorrow morning," she said, still not coming into the dining room, "if that's the answer you wanted."

"Okay," Eric said cheerfully. "I just wondered."

There seemed to be kind of an epidemic of splitting up going on. But with Mom I knew that unless I wanted my head on a platter, it wouldn't be wise to say anything at all. I didn't.

Saturday morning Elliott came to get his stuff. He was cheerful, but a little nervous looking. "Hi, Jo," he said.

I didn't know what to say exactly. I was kind of curious what had happened. You'd imagine grown-ups don't fight about such dumb things as teenagers do, but sometimes I wonder. "Are you going to take your wok?" I said.

"Your kitchen supplies are packed in a box," Mom announced coolly.

"Thank you," Elliott said. He was looking at Mom a little uneasily, as though he wanted to say something more, but didn't know how to put it. Finally he said, "Beth, could I just have a word with you? In private?"

I started ducking out, when Mom said, "Jo, come back here! I don't want any of this behind-closed-doors stuff. What is it?" she said, glaring at Elliott. "What else do you have to say?"

He looked nonplussed. "Nothing," he said softly. He straightened up and started out the door. After he'd gotten into the elevator, I looked down and saw he hadn't taken his box of kitchen supplies.

"Mom, he forgot some of his stuff, his wok and all that."

"Oh, the hell with his fucking wok!" Mom said.

"I can take it down to him," I said.

She vanished, so I went down in the elevator. Elliott was just getting into his car, which was double-parked in front of our building. "Hey, here's your cooking stuff," I said.

He looked up, startled. "Oh, thanks, Jody," he said in a kind of quiet, beaten-down voice. He took the box and put it in the back of the car. "Tell me," he said a little awkwardly, "has, uh, Beth said anything about—well, about how all this came about?"

I shook my head. I didn't want to say I was afraid that if I asked she'd have my head on a platter, because that might not sound too nice.

"I feel she's—well, she seems to be overreacting a little to something that—"

"Yeah, she does that," I said, smiling.

He tried to smile too, but he didn't look very cheerful. "I just thought—well, I thought I'd give you my phone number. I'll be staying at a hotel on East Sixty-ninth, just till I sort of get my bearings and so on. So if Beth should, well, if she needs to get in touch with me for any reason, she can." He took out a pen and wrote the number on a piece of paper.

I really wished I could say something cheerful to

him, but I just said, "I'll give it to her . . . maybe when she's in a better mood."

"Thanks. . . . Well, it's been enjoyable getting to know you, Jody. I wish we'd had more time to talk about things. I always meant to introduce you to my son, William. I thought you and he might have had something in common, but . . . well, I suppose you don't need me for that. You can take care of yourself."

I shrugged. "I hope so."

"Have a good year at college."

"Thank you. I'll try."

He got into the car, put on his sunglasses, and drove off.

It was true what he'd said. I didn't feel we really had gotten to know each other that well, but what I knew of him I'd gotten to like. I mean, I still thought some of his theories were a little screwy, but maybe he thought some of my theories were a little screwy.

For the next week I stuck to my policy of not mentioning Elliott. Mom's mood veered from her usual screaming bit to, by the end of the week, a more subdued, not-talking-that-much-one. Eric seemed completely unaffected. He bounded around the apartment cheerfully, whistling, full of high spirits. He's dating a girl, the one he met last summer who was a mother's helper near where he was a mother's helper. Every Saturday he disappears around seven, looking for him, fairly clean and presentable. I hope he's taking to heart all the good advice I gave him about not lying to girls to get them into bed.

Saturday night Mom and I were alone in the apartment together. Somehow the symmetry of our both having fallen victim to the same disease at roughly the same time didn't seem to bring us closer together. I think I read somewhere that it usually doesn't. Actually, I was feeling a little better. I'd still have moments of feeling really low about Lyle, but in between I'd look around and notice that it was a beautiful spring day and the sun was shining and it was kind of dumb to be that brokenhearted.

They always say opposites attract, which in the case of Lyle and me would certainly seem to be true. I mean, we were certainly opposite enough in a lot of major ways. Though in some things I felt we were alike too, and I couldn't quite figure out if we'd lasted even as long as we had because of the opposite things or the things that were alike.

My upbeat mood lasted till around ten in the evening. I got into one of my rare cleaning-up moods and went through all my papers, throwing things out with abandon, even doing things like putting exams in one place, term papers in another, and all of that. While I was doing it, I kept feeling really proud of myself. I wanted to drag Mom in and show her, since she had proposed a similar project many times over the year. But there was neither hide nor hair of her. Finally, at eleven, I decided I'd had it and went into the living room to look at a movie on TV. It was an old Hitchcock movie. I felt in the mood for slumping down with a glass of root beer and concentrating on something pleasantly escapist for a while.

The TV wasn't there. I wasn't afraid it had been stolen. Our TV is portable, on a little table with wheels, so whoever wants to watch it can wheel it into his or her room. I rarely wheel it into mine because the reception is lousy there, but Eric does sometimes, and so does Mom. However, the rule is you're supposed to wheel it back when you're done with it, which both of them forget most of the time.

I looked into Eric's room, and since it wasn't there, I knew it had to be in Mom's bedroom. For a minute I wasn't sure if I should go in. The door was closed. Then I figured what the heck and knocked.

"Jo? Come on in."

I opened the door. Mom was sitting in bed, knees up, watching the same movie I had thought of watching. She was wearing her glasses, which she only wears for movies and things that are far away.

"I was going to watch that," I admitted, "but, you know, if you feel like being alone . . ."

"Uh-uh. Come sit next to me." Mom looked pretty. Her hair was loose and she was wearing this

236

nightgown I really like. It's shocking pink with orange and purple flowers on it. I think Elliott got it for her for Christmas. I think if I ever progress to actual nightgowns, that's the kind I'd like, not those sexy black-lace numbers that make you look like the cover of a Gothic novel.

We sat and watched together. I was glad to have company. I've never liked sitting in the living room all by myself watching TV. When it was over, Mom got up and snapped it off. Then she lay back on the pillow and yawned. It was after one. "Oh, Lord," she said. She smiled at me. "So, here we are."

"Mom, the thing is . . . when Elliott left, he gave me his phone number. He said he was staying at some hotel, and in case you . . . well, I just thought you'd want to know."

"I just can't get over why he would *lie!*" she said.

"What'd he lie about?"

"It was so pathetic! I went to this party for a writer we represent, and there was Pam, the supposed arch bitch or witch. She knew the writer too. And we got talking, and she was this lovely, this wry, warm, funny woman! Elliott used to say if she met me, she'd tear me from limb to *limb* and, on the contrary, she didn't seem the least bit resentful or anything. She even has a guy who seemed perfectly nice. And that whole spiel about her draining him financially. I mean it's just not *necessary*. Why invent a phony story like that?"

"To win you over?"

"That's so dumb! To start a relationship on a lie is the worst possible. But look, it's not just him. I fall for all these stories because I want to! Because I swallowed all that garbage about 'coddle their egos, they're so sensitive, they'll crumple if you look at them cross-eyed.' Don't do that, Jo!"

I didn't know whether to mention that her advice of a week ago had been the exact opposite. Maybe she could tell I was thinking that, because Mom said, "I know I've set you a lousy example, going from one man to another, but you know the old thing—do as I preach, not as I do. What's wrong with celibacy? Leaping from one guy to the next— who needs it? Who *needs* all of that?"

"Sure," I said.

20

The next Friday Uncle Howard was giving a party.
Mom said she was going and said I could come too
if I wanted. I decided I would go.

Uncle Howard teaches art history at Columbia—in fact, I think he knew Philip at college, and
that might have been how Mom met Philip. He's
younger than Mom by a couple of years, but somehow, especially lately, it seems to me he looks
older. His hair is more gray. He's about Mom's
height, sort of thinnish, and he dresses very nicely,
not in a far-out way, but as though he gave some
thought to what he put on his body in the morning,
which is not the case with most of the other members of our family. He lives by himself in a not too

big apartment, but, unlike Philip's, it's very sunny and bright, with Lucite furniture and Persian rugs and a big carved Indian in the hall.

When we were little, Uncle Howard mostly ignored Eric and me. He has this theory that children, no matter what their personalities, are beasts and aren't worth associating with until they're twelve. But when we were twelve, he suddenly went almost to the other extreme and would take us to museums with him and even on overnight trips to Boston. He might have done it a little more with Eric than with me, but I went along a lot too. I like him, except sometimes he can be sort of sarcastic, and if you're in a vulnerable mood, that can be a little hurtful. But at parties he's usually pretty genial and goes around talking to everyone and asking if they're doing okay and have enough to drink. I know, because since we turned sixteen, he's always included us in his invitations to Mom, and even though we don't always go, we sometimes do.

I had dressed carefully, because when I go out with Mom, I have to tread a kind of careful line. If I wear something at all low cut or tight (in her opinion), she'll say it's too "provocative" and if I wear something old and comfortable, she'll say I look like a slob. So I wore this light-green silk blouse that she got me for my seventeenth birthday and a pair of green slacks. The blouse isn't really see-through because it has a lot of flowers on it.

It's OK If You Don't Love Me

Anyway, since Mom got it for me, she couldn't very well protest.

I felt a little out of it at the party. I guess it was my mood. I didn't feel that gay or jovial, more sort of misanthropic. I went over in the corner and started strumming a guitar someone had left around.

This man with a black beard said, "I play the banjo."

"Oh." I looked up.

"Are you Howard's niece?" he said.

I nodded. "How can you tell?"

"Well, he said his niece was coming, and you're the only one here who looks young enough to be someone's niece."

"I'm eighteen," I said, trying to sit up straight.

He started talking about something, and I listened, but at the same time I noticed Mom across the room. She was standing in one corner, a drink in her hand, looking up at some guy. I don't think I mentioned that last week Mom suddenly cut her hair. It's around shoulder length now, maybe a little above, and she wears it parted in the middle. I can't exactly get used to it, though everyone says she looks great. I guess having seen her the other way for so many years, it seems strange to me. She was talking to this guy, but when she stopped talking and just listened, her face would get this faraway, sort of sad expression, like she wasn't really listening. I felt bad seeing that expression on her face. Probably she didn't even know it was there, and maybe if she hadn't been my mother, I wouldn't have noticed.

"You wouldn't feel like ducking out of here and going somewhere for a drink?" the man in the black beard said.

"Um . . . well, I came with my mother."

"Your mother?"

"She's Uncle Howard's sister. I mean, that's how come I'm his niece."

"Where is she?"

"Over there. In that corner. She's the one in the red dress."

"Well, just tell her you'll see her later."

"Okay." I went over to where Mom was and said I was going to go for a drink with the man in the black beard.

Mom didn't look very happy about it. "Jo, it's pretty late. It's past midnight."

"I won't turn into a pumpkin."

"I don't know. Who *is* this guy?"

"His name is Jim, I think."

I knew Mom was thinking I was going to go off and be seduced—she always thinks that. "Listen, I'll be okay," I said.

"I just don't know."

Suddenly I thought: Really, why do it? I didn't feel that much in the mood. So I went back and told that to the man, whose name turned out to be Gerald. "My mother thinks it's a little bit late," I said.

He got a kind of sarcastic expression. "She does, huh?"

"*And* I'm sort of tired."

"Uh-huh." He kept looking at me sort of intently. "Well, fine. Let me just get your number."

"My number?"

"Your phone number."

Mom and I went home in a cab at one. "Did you have fun?" she asked.

"In a way. I wasn't that much in the mood."

"Me neither. Look, Jo, I'm sorry about that guy. If you really want to do that kind of thing, it's up to you."

"I wasn't planning on *doing* anything," I said indignantly. "He just wanted to go for a drink."

"Right. Well, I guess what really got me was I heard these two men talking about you. It was when you were playing the guitar, and one of them said, 'She's pretty good,' and the other one said, 'I bet she's good at a lot of things.' I felt so mad! I felt like going over and saying, 'Hey, wait a sec, that's my little girl you're talking about.'"

I laughed.

"Only you're not anymore. I have to keep reminding myself of that. Thanks for coming with me, though, Jo. It would've been pretty dreary if I'd gone alone."

"It was fun," I said. I really was glad that I hadn't gone for a drink with the man in the black beard. Given the dopey things I can do at times, maybe it was just as well.

When we got back home, I got straight into my pajamas and went to bed. But somehow, though it was late, nearly two, I couldn't fall asleep. I thought maybe it was horniness and tried masturbating, but that didn't seem to work. Sometimes I feel masturbating isn't all it's cracked up to be. I mean, I think it's good it exists but I always feel kind of depressed after I do it. Maybe that's just guilt of some kind. I don't know. Maybe I just don't have an active enough imagination. I mean, if I could do it really imagining I was with someone, that might be good. But I always know I'm not, that I'm just lying there all by myself and that seems to make it sort of lonely.

Finally, at two thirty, I got up and had some milk and graham crackers with honey, which is a snack I like late at night. I suddenly got this tremendous urge to talk to Lyle. The thing is, in Renee and Wesley's apartment there's only one phone, and it's in the living room. So I knew if I did call, I wouldn't wake them up. If the phone was in their bedroom I'd never have even thought of calling him. I picked up the receiver and then put it back on the hook. I got back into bed. Then a few minutes later I got up again, went back into the kitchen, and dialed.

The phone rang about four times before it was picked up. Lyle's voice, sort of slow and sleepy, said, "Hello?"

"Hi, it's me."

"Jo? What're you doing calling so late? It's the middle of the night."

"Yeah, I know. I'm sorry. I guess I must have woken you up."

"Well, I . . . here, wait a sec, let me move the phone around. Did something happen?"

"What do you mean?"

"No, I just wondered why you were calling."

"No special reason."

"Oh. . . . How've you been?"

"Okay. . . . How have you been?"

"All right."

"Listen, Lyle, I'm sorry, I just got home late from this party and I—well, I'm sorry I woke you up."

"That's okay. . . . What have you been up to, Jo?"

"Nothing special. . . . Repenting for my sins."

I wished I could see Lyle's face, to see if he was smiling or just had that grim, angry look he had had when we had our fight. But then there was a long silence. The dumbness of having called him began to seem really overwhelming. "Well, thank you for calling," he said very formally.

"That's okay," I said.

When I got back into bed, I felt around ten times worse than before. Mom was right—at least if I'd written a letter, but to wake someone up in the middle of the night! What was the point of *that?*

I think it must have been around three when I finally fell asleep, but when I did, I sacked out completely into this heavy black kind of sleep, no dreams, nothing. I was glad. I didn't even feel up to dreaming.

21 ✠✠✠

In the morning came one of the great shocks of all time. I got out of bed around eleven, yawning, and staggered into the kitchen, expecting to see Mom or Eric or maybe both of them. Instead there was Elliott standing in front of the stove making french toast. And inside, sitting around the dining-room table, were Mom, Eric, and that girl he's been dating whom I met once before, Fiona Lobsenz.

I looked around groggily. I felt a little like Rip Van Winkle, like maybe I'd overslept by about ten years or maybe the opposite, maybe time had gone backward in some weird way. "Uh . . . hi," I said to Elliott.

"Will two slices be enough for you, Jody?" Elliott

said, perfectly calmly. "I can throw on another if you're really hungry."

"No, two is fine." I stood there, immobilized, watching him. "When did you, uh . . . return?"

"Oh, I slipped through the keyhole in the dead of night," he said smiling slyly.

I followed him into the dining room. "This french toast is really delicious, Mr. Epstein," Fiona was saying. She was a tiny girl, under five feet, with reddish brown curly hair and freckles and big blue eyes. Every time Eric said anything, she would look at him like he'd just created the earth and moon. I guess that would have been hard to take under any circumstances, but it seemed especially so at the moment.

Evidently Elliott decided to let Fiona assume his name was Mr. Epstein. Really it's Jarco.

"I suppose Eric has gotten his interest in cooking from you," Fiona said to Elliott.

Mom and I looked at each other, this being the first either of us had heard about Eric being interested in cooking. Usually you have to practically hold a gun to his head to get him to make anything more than spaghetti.

"I find it relaxing after a day at work," Elliott said, letting that illusion remain untouched also.

"I wish my Dad would," Fiona said. "He's a chemist and he claims cooking is too much like what he does all day, you know, pouring things from one test tube to another."

"Excuses, excuses," Mom said. But she had a pretty cheerful expression on her face. "Did you sleep well, Jo?"

"Yeah, pretty well."

"I'm sorry Fiona and I missed the party," Eric said. "We were going to go, but it got sort of late."

"It was nothing that special," I said.

Elliott brought in my french toast and set it down in front of me. I had this peculiar feeling, like maybe I'd undergone some lobotomy overnight and there was a perfectly good explanation for all of this, which everyone knew but me. They were all smiling. Everyone looked like they were in a very jolly mood. Every time someone made a joke, everyone would roar with laughter, even if it was something pretty dumb. Okay, I did, I have to admit, feel left out. It was like seeing the last four animals pair off and disappear into the ark as the rains started to fall.

After breakfast I went back into my room to try and get my head together. Mom peeked in and said, "Hon, Elliott and I are going bike riding. We'll see you later."

I looked at her. "You've just set a new world's record for celibacy . . . twelve days."

"Jo, don't be a smart-ass. We'll see you later, okay?"

After Mom and Elliott left, I wandered around the apartment. Eric's door was closed, but it was clear they were in there. I decided to go see Philip. According to his answering service he'd returned the week before. Just to make sure I called, and he said, "Sure. Come on over, Jo."

I walked up Riverside to Philip's house. It was a gorgeous day, sunny, blue sky, the whole works. I imagined Mom and Elliott blithely biking through the park and felt a little mild regret at my parting crack.

"Philip, something really *weird* is going on at our house," I said as he led me into the apartment.

"What's that?" he said. Then he said, "Jo, I think you met Marya once, didn't you?"

I looked up. There, squatting on the floor in front of a chessboard, which was open on the coffee table, was the woman I'd seen that time Philip and I went to the photo gallery. She was squinting at the board intently. "Hi, Jody," she said, not looking up.

"Uh . . . hi," I stared at her. I was dumbfounded. I remember Elliott once said that the reason some people become paranoid is that occasionally life conspires to make a series of things happen that, though they're completely coincidental, make that person feel they're up against just too much. Usually you can say to someone, "Oh, it's just your imagination," but sometimes a series of disasters follows one another that it's hard to explain away. *Philip* with a girl! Why couldn't this have happened, if it had to, a year ago or a year from now or, best of all, never? And the awful part was that at one glance I could tell that Marya Berger was just the person for Philip. She was dressed in Oshkosh overalls and a man's shirt, was barefoot, had shaggy blond hair and a kind of funny but appealing face. Just the kind of woman someone like Philip would notice, a little self-absorbed, a little odd. And the way she stared at the chessboard, I suspected she was a very good player, not to be distracted easily.

"Do you mind if we just finish this one game?" Philip said. "I think Marya is about to edge me off the board."

She just smiled to herself, but I could see that unless Philip did something fast, the game would be over rather rapidly.

I sat there looking at both of them. Philip looked exactly the same, his hair sort of stringy, his clothes sort of wrinkled. I started to wonder, though. Mr. Meleo once said in Sex Ed. that behind every relationship is a fantasy that a person has of that relationship. The fantasies may be completely different, even contradictory, but they determine a lot of the way people react. I still didn't think that Mom had ever been right that there was anything sexual between Philip and me on either side, even subliminally. But, God, I did feel horribly blindly jealous of Marya Berger. I think my fantasy about my relationship with Philip wasn't that we would ever make it together but more that I would always be first with him, the favorite. Maybe it was because when he and Mom split, it was me he continued to see, not her, and I thought it would go on that way indefinitely. It wasn't very fair, I admit, because I imagined me going off and having affairs and so on, but Philip was to just remain there, to be someone to talk to or turn to whenever things got bad.

And here was Marya Berger, sitting there very comfortably and at home, with Philip gazing at her fondly. It felt like a blow below the belt.

"What's so weird at home?" Philip asked when they were done.

"I don't know. I can't exactly figure Mom out. The week before last she and Elliott had this big fight and she said she was resolved on celibacy, and this morning there he is right in our kitchen making french toast!"

Philip laughed. "Well, people do resolve these things."

"It's just so hypocritical!" I said. "She should act the way she says."

"Jo, don't be such a moralist."

I turned red. "No, it's like the thing with me and college. She always goes around saying she believes in one thing and the next day she's doing something completely different."

Marya said, "Don't you like Elliott? Is that the trouble?"

"No, it's not that. I do, really."

They were looking at me with these sympathetic she'll-grow-out-of-it expressions. "How's Lyle?" Philip said.

I swallowed. "Uh . . . he's okay."

I knew Philip could tell by the way I spoke that something must have happened, because he very dexterously changed the subject.

I played Marya a few games of chess while Philip went inside to do some work. She was a lot better than me. Of course, I haven't played much lately, but I have the feeling she still would've been better. After the third game she said, "God, I better get going! I'm supposed to be downtown at five."

She and Philip asked if I felt like going downtown with them, but I said no. I decided to wend my way home.

No one was home. The apartment was completely silent. I started into my room, when I saw a note in Eric's handwriting. He'd taped it onto the refrigerator. *Meet Lyle at the court,* it said.

It didn't say anything about *what* court—the one at 120th and Riverside or the one at 93rd and Central Park West. And it didn't say what time I was supposed to meet him. It didn't even say when he'd called. When I leave a message like that for Mom, she usually hits the ceiling, but since Eric wasn't around, there wasn't anything I could do about it.

I changed into my tennis stuff and took the bus up Riverside. When I got to the courts, I could see Lyle playing. He was playing doubles with three other men. Two of them I'd seen around, but the other one I didn't know. I can always spot Lyle because he never wears white, he only wears the same faded navy-blue shirt and khaki shorts. Quietly I walked over to the side of the courts and sat on the hill, looking down, watching him play.

He didn't see me; he was too intent on the game. I began feeling excited, despite myself, and then mad that just a little call from him could have that effect on me. It's funny about couples. I guess it's just impossible to figure out why sometimes it works and sometimes it doesn't. It seems like even when you get older, like Mom, you still don't know that much more. You just go on hoping for the best. It's not that I think the only relationships worth anything are the kind that last for all time. Maybe it's sort of romantic, to want that. But I wish I could be looking back ten years from now so I could know if Lyle will be someone important, someone who's still there, or someone whom I'll just remember because he was the first. Not the first in one sense, but the first in terms of being all-out in love.

I wonder what it'll be like if it turns out that there is a heaven after all and God, as I've always suspected, turns out to be a woman. I imagine She'll look like Golda Meir, stocky and wrinkled and wise, with kindly penetrating eyes. All the women in the world who thought of themselves as feminists will have to line up and take their turn justifying all the times they were ever crazily, dopily in love. I hope She will turn out to be a tennis player. Because, if I were talking about Lyle, I think I'd have to say, "If you saw his backhand, you'd understand."

I hope that will make sense to Her.

PRAYing with
Celtíc
Saínts,
Prophets,
Martyrs,
and Poets

❖

Praying with

Celtic

Saints,

Prophets,

Martyrs,

and Poets

❖

June Skinner Sawyers

SHEED & WARD

Franklin, Wisconsin

As an apostolate of the Priests of the Sacred Heart, a Catholic religious congregation, the mission of Sheed & Ward is to publish books of contemporary impact and enduring merit in Catholic Christian thought and action. The books published, however, reflect the opinion of their authors and are not meant to represent the official position of the Priests of the Sacred Heart.

2001

Sheed & Ward
7373 South Lovers Lane Road
Franklin, Wisconsin 53132
1-800-266-5564

Printed in the United States of America

Cover and interior design by Robin Booth
Cover art: A detail of a painting of Saint Clare created by an anonymous artist soon after her canonization in 1255. The artist was seeking to portray her spiritual rather than individual likeness.
Author photo by Theresa Albini

Library of Congress Cataloging-in-Publication Data

Sawyers, June Skinner
    Praying with Celtic saints, prophets, martyrs, and poets / June Skinner Sawyers.
        p.cm.
    Includes bibliographical references.
    ISBN 1-58051-094-9
        1. Celts—Religion. 2. Christian biography—British Isles. 3. Christian
        biography—United States. 4. Christian saints, Celtic—Biography. I. Title.

BR737 .C4 S39 2001
270'.089'916—dc21

2001020107

1 2 3 4 5 / 04 03 02 01

❖

In loving memory of my mother,
Elizabeth Muir Lawson Porter Sawers
(October 30, 1920–December 4, 2000)
. . . my favorite person in the history of the world.

Contents

Acknowledgments

Special thanks are due to Jeremy Langford for his patience and understanding, especially during the difficult final weeks of the project. His support, along with the presence of all the saints and poets mentioned in the book, proved to be able traveling companions. I couldn't have done it without them. Thanks also to Kass Dotterweich for editing with such grace and good humor.

Several reference books were particularly useful, especially the revised and updated edition of *Butler's Lives of the Saints* and Robert Ellsberg's *All Saints*. For anecdotal information on the saints' often confusing, sketchy, and contradictory lives, I recommend *The Spirituality of the Celtic Saints* by Richard J. Woods, and *Wisdom of the Celtic Saints* by Edward C. Sellner. For a complete listing, consult the bibliography at the end of this volume.

Introduction

P raying with Celtic Saints, Prophets, Martyrs, and Poets contains the stories of a remarkable group of pilgrims, wanderers, and seekers; poets, artists, and sages; saints, prophets, and martyrs. Their stories are our stories. Whether Saint Patrick or Saint Brigid, Flannery O'Connor or Archibald MacLeish, they share the same self-doubts, the same fears, the same dreams.

By examining ancient Celts and modern Celts, Old World Celts and New World Celts, it is my hope that *Praying with Celtic Saints, Prophets, Martyrs, and Poets* will reveal how the elusive and stubborn Celtic spirit has survived through the centuries and how it can—and indeed does—still touch us today. For despite being separated by time, Saint Kevin and Seamus Heaney share a common emotional bond. The past lives in the present, the present in the past.

The people you will meet in *Praying with Celtic Saints, Prophets, Martyrs, and Poets* are not airy-fairy types. They are flesh-and-blood human beings with a refreshingly earthy and practical approach to living. I have tried to preserve the Celtic sense of mystery while revealing the human elements behind the myths, behind the legends. I have also attempted to humanize well-known but essentially aloof historical figures—for example, how much does the typical person know about Patrick and his struggles—while cutting down to size, so to speak, modern pop-culture Celts who are more accustomed to the limelight than the hermit's lonely cell. In this way, I hope that the reader will not only discover an authentic and abiding Celtic spirit that stretches from centuries ago to the present but also will learn how the dilemmas of these ancient figures can apply to the way we live our lives today.

What exactly do we mean by Celtic spirituality? Why is it so popular today? What makes it relevant?

The Celts had a deep reverence for the land and for nature itself. Ritual was an important part of their daily life. More important, though, was the belief that God resides everywhere, in everyone, and in everything. At heart, they were poets, and it is this poetic spirit, shining through their spirituality, that people find so appealing today.

The origins of Christian monasticism date back to fourth-century Egypt and Syria and were then introduced to Western Europe through the writings of Athanasius and John Cassian, as well as the life of Martin of Tours. They all had a profound influence on Celtic Christianity.

But let me pause right there. The concept of a Celtic Church is a misleading and highly erroneous one. There was no Celtic church per se in the way there is a Roman Catholic or a Presbyterian Church. The Celtic "church" was part of the universal Church; there was no separation back then. What set the Celts apart from their Roman counterparts amounted to ritual, custom, and administrative differences.

On the other hand, I believe it is fair to say that Celtic Christianity, the form of Christian worship performed by the Celtic peoples, does have a distinctive personality. (The concept of Celticity, of "being Celtic," is a very complex one and exceeds the boundaries of this book.) There are several important themes in Celtic spirituality that are worth a brief mention.

Asceticism and a strong use of ritual were key features. Irish asceticism in particular was inspired by the stories of the Old Testament (see Genesis 12:1). Abraham's journey encouraged Saint Anthony, another early influence, to seek a life of solitude in the Egyptian desert, which in turn further inspired the Irish monks.

The Celtic predilection for pilgrimage and penitence derives from the essentially monastic nature of early Irish Christianity, with its emphasis on self-discipline and sacrifice. The Celts were born martyrs. They even applied colors to the various types of martyrdom. Red meant giving one's life for Christ, and green consisted of freeing oneself from temptation and evil desire, whether by fasting or repenting for past sins. White represented one's willingness to leave home and family by going into exile. Celtic Christianity could be hard and demanding. Withdrawal and solitary contemplation were particularly appreciated among the Celts.

The Celts were also a highly creative people. Anyone who has admired the Book of Kells and other illuminated manuscripts knows of the delicate intricacies of Celtic art. And since the oral tradition played such an important part in the lives of the Celts, as best personified by the ancient bards, poetry and the spoken word were highly valued. In the Celtic realm, it was left to the poet to better understand the mysteries of the world, to make sense of the universe. And yet they did not have all the answers. To the Celtic poet, much was left unsaid.

There are other qualities as well: a mindfulness, a being present in the moment, a celebration of place, and a sense of unity with all of the earth's creatures. It is an all-encompassing spiritually that, at its fundamental best, is life affirming.

And maybe there's something else going on that's hard to pin down, an ineffable characteristic that pulls us in. "[I]t is precisely the 'otherness' of early medieval Celtic Christianity that makes it attractive to us . . . ," concludes historian Oliver Davies.

> Let us adore the Lord,
> Maker of marvelous works,
> Bright heaven with its angels,
> And on earth the white-waved sea.
>> "THE LORD OF CREATION," Ninth-Century Irish Poem

I believe the secret of the Celtic Christians' appeal can be found in the paradoxes and contradictions and little inconsistencies—the soldier-saint, the poet-warrior—that play such a prominent part in the stories. An irresistible combination of robust spirituality and graceful elegance allows us to fully enter their world. Although always searching for something, the ancient Celts would willingly embrace the unknown, the great mysteries. They didn't always have to know all the answers. They had a simple faith.

And somehow, they knew that no matter where the road takes us, we will always return home.

A NOTE ON SELECTIONS

The selections in *Praying with Celtic Saints, Prophets, Martyrs, and Poets* are arranged alphabetically. Each selection is preceded by a quotation from or about the person, followed by the story, and ending with a reflection for the day. When appropriate, I include a list of important sites as well as suggestions for further reading.

Davío Aдam

VICAR
(1936-)

The Presence of God is an eternal fact.
He never leaves us alone or forsakes us.
It is when we lose sight of Him that we falter
and sink beneath the waves.
DAVID ADAM

David Adam, currently the vicar of Holy Island (or Lindisfarne), is one of the leading figures within the modern Christian Celtic tradition. Although he is not a Celt—like many followers, he came to it as an outsider—his work is inspired by the writings of the ancient Celts. In his hands, the age-old wisdom seems as fresh and invigorating as a cool breeze on a spring morning. More than this, he gives the stories and tales a new twist and a strong personal touch.

Born in Alnwick, Northumberland, in the north of England, Adam worked as a coal miner before being ordained. For more than twenty years he served as the vicar of Danby in North Yorkshire, where he discovered he had a talent for composing prayers in the Celtic tradition.

Adam prefers to walk, as he says, "on the edge of things," to discover something within himself—within ourselves—in the shadow world, in the in-between world. When something

1

appears just beyond our reach, "beyond the border," that is the place where Adam finds the human spirit at its best, when it is most alive. The Celts believed every living and nonliving thing on the planet is dependent on one another. Everything is intertwined, everything circular. The beginning leads to the end, the end to the beginning. The earth is constantly moving, the tides ebbing and flowing, human lives dying and being born.

Adam refers to Jesus as someone who constantly crossed borders between different ethnic groups, different classes of society, the known and the unknown, the visible and the invisible, heaven and earth, life and death.

One of Adam's most common themes is to find strength through faith. He tells of a time when life became "increasingly hard," so hard that he ran away to the Cheviots, those gently rolling hills that form the natural boundary between Scotland and England. "The morning was spent winding down, . . . The afternoon was filled with the sound of the cuckoo," he writes. "Suddenly the valley darkened; it was only a cloud, but all my troubles returned with it."

He clambered up the summit of the nearby hilltops, "climbing over a great heap of stones into a Bronze Age fortress." There he sat, getting his breath back and looking out toward the North Sea to Holy Island, the island that would one day become his spiritual and physical home. He could see that a storm was brewing and coming his way, or so he thought. But, to his surprise, it never came. "The hills seemed to break the clouds and divide them: the storm went to the north and south, but it did not come over me. In that ancient circle built to protect ancient man, I suddenly felt protected. I was surrounded by the Presence and Power of God."

Here in the Cheviot Hills, surrounded by the elements, by the wind and the sky, Adam affirmed his faith in God and said aloud:

> Circle me O God
> Keep hope within
> Despair without.

Adam is an explorer. He does not seek Jesus, but rather hopes to discover him, to share and learn. Christ, then, becomes not a stranger, but a friend. "It is when we open ourselves to the other who comes to us that the great Other also seeks to enter our lives." Adam believes in total immersion in the faith; no halfhearted approach for him. He wholeheartedly recommends activities that involve our whole being, whether it be the simple act of reading a book or participating in a sport.

All things must come to an end. And yet there is something about the human condition that refuses to let go without a fight. Adam refers to the human race as "seekers." "We seek something that is still beyond us, an inner urge . . ."

David Adam himself is a seeker: a seeker of life, a seeker of the spirit. Although he does not always know what he seeks or where to seek, as vicar and as human being, he seeks every day of his waking and non-waking life, now and forever.

REFLECTION

David Adam is a spiritual fringe dweller, a dweller on the fringe of things. Where do you fit in? Do you, like Adam, find comfort and solace living in what he calls the "marginal lands," or do you prefer a safer and more predictable environment, where risk is kept to a bare minimum and the future seems all but secure?

FOR FURTHER READING

David Adam. *Border Lands: The Best of David Adam's Celtic Vision* (Franklin, WI: Sheed & Ward, 2000).

Aíðan

BISHOP AND ABBOT OF LINDISFARNE
(580–651)

He cultivated peace and love, purity and humility:
he was above anger and greed, despised pride and conceit;
he set himself to keep and teach the laws of God,
and was diligent in study and in prayer.

BEDE

Often called the "Apostle of Northumbria," Saint Aidan arrived in Lindisfarne, also known as Holy Island, from Iona in the year 635. He came at the request of King Oswald, who required the services of a bishop to help convert the pagan population. It was there, at Lindisfarne, close to the royal residence of Bamburgh, that Aidan established a bishopric.

Using Lindisfarne as his base, Aidan founded additional religious outposts in other areas of the north, including, most famously, a monastery in Melrose in the Scottish Borders. An Irish speaker, he used Oswald as his interpreter when addressing the Anglo-Saxon court. Lindisfarne, cut off from the mainland twice a day, was a remote and austere place, perfect for someone of Aidan's quiet demeanor and serious disposition.

Born in Ireland, Aidan studied under Saint Senan on Scattery Island before becoming a monk at Iona. Aidan replaced Corman, the first missionary bishop to the Angles, a rigid man who referred to the native population as barbaric and hopelessly stubborn—indeed, too stubborn to teach.

Aidan felt Corman's behavior to be unduly harsh and unreasonable as well as unwarranted. In contrast, Aidan's warmth and intelligence convinced the elders that he, Aidan, was the perfect man for the job. He was kind and compassionate, a devoted teacher who committed himself to his new land and the people he served. He taught by example; what he said and what he did were one and the same.

Shortly after Aidan arrived, he built a school, a mission, and a church. Everyone, regardless of their station in life, received the same high level of education. Thus, he treated everyone, whether lowly beggar and the highest of kings, with the same respect and dignity he sought for himself.

Aidan loved to walk, to meet people, to bring some element of joy to those he encountered in his daily travels. He circumnavigated the island on foot. Having no interest or need for earthly possessions, he would routinely hand out gifts or monies, received in his various journeys, to the poor and the needy.

One day a king named Oswin gave Aidan a horse as a gift, a literal "gift horse." The king knew Aidan was an avid walker but, should the occasion arise, such as, he mused, an emergency or the crossing of a large body of water, the horse would be an asset. Shortly thereafter, Aidan met a beggar on the road, who asked for alms. Rather than presenting a few tokens or a mere handful of coins, Aidan stepped down from his horse and offered the animal to the shocked man. When the king discovered what Aidan had done, he was more than slightly taken aback and, truth be told, vaguely insulted. "Why," he wondered, "would Aidan give a royal horse to a mere beggar?"

"Surely," Aidan replied, "this son of a mare is not dearer to you than that son of God."

Left speechless by Aidan's straightforward answer, the king took some time to collect his thoughts before, ultimately, asking Aidan for his forgiveness. How could he, a king, be so selfish?

Aidan had that effect on people. In his gentle and nonconfrontational manner, he made others think about their motives, about how and why they behaved a certain way. And all of this soul-searching on their behalf may have been prompted by nothing more than a simple question or gesture. But this came to him naturally, with no affectations, no secret agendas. He was a beloved figure—humble to a fault—who managed to bring the best out of almost everyone.

Aidan died on August 31 in 651. He was buried in the cemetery in Lindisfarne, although his remains were later moved to a larger church on the island.

Today, an eleven-foot statue of Aidan stands near the Lindisfarne Abbey ruins. In one hand he holds a crozier, indicating that he is a bishop; in the other he holds a torch. Even now, he continues to light the way.

REFLECTION

We live in an increasingly selfish society. When was the last time you put someone else's interests and wishes ahead of your own? How did that make you feel?

SITES ASSOCIATED WITH AIDAN

Statue of Aidan
Lindisfarne, England
The statue is located on the grounds of the priory on Lindisfarne and was erected in 1958 for the visit of Queen Elizabeth.

Lindisfarne Priory Museum
Lindisfarne, England

A fine museum recalls the history of this most holy of islands, from its monastic past to the present day.

FOR FURTHER READING

David Adam. *The Holy Island: Pilgrim Guide* (Norwich: Canterbury Press, 1997).

Jane Hawkes. *The Golden Age of Northumbria* (Morpeth, Northumberland: Sandhill Press, 1996).

Iain Macdonald, ed. *Saints of Northumbria: Cuthbert, Aidan, Oswald, Hilda* (Edinburgh: Floris Books, 1997).

Andrew

SCOTLAND'S PATRON SAINT
(?–60)

. . . present me to my Master, that he who redeemed me
on thee may receive me by thee.
ANDREW

Saint Andrew is the patron saint of three very different countries: Scotland, Russia, and Greece. Much of his story is based on conjecture, with more than ample doses of tradition, legend, and even, as one source puts it, "devotional patriotism" as part of the frothy mix.

Andrew was born in Bethsaida, a small town and important fishing port on the Sea of Galilee, near the Jordan River. His father was a local fisherman, as was Andrew and his brother Simon Peter.

Andrew followed the preaching of John the Baptist. One day, while fishing in the Sea of Galilee, the siblings encountered Jesus, who called out to them while they were casting their nets and invited them to become "fishers of men." Andrew, according to tradition, was the first to respond and, for this reason, has been called "the first missionary." According to the Gospel, it was Andrew who introduced to Jesus a young lad who somehow managed to share five barley loaves and two small fishes with five thousand men (see John, 6:8).

Andrew preached in many lands, including Cappadocia, Bithynia, Galatia, Byzantium, and especially Scythia, or modern Russia—he is credited with converting many Scythians to Christianity. Andrew is also strongly linked with Greece. Tradition tells us he died in the Greek town of Achaia in A.D. 60 as a martyr under orders of Aegeas, the Roman governor who made it his official duty to persecute Christians at whatever cost and whenever possible.

Like Jesus, Andrew was crucified, bound to a diagonal cross with cords. There he hung for three tortuous days. Despite the pain and agony he was forced to endure, however, he continued to preach to the crowds—attempting to bring converts to the cause—until his dying breath.

Initially, Andrew was buried in Patras, where his body remained for some three centuries. Then his remains were taken to Byzantium, which later became known as Constantinople. In 357 his bones were moved to a church that was erected in honor of the Twelve Apostles. Finally, in the thirteenth century, his bones were moved once again, this time to the Cathedral of Amalfi, where most of them remain to this day.

How Andrew's story made its way to Scotland is a rather fanciful one. Reportedly, in 370 a Greek monk by the name of Regulus had a vision imploring him to take Andrew's relics to a far-distant land in the west. And so the Greek dutifully set off on his journey, accompanied by a priest, two deacons, eight hermits, and three virgins. With them they carried three fingers of Andrew's right hand, an arm bone, one tooth, and a kneecap. A terrible storm forced the ship aground somewhere in the east of Scotland at a place called Kilrymont, where the town of St. Andrews now stands. Here the Pictish king gave them refuge, and the relics were laid to rest in a local church, allegedly established by one of Saint Columba's disciples. But there's more to the Pictish angle.

Around this time, a major battle took place between the Saxon Athelstane and Angus, King of the Picts. On the eve of the confrontation, Andrew appeared to the king in a dream, assuring him of victory over the Saxons. As the battle was about to begin, a white, X-shaped cross swept across a blue sky. To this day a white cross on a blue background—a saltire—forms the flag of Scotland. The Picts, indeed, won, and in order to give his thanks, King Angus offered the church that housed Andrew's relics many gifts, including a handsome case to securely hold the remains, as well as a large tract of land.

Still another story says that Andrew's bones were brought to Scotland a century later by Rule, or Riaghuil, a missionary from Ireland.

Eventually a cult of Saint Andrew developed. In medieval times thousands of pilgrims flocked to St. Andrews, finding sympathy and inspiration in the story of Andrew's own struggles and ultimate sacrifice. In 1472 the town of St. Andrews became an archbishopric.

St. Andrews developed in to a renowned pilgrim center for absolution of crimes, cures for common illnesses, and even miracles. Pilgrims wore special badges—called pilgrim badges—that depicted the crucifixion of Saint Andrew at Patras, Greece, on an X-shaped cross. The badges consisted of four stitching holes that could be sewn to hats or other articles of clothing. They were easy and cheap to make and cast in an alloy of tin and lead in one piece or two-piece molds.

In the twelfth century the Church of St. Rule was built to house the shrine of Saint Andrew. Today the area around the cathedral continues to attract modern pilgrims, both of the secular and spiritual varieties.

REFLECTION

Andrew's life is a tribute to patience, perseverance, and quiet grace. Where does one's strength come from? How much suffering can one person endure? Why do some surrender while others go on? Can you think of a time when you wanted to stop yet somehow found the inner strength to continue?

SITES ASSOCIATED WITH ST. ANDREW

St. Andrews Cathedral
St. Andrews, Scotland
Now in ruins, this magnificent structure stands on the edge of the sea. Nearby are what remains of St. Rules and St. Mary's Churches.

St. Andrews Museum
Kinburn Park, Doubledykes Road, St. Andrews, Scotland
An excellent museum that explores the heritage of the city, from medieval times to the present day. Don't miss the display on pilgrimage to St. Andrews.

FOR FURTHER READING

Peter Yeoman. *Pilgrimage in Medieval Scotland* (London: Batsford/ Historic Scotland, 1998).

Antony

ABBOT
(c.251–356)

Who sits in solitude and is quiet
hath escaped from three wars:
hearing, speaking, seeing.
Yet against one thing shall he continually battle:
that is, his own heart.
ANTONY

ntony changed his life forever—abruptly, completely, irrevocably—to pursue a vision. Those who knew him and loved him probably were baffled by his sudden transformation. And yet change he did. By changing his fate, he also altered, or at least profoundly affected, the course of Western spirituality. Antony, and the Desert Fathers, had an undeniably crucial effect on Ireland in particular. He dedicated himself to a life of poverty and self-discipline, a life intent on helping the poor.

The desert was a place of spiritual power. After all, it was the place where God had revealed himself to Moses and to Elijah. And it was the place where Jesus had fasted for forty days and forty nights.

Most of the stories of the Desert Fathers were translated into Latin from their original Greek during the fifth, sixth, and seventh centuries. What's more, the Desert Fathers and the Celtic tradition are linked historically and spiritually. Indeed, the figure of Saint Antony of Egypt appears on many Celtic high crosses, those wonderful symbols of grace and elegance that dot the Celtic landscape. Whether body or soul, intellect or emotion, to the Desert Fathers there were no artificial boundaries, just like to the Celts there was no boundary between this world and the next. The early Celtic saints and monks withdrew into their own "deserts," their own watery abodes by the sea. Moving easily and effortlessly between the known world and the unknown world was to the Celts as natural as breathing.

Born in Egypt, Antony was the son of wealthy Christian parents who died when he was eighteen. At that time, he assumed control over the family estate and accepted responsibility for his younger sister. Antony was not particularly religious, but his life changed when, attending church one day, a biblical passage from the Gospel struck a chord. Jesus said: "Go sell what you possess and give to the poor, and you will have treasure in heaven." It was as if Jesus himself spoke to him directly.

Shortly thereafter, Antony sold most of his possessions and donated the rest to the poor, keeping only essential items and funds for himself and his sister. Subsequently, he arranged for his sister to enter a convent, hence freeing himself from all responsibilities. He then dedicated his life to God.

Because there were few monasteries around at the time, Antony sought advice from holy men whenever he could, such as the local hermit who gave him lessons on how to live in solitude. He initially moved to the outskirts of villages but eventually decided to follow Jesus' example and live in the desert. He found shelter in small huts and caves, and it was here where he spent his time praying, studying, and working, surviving mostly on dried loaves of bread, brought to him by friends, and water from the well. A typical hut was made of stone and covered by a roof made of branches, comparable in some ways to the Celtic beehives that were especially popular in the west of Ireland.

Antony lived in solitude for some twenty years, rarely seeing another human soul during that long and sometimes tortuous sojourn. Although friends brought him supplies of bread and water, they never addressed him face to face. After occasionally hearing the bloodcurdling shrieks and screams of a frightened soul behind locked doors, however, Antony's friends became so concerned for his welfare that they broke down the doors of his hut, expecting to find an emaciated figure. Imagine their surprise when the person who emerged seemed in every way healthy, robust, and full of insight and wisdom on how to lead a contemplative life. Antony had apparently confronted his demons head on—and had survived to tell the tale.

The dangers of the desert were ever present, however. Hunger, thirst, lack of sleep, and the threats to his physical well-being from predators such as lions, crocodiles, and poisonous snakes all took their toll. Worse, Antony was haunted by visions of devils. Psychological warfare did, indeed, take place, as if a battle for his soul was waging inward. And yet he soldiered on and, in the end, won the battle.

After his period of self-imposed isolation ended, Antony welcomed a community of monks to join him in the desert. Serving as abbot of this makeshift monastery, he received and played host to countless pilgrims who sought him out for his wisdom and compassion. For a short period of time, he even settled disputes, preached sermons, and healed the sick. He played the role of public figure.

Considered by many to be the ideal Christian, Antony lived to the age of 105, or so the story goes. During his own lifetime his experience in the desert influenced thousands of men and women to seek religion. Most of all, thanks to his example, they sought solitude, not as a way to escape from society but as a way of knowing oneself better, as a way to live an uncluttered life. After all, to possess goods is to be possessed by them; the Desert

Fathers, however, had nothing left to lose. They had already given up everything. Antony, the most famous of the Desert Fathers, epitomized the life of a true ascetic. A thirst and a longing for certainty, purpose, and some kind of meaning: this is what he found in the desert, and this is what he ultimately found within himself.

REFLECTION

The Desert Fathers believed that only by having self-awareness will we be able to truly know ourselves. Antony gave up everything to pursue his vision. Could you give up all your worldly possessions for your faith? for a cause? for a person?

FOR FURTHER READING

Athanasius. Robert C. Gregg, trans. *The Life of Anthony and the Letter to Marcellinus.* Classics of Western Spirituality (New York: Paulist Press, 1980).

Peter France. *Hermits: The Insights of Solitude* (New York: St. Martin's Press, 1996).

Gregory Mayers. *Listen to the Desert: Secrets of Spiritual Maturity from the Desert Fathers and Mothers* (Liguori, MO: Liguori Publications, 1996).

Helen Waddell, trans. with an introduction. *The Desert Fathers.* Vintage Spiritual Classics. Preface by M. Basil Pennington (New York: Vintage, 1998).

Bede

MONK
(673 – 735)

Before the inevitable journey no one can be
So wise that for him it will not be necessary
To consider, before his going hence,
What, for his soul, of good or ill,
After his death-day, the judgement will be.

BEDE

the Venerable Bede, considered the Father of the English Church and the greatest historian of the early Middle Ages, lived a quiet and contemplative life. He spent most of his time writing, translating, studying, and reflecting. He wrote books on natural history, the writing of verse, and the work of his saintly predecessors, including Saint Aidan and Saint Cuthbert. His *Life of Cuthbert*, in particular, is perhaps one of the finest examples of hagiography available today, a distinctive literary form that emphasized that the subject was a man of God and thus adept at performing saintly duties and miracles. Many of these so-called miracles were apparently modeled after stories from Scripture.

It is unlikely that Bede ever traveled much beyond his beloved Northumbria, in the north of England. Born at the monastery of St. Peter's at Monkwearmouth—it was not unusual for infants and children at that time to be raised in religious institutions—Bede was placed under the care of its founder, Benedict Biscop, at the tender age of seven. In 682 a second monastery was built at nearby Jarrow, dedicated to Saint Paul and operated under the capable auspices of Abbot Ceolfrith. Two years later, Bede was transferred to this monastery, where he would grow from boyhood to manhood, learning Greek and Latin and a smattering of Hebrew. Above all, it was there that he studied the Bible. He was made a deacon at the age of nineteen and a priest when he turned thirty.

Bede lived a long life; most people would probably consider it an uneventful life, but this was not so. For Bede lived a life of the mind. His works were populated by all the great heroes and saints of his day and of legend. He spent virtually his entire life in one place—St. Paul, where he studied, taught, wrote, and ultimately died.

Among his many works are Bede's *Lives of the Abbots* and, his most famous, *History of the English Church and People*, a masterful account documenting the arrival of Christianity in the British Isles and recounting the stories of its early saints and missionaries.

The monastery at Jarrow housed an excellent library that was endowed by Biscop, a Northumbrian nobleman who served in the court of King Oswy and who later, as a monk, actually founded the monastery.

The twin monasteries of Monkwearmouth and Jarrow were large and wealthy. The buildings that comprised the monastic estate, which at times varied from 60 to 120 acres, were built of stone and said to emulate buildings in Gaul and Italy.

Bede died on May 25, 735, and was buried in Jarrow. At the time of his death, he was working on an English-language translation of the Gospel of John. Eventually his remains were removed from Jarrow and placed in the same coffin as Cuthbert's. Finally, his relics were placed in their own tomb at the Galilee Chapel in Durham Cathedral.

REFLECTION

Most of us struggle through life, not sure which route to take along the journey. Bede received a true gift: to have a purpose in life—to know where one's talents lay—at a young age. When did you know what your life purpose would be? Do you know now? If not, what are you doing to achieve that goal?

SITES ASSOCIATED WITH BEDE

Durham Cathedral
Durham, England
This Romanesque cathedral contains the tomb of the Venerable Bede.

Bede's World: The Museum of Early Medieval Northumbria
Jarrow Church Bank,
Jarrow, England
The story of the life and times of the Venerable Bede, one of the greatest scholars of the early Middle Ages. Jarrow Hall contains a variety of exhibitions on Bede as well as a miniature model of St. Paul's.

FOR FURTHER READING

Jane Hawkes. *The Golden Age of Northumbria* (Morpeth, Northumberland: Sandhill Press, 1996).

J. F. Webb, trans. *The Age of Bede.* Edited with an introduction by D. H. Farmer (London: Penguin Books, 1998).

Blasket Island Poets and Storytellers

The cock is crowing and the dawn is breaking,
And my love, he himself, going home away from me.
GREAT BLASKET LAMENT FOR THE DEAD

The like of us will not be seen again.
TOMÁS Ó CRIOMHTHAIN, GREAT BLASKET POET

The Blasket Islands lie off the coast of Kerry in the far southwest corner of Ireland, separated from the Irish mainland by a scant three and a half miles of treacherous waters. It might as well be the other end of the earth, however, so different are the two areas. The islands never contained more than two hundred people; at its peak, in 1916, the population swelled to 176.

The Great Blasket, the largest of a group of six islands, is only five miles long. It is a small island, now uninhabited, but for generations it nourished the minds and souls of a marvelously imaginative population of poets, storytellers, singers, and musicians. The islanders preserved the ancient tales of an oral tradition, including legends—some reportedly older than *Beowulf*—poems, songs, and folklore.

The islanders spoke Irish, but more than this, the Irish they spoke was almost medieval in thought and execution. It was blunt yet rich in allegorical associations. Clever turns of the phrase were much appreciated in this conversation-rich culture. The language was also known for its elegance and grace, for its lyrical quality.

Often cut off by the unpredictable vagaries of the weather, the islanders relied on one another for emotional sustenance while being economically dependent on the Irish mainland for the bare necessities of life. For centuries, they lived in glorious isolation, untouched by the cruelties of the modern world—or, as Cole Moreton writes, "They lived on an island of stories."

Maurice O'Sullivan (1904-1950), Tomás Ó Criomhthain (1854 or 1856-1937), and Peig Sayers (1873-1958) wrote autobiographies of what it was like to live in this remote corner of Western Europe. O'Sullivan penned *Twenty Years A-Growing*, Ó Criomhthain, *The Islandman*, and Sayers, *Peig*—all published in their original Irish between 1929 and 1935. The books are known for their directness, subtle wit, and acute sense of observation. And all describe without fail the natural beauty of the island. Ó Criomhthain lived on the Great Blasket all of his years, O'Sullivan spent some time away, while Sayers came to the islands as an adult.

Their stories tell of fishing, seal and whale hunting, attending wakes and weddings, matchmaking, the danger of making a living by the sea, and bidding farewell to relatives and friends off to make their fortune in America. In other words, they tell of the ordinary drama of everyday life. Music, too, brought the community together. More than just a mere pastime, it drew from and enhanced island culture.

O'Sullivan was one of the best known of the island storytellers. Born and bred in the Great Blasket, he left the island for the Irish mainland when still a young man to join the Civic Guard in Dublin, although he soon discovered it was not to his liking. Tragically, he drowned in 1950.

Ó Criomhthain chronicled, through tales and stories, the passing of a way of life. Originally published in 1929, *The Islandman* was successfully translated into many languages.

And then there was Peig Sayers. Not a native of the island, she turned out to be the grandest storyteller of them all. She could recite more than three hundred folk tales, ranging in theme from the bawdy to the saintly, from exciting adventures to moral fables. Her autobiography, *Peig*, was published in 1936.

Theirs was an egalitarian society, where time meant something altogether different than it does to you or me. Rather than watching a clock, the islanders' lives were dictated by the wild rhythms of the sea and by the cyclical turning of the seasons, by the ceaseless wind and the breaking of the waves. Yet everything fell into place.

These poets and storytellers often dreamed of a land without suffering, of a place at the edge of the horizon beyond all mortal reach, where no one grows old. They looked westward. To some it was the mythical Tir na nOg, or Land of Youth, to others it was the Land of Promise. And to a generation of Blasket islanders it was simply America. Writes Maurice O'Sullivan:

> I looked west at the edge of the sky where America should be lying, and I slipped back on the paths of thought. It seemed to me now that the New Island was before me with its fine streets and great high houses, some of them so tall that they scratched the sky; gold and silver out on the ditches and nothing to do but to gather it. I see the boys and girls who were once my companions walking the streets, laughing brightly and well contented. I see my brother Shaun and my sisters Maura and Eileen walking along with them and they talking together of me. The tears were rising in my eyes but I did not shed them. As the old saying goes, "Bitter the tears that fall but more bitter the tears that fall not" (*Twenty Years A-Growing*).

Slowly, the islanders left . . . for the Irish mainland, or for Britain, and especially for the United States. Many settled in Springfield, Massachusetts. The population dwindled so rapidly, in fact, that by 1953, only twenty-two people remained. On the verge of starvation, the desperate islanders agreed to be evacuated to the mainland. Thus, on November 17, 1953, a Dingle fishing boat, significantly named in honor of a martyred saint, the *St. Lawrence O'Toole* carried the four remaining families to their new homes—"four newly built cottages," reported the front page of *The Kerryman*—in the village of Dunquin.

Ironically, the words of the island poets inadvertently led to their island home's demise. When word got out about this seemingly island paradise where stories fell effortlessly from the lips of peasants, it didn't take long before visitors outnumbered the natives. Until all that remained were memories and, like a fleeting dream, it did not last. But it was all in the telling.

REFLECTION

To the Blasket islanders, the spoken word was everything. The stories and tales they shared with one another contained the wisdom and heritage of generations past, linking them forever to their forebears. Do you have your own family stories? Do you share them with family members?

SITES ASSOCIATED WITH THE BLASKET ISLANDS

The Blasket Centre

Near Dunquin, County Kerry, Ireland

Overlooking Blasket Sound, the center features a permanent exhibition on island life and history. It includes a restaurant and small bookshop. Boats from Dunquin and Dingle can take visitors across to the islands during the summer months.

FOR FURTHER READING

Cole Moreton. *Hungry for Home: Leaving the Blaskets: A Journey from the Edge of Ireland* (New York: Viking, 2000).

Tomás Ó Criomhthain. *The Islandman*. Translated by Robin Flower (London: Oxford University Press, 1978).

Maurice O'Sullivan. *Twenty Years A-Growing*. With an Introductory Note by E. M. Forster (Nashville: J. S. Sanders & Co., 1998).

Peig Sayers. *An Old Woman's Reflections*. Translated by Seamus Ennis (London: Oxford University Press, 1978).

Joan and Ray Stagles. *The Blasket Islands: Next Parish America* (Dublin: O'Brien Press, 1988).

RECOMMENDED LISTENING

Beauty an Oileain: Music and Song of the Blasket Islands (Claddagh Records). Songs and music performed by the islanders themselves.

Bono

ROCK MUSICIAN
(1960-)

Grace makes beauty out of ugly things
U2

orn in Dublin in 1960, Paul Hewson, otherwise known as Bono, is the lead vocalist and, along with guitar player The Edge (Dave Evans), the chief lyricist of the most popular rock band ever to emerge from Ireland.

With the exception of Adam Clayton, all members of the band practice a brand of charismatic Christianity that enhances their work rather than detracts from it. They don't hit you over the head with their beliefs; they are not proselytizers or preachers. On the contrary, anyone can fully appreciate their music without having any knowledge whatsoever of the artists' religious proclivities. But for those who prefer some lyrical substance, the spiritual dimension certainly provides added weight to their music.

Founded in late 1976 by Larry Mullen, Jr., even from the beginning U2 was no ordinary band. Each of the four very different and strong-willed individual members brought his own talents and viewpoints to the whole. It was Bono, though, who, within a very short period of time, assumed the leadership role.

Born on May 10, 1960, in north Dublin, Bono is the product of a "mixed" marriage—the son of a Protestant mother and a Catholic father. His father in particular had an interesting background: a postal worker with socialist tendencies who also dabbled in acting, painting, and the music-hall tradition. When Bono was fifteen, his mother died, and he took his unfocused anger to the streets before finding solace and peace of mind in Christianity.

U2 has always been a band with a message: no matter how dire the circumstances may be, no matter how bleak the future may appear, don't give up. Don't surrender to the darkness. With other bands, the same message may seem trite and contrived. But coming from U2, you know they mean it: their style of rock 'n' roll is not used as self-gratification but as inspiration to do good.

U2's lyrics reveal this essentially optimistic viewpoint. In fact, biblical metaphors are interspersed throughout their diverse songbook. In songs such as "Rejoice," "Scarlet," and "40," for example, the band exudes a quiet Christianity. Whereas "Gloria," which includes a prayer in Latin, manages to recall both the Church and fellow Irishman Van Morrison's randy hit of the same name back in the sixties. But that's the essence of U2: spirituality and sensuality, doubt and faith, all wrapped up in one irresistible musical package.

In "Drowning Man," the narrator surrenders to a higher love, to a higher calling. Bono himself has described this work as a psalm, a rock 'n' roll psalm perhaps, but a psalm nevertheless. Written from the point of view of a David railing against God or the forces of nature, the song is about losing control and the attempt to get it back. It's about feeling overwhelmed by the enormity of everyday life. It's about searching for ecstasy. If one doesn't achieve it, at least one has tried. It's about all of these—and none of these, for, like many U2 songs, it's about what you, the listener, bring to it.

A further look at "40" reveals a gentle hymn of resignation, with lyrics partially lifted from Psalm 40: a song as incarnation and a bit of a prayer.

You have multiplied, O LORD my God,
  Your wondrous deeds and your thoughts
    toward us.

PSALM 40, 5:1–2

Undoubtedly, U2's most popular recording to date, "The Joshua Tree," is also their most spiritual. If the Desert Fathers found solace in the arid Egyptian desert, then U2 found renewal—a spiritual renewal—in the deserts of the American West, where the Joshua tree, a giant cactus and one of the oldest trees in America, came to represent everything that was ancient, wise, and good. According to Irish writer Mark J. Prendergast, it was named by early Mormon settlers and symbolized, for them at least, the struggle of the Old Testament prophet Joshua to reach the Promised Land. In the nineteenth and twentieth centuries, America remained the Promised Land, especially for the countless Irish emigrants who came to its shores.

Whether it's the spiritual doubt of "I Still Haven't Found What I'm Looking For" or the bleak uncertainty of "With or Without You," the songs of U2 offer many interpretations, which makes for a satisfactory listening experience. In song after song, Bono may be addressing Christ himself or perhaps a loved one, we can never be sure. But it is this very ambiguity that enriches the music. Each listener brings to the songs what he or she wants, and each is amply rewarded in the end.

REFLECTION

U2 has always been the most idealistic of rock bands. In a cynical age and in an industry more known for manipulation than good Christian charity, that comes as a refreshing anecdote to despair. In their view, rock music can change the world—for the better. Has a work of art ever profoundly affected you so strongly that you thought you could change the world? or at least your small corner of it?

FOR FURTHER READING

Mark J. Prendergast. *Irish Rock: Roots, Personalities, Directions*. Dublin: O'Brien Press, 1987.

Niall Stokes. *Into the Heart: The Stories Behind Every U2 Song*. New York: Thunder's Mouth Press, 1997.

RECOMMENDED LISTENING

October (Island, 1981).

War (Island, 1983).

The Joshua Tree (Island, 1987).

All That You Can't Leave Behind (Interscope, 2000).

Brendan

Abbot
(c.486-578)

Is not the Lord our captain and helmsman?
Then leave it to Him to direct us where He wills.
Brendan

Brendan was one of the Celtic world's greatest of travelers. Although he journeyed widely throughout the known world, he is best known for his famous sea voyages. The inspiration for the voyages came from the Desert Fathers, although Brendan sought, in his case, "a desert in the ocean."

Brendan was born on the west coast of Ireland, near Tralee. His name means "fair drop," referring to a drop of rain that fell from heaven on the day he was born. Before his birth, his mother saw a vision: her bosom was full of gold, her breasts shone like snow. She was told that this vision was a sign that she would give birth to a special child, a child who would be filled with the endless grace of the Holy Spirit.

For nearly half a dozen years Brendan stayed at a convent run by Saint Ita, his foster mother—it was quite common then for children who were deemed spiritually worthy to be educated by saints—at what is now Killeady in County Limerick. He later studied under the famous teacher, Saint Enda, and eventually rose to become an abbot. But it was Bishop Erc in County Kerry who baptized him as a child and served as his true mentor. Erc probably taught him Latin, with perhaps a smattering of Hebrew. From Erc he also mastered the Old and New Testaments.

A restless child, Brendan wished to explore his saintly isle of Ireland. So Erc granted him permission, with the directive: "Come back to me and bring the rules with you, that I may ordain you when you return." After learning the rules of the saints and their customs, and committing to memory their devotions, he dutifully returned to Erc to be ordained.

Brendan began to travel shortly thereafter to such places as Strathclyde, Cumbria, perhaps, and Wales. Yet his main center of activity remained the western part of Ireland. Mount Brandon on the Dingle peninsula, for example, is named in his honor. In 559 he founded the monastery at Clonfert—and eventually founded several other monasteries, including Ardfert in Kerry, Inishdadroum in Clare, and Annadown in Galway.

But Brendan was never satisfied staying in one place. And yet he didn't want to travel just for the sake of traveling. Rather, he yearned to travel for the Lord, and so he asked the powers that be to offer up an unknown land that he could visit, far away from his native shore. Indeed, from an early age the precocious Brendan was obsessed with the notion of finding the Promised Land of the Saints, a variation of the old Irish Land of Eternal Youth, or Tir na nOg. It didn't really matter the destination, though, for the journey itself became almost a leap of faith, fraught with inherent dangers that added immeasurably to its general appeal. He visited Saint Enda of Aran, Saint Jarlath of Tuam, Saint Finnian of Clonard. and perhaps Columba on Iona, and, at various times, he traveled to Brittany, Orkney, and Shetland, and even as far as the Faroes.

After five years of traveling, Brendan returned to Ireland. While back home, he performed many miracles, healing the sick and setting free the incarcerated. He made a visit to his foster mother, Ita, who told him that the only way he would be able to find the land he was seeking was to build a boat made of timber.

And so Brendan went to Connacht, on the west coast of Ireland, and built a large boat of timber. From there, he and his companions embarked on yet another voyage across the great ocean. One day, as if by accident, the party came upon the mythic Land of Promise.

Here, at long last, they found what they had been looking for: a land without sickness or disease, a land of constant pleasure and contentment, where food was always plentiful and meadows bloomed with the sweetest of flowers.

It was this second and more famous voyage that may have brought Brendan and his sixty-man crew to as far away as North America. If this is true, they would have reached the New World some one thousand years before Columbus and four hundred years before the Vikings.

The publication of *The Voyage of Brendan* in the tenth or eleventh century led to the cult of Brendan. Today, the tales of Brendan's sea voyages are among the most popular works of the Middle Ages, surviving in more than one hundred Latin manuscripts, as well as in English, Spanish, French, German, Italian, and other languages. *The Navigatio*, as it is also called, is sheer fantasy, of course—the product of an extremely vivid imagination—but as compellingly delightful as anything coming out of the Hollywood studios. With its tales of sea monsters and celebrating Easter on the back of a great whale, how could it be otherwise?

When Brendan returned to Ireland, he settled in Clonfert, in County Galway, where he lived a long life, completing some ninety or so years on this earth. He died in 575 (some sources say 578), reportedly at the home of his sister, and was buried at Clonfert with great honor and dignified pageantry.

REFLECTION

Brendan was a restless soul, never content with what he had or where he was. To him, the most significant part of his travels was not the final destination, but the journey itself. What's important to you? The actual arrival or the experiences gained along the way?

SITES ASSOCIATED WITH BRENDAN

Clonfert
County Galway, Ireland
All that remains of the monastery founded by Saint Brendan is a ninth- or tenth-century Irish Romanesque doorway and a tiny twelfth-century cathedral.

Craggaunowen, The Living Past
County Clare, Ireland
Features recreations of ancient Irish dwellings and items associated with Tim Severin's *Brendan*, the leather boat that made its way across the Atlantic in 1976–1977, which was built in a boatyard in County Cork.

Sixmilebridge
County Clare, Ireland
This outdoor living-history museum includes a reconstruction of the living conditions of the early inhabitants of Ireland, and features the *Brendan*, the boat that Tim Severin and his companions used to sail from Ireland to America in the 1970s.

FOR FURTHER READING

John J. O'Meara. *The Voyage of Saint Brendan: "Journey to the Promised Land."* Translated from the Latin (Gerrards Cross, Buckinghamshire: Colin Smythe Limited, 1991).

Tim Severin. *The Brendan Voyage* (London: Little Brown, 1996).

Brigid

ABBESS OF KILDARE
(c.450-c.525)

I would like to have the men of Heaven in my own house:
With vats of good cheer laid out for them.
I would like to have the three Marys, their fame is so great.
I would like people from every corner of Heaven.
ATTRIBUTED TO BRIGID

he most famous female Irish saint, and second in popularity only to Patrick, is Saint Brigid, patron of poets and healers, travelers and pilgrims, animals and midwives. In the Scottish Highlands she was known as "Mary of the Gaels," and in London there is a famous church, St. Bride, named in her honor. In recent years, a group of Irish American women in Chicago have given "Brigid Awards" to women of Irish heritage whose sense of justice, generosity, and compassion emulate that of the noted saint.

Yet, Brigid was no plaster saint, no untouchable icon of a distant and rigid institution. Rather, she was the original Earth Mother, all flesh and blood, an earthy, robust woman with a healthy sense of humor, whose sole wish was to bring joy and goodness to her fellow earthly travelers. It was said that she could transform water into beer and make salt from a stone. How can one help but like and admire her?

Brigid straddled two quite different traditions—a nascent Christianity and a very old pagan religion—yet so versatile and adaptable was she that she could serve as a go-between of sorts, assimilating quite comfortably between the two. A transitional figure, she possessed the same name as the goddess Brigit, meaning "the exalted one." Brigid was associated with wisdom, poetry, fire, and the hearth.

Brigid was the daughter of Dubthach (sometimes spelled Dubhthach), a pagan aristocrat from Leinster, and a Christian slave named Broicsech (or Brocseach)—some accounts, though, claim she was of noble parentage. At sunrise one day, Broicsech, who was holding a vessel containing milk, gave birth to a daughter whom she named Brigid. According to legend, the attending maidservants washed the infant in milk. Later, prodded by his jealous wife, Dubthach sold Broicsech to a poet who in turn, sold her to a druid.

Brigid was apparently baptized at an early age. Some accounts say she was converted to Christianity by Saint Patrick while she was still a child. A druid once prophesied: "Marvelous will be the child . . . No one on earth will be like her." And so he was right.

One day, years later, when her mother went to milk the cattle, she left Brigid alone in the house. While she was gone, the house caught fire, as a single flame shot skyward toward the heavens. When neighbors came to rescue the girl and found that the fire had dissipated, they took this as a sign that the child was sent by the Lord.

As she grew older, Brigid offered her considerable powers to those in need—whether human or animal. She tended sheep, cavorted with birds, fed the poor.

One day Brigid and her mother went to her father's house. Whenever possible, she would take from her father his wealth and possessions and give it to the poor. At one point, for example, she gave a leper, who had come to her seeking spiritual assistance, her father's sword. After her father learned of her "gift-giving," he was so angry that he brought her to the court of the king to try to sell her—no disobedient daughter would be allowed to stay under his roof.

When the king asked her why she had stolen and given away her father's sword, Brigid simply explained that if she had all the wealth and power in the world, or at least in all of Leinster, she would give it all to the Lord. Taken aback, the king remarked, "It is not right for us to deal with this young woman, for her merit before God is higher than ours." Thus was Brigid saved from a life of slavery.

Eventually, this most devout of women was ordained by Bishop Mel of Ardagh. She went on to found a famous monastic city, a double monastery, for both men and women, at a place called Kildare, or "the Church of the Oak." According to legend, Kildare had once been a pagan sanctuary, where a ritual fire had been kept perpetually burning "by an order of virgins." Clearly, Brigid had chosen a most unusual site for her monastery. In due time, under her leadership, this became one of the richest and most powerful monasteries in Ireland, as well as an international center for pilgrims worldwide.

Brigid also founded a school of arts and letters at Kildare. Kildare even reportedly produced its own illuminated manuscript, which, had it survived, some say would have rivaled the famous Book of Kells.

Brigid was an evangelist for Christ, and her mode of transportation was a chariot. So forceful and persuasive was her personality that she negotiated the release of hostages (tribal conflicts were quite common in her day), healed the sick and lame, helped the poor, and restored sight to the blind and speech to the mute. Brigid died in 525. Years later, in the ninth century, her relics were moved to Downpatrick because of the threat of Viking raids.

In life and death, Brigid of Kildare remains one of the most beloved of Celtic saints.

REFLECTION

If anyone could be called selfless, surely it is Brigid. Should you be fortunate enough to receive an economic windfall, what would you do with it? Would you, like Brigid, give generously to the poor, or can you think of other ways you would share your good fortune?

SITES ASSOCIATED WITH BRIGID

St. Brigid's Cathedral
Market Square, Kildare, Ireland
St. Brigid's round tower and St. Brigid's Cathedral, a restored medieval cathedral, are at the top of a hill, commemorating the saint who established a monastery on this site in the late fifth century. St. Brigid's statue is located in the center of town. There's also St. Brigid's Holy Well and St. Brigid's Celtic Cross within the vicinity.

George Mackay Brown

Writer and Poet
(1921–1996)

We are all one, saint and sinner.
GEORGE MACKAY BROWN (*For the Islands I Sing*)

George Mackay Brown was a native son of Orkney, the far-away islands located north of the Scottish mainland. He lived there most of his life, and it is the legends and myths of those northern lands and the timeless rhythm of the sea that infuse his writing.

Born in the Orcadian town of Stromness in 1921, Brown studied at Newbattle Abbey under the renowned Scottish poet Edwin Muir, his mentor and a fellow Orcadian. He also read English at Edinburgh University, where he did postgraduate work on the Jesuit poet Gerard Manley Hopkins. Brown was a prolific writer in various genres: novels, short stories, essays, poetry, and plays. Perhaps Muir best summed up Brown's work when he described it as a mixture of "strangeness and magic rare anywhere in literature today."

Brown's works include the novels *Vinland, Beside the Ocean of Time, Greenvoe,* and *Magnus;* the short story collections *Hawkfall, Andrina and Other Stories,* and *A Time to Keep;* the essays *An Orkney Tapestry,* and the poetry collections *Loaves and Fishes, Fishermen with Ploughs,* and *Voyages.*

Born the youngest child of a dirt-poor family, Brown contracted tuberculosis at an early age, a condition that would haunt him the rest of his life. But it would also allow him to spend vast amounts of time, a "desert of time" he would call it, in solitude. He converted this excess of time in two directions: to alcohol, which offered insight into the complexities of the mind as well as a range of health concerns, and, on a more productive note, to the glory of putting words down on paper.

Brown was a deeply religious man, a religion that combined the Norse ancestry of the Orkney Islands and his intense attachment to mysticism. As a boy, he was thrilled by the stories of the Old Testament. Later, as a young man, he observed, at first from afar, the mysteries of the Catholic Church and, eventually, became enchanted by the wondrous power of its rituals, icons, and customs and by the miraculous sweep of its two-thousand-year-old history. Here, he felt, was a Church for the ages, a Church that could combat the erosions of time. Ultimately, though, it was the power of words that convinced him to convert to Catholicism in 1961: the richness of the words belonging to the Welsh poet George Herbert, the uncertainty and doubt that dogged Graham Greene's collection of wayward priests and forsaken sinners.

Coupled with this, Brown returned to the legends and folklore of his own native Orkney, with its magnificent stories inspired by the great Scandinavian sagas, a curious mixture of piety and barbarism. In particular, it was the straightforward narrative of the *Orkneyinga Saga* that appealed to him the most: of the rivalry between Earl Thorfinn and Earl Rognvald; of the feud between Earl Hakon and Earl Magnus; of the pilgrimage of Earl Rognvald the Second to Jerusalem, Byzantium, and Rome. The language was terse and spare, the emotions primitive and elemental.

In his novel *Magnus*, his interpretation of the life and martyrdom of Saint Magnus, Brown turned directly to Orcadian legend. An atypical Viking, Magnus refused to participate in any type of warfare, choosing instead to read from his Psalter and chant the psalms. At this point, Magnus and his ambitious cousin, Hakon, were both joint earls of Orkney. Jealous of his cousin's popularity, Hakon met with Magnus on Easter Monday 1117, on the Orcadian island of Egilsay. One came with peace in his heart, the other with murder on his mind. With the single stroke of an axe to the forehead of gentle Magnus, Hakon assured his ascension to power.

But that wasn't the end of the story. Strange things began to happen—for example, people were cured of illnesses at the site of the murdered earl's tomb—and soon the cult of Magnus spread throughout the land, with the location of his burial at Birsay becoming a place of pilgrimage. The magnificent St. Magnus Cathedral in Kirkwall bears his name, as does the arts festival that, centuries later, classical composer Sir Peter Maxwell Davies helped cofound in 1977. And in a twist of cruel fate, the man who built the great cathedral, Magnus's nephew, Earl Rognvald Kolson, also had built a fine Norwegian ship that carried him and his companions on a holy pilgrimage to Jerusalem. Alas, like many men of his time, this scholar-pilgrim-poet died a brutal death in Caithness, on the Scottish mainland.

All these stories added immeasurably to Brown's art. As an adult, he looked back at his childhood in idyllic terms. Edwin Muir has referred to one's first childhood as "the only time in our lives when we exist within immortality," of "one day endlessly rising and setting." Most of all, he deeply loved the little town where he was born and raised, describing it in words worthy of a Dylan Thomas:

> The snow had fallen all night—the storm has blown itself out. I open the door to a transfigured world, a white enchanted Stromness. All the roofs wear tilted white bonnets. The old wives shake their shawls, lamenting, "Oh, what awful weather!" I walk, I sink above my boots in thrilling whiteness.

All sounds are muted. The cat shakes a paw. The
birds leave prints, hopping from crumb to crumb.

And the stars flashing like jewels in the early
evening—all night long till the late dawn wells in
the south-east, over Scapa Flow.

The moon hung like a Chinese lantern over the
chimney pots.

PORTRAIT OF ORKNEY

Brown loved a good story, well told. Fortunately, Orkney is
full of good stories. In *Portait of Orkney*, he tells about two fiddlers
returning home late one summer night from a country wedding.
Their journey took them past a cluster of green mounds or
howes where, it was said, trolls dwelled. In Orcadian folklore,
trolls were mischievous creatures who often kidnapped their
human prey. A few, however, were also known for their goodness and love of music.

So there the young fiddlers stood, giddy with the drink and
camaraderie of friendship, talking loudly and laughing under the
perpetual twilight of an Orcadian summer evening. Suddenly,
one of the fiddlers completely vanished, his fiddle now silent.
Terrified, the friend ran to the safety of his home. Years later,
when the fiddler happened to be walking the same path at the
stroke of midnight in the heart of summer, he heard the sound
of familiar footsteps. Turning in the direction of the noise, he recognized the face of his fiddler friend who had disappeared so
many years ago. The young man, a veritable Dorian Gray, had not
aged a day.

Brown relished the timelessness of this story, of its artfulness
and its appreciation of artistic expression. Brown's work was of an
archetypal nature, deriving its terse and plainspoken style from the
ancient sagas themselves. He had utmost respect for the rituals of

life and the humble acts of ordinary men and women—laborers, fishermen, farmers—who featured prominently in his tales. Often, the same characters appear over and over again in his stories, embroiled in a daily struggle for survival that is "at once brutal and holy."

Orkney's favorite son, George Mackay Brown, died in 1996. For most of his life, he had prowled the steep steps and twisting streets of his little town. At his most eloquent, he embodied the best of what Orkney had to offer: a huge heart, an expansive spirit, and a spiritual grace that spanned the ages and bridged cultures.

REFLECTION

George Mackay Brown's stories are very much steeped in a strong sense of place. Community and family and tradition meant a lot to him. He found great solace, too, in religion and in the customs and rituals of the Church. How important is tradition to you? Do you take time out of your day to incorporate your own little rituals and traditions into daily living?

SITES ASSOCIATED WITH GEORGE MACKAY BROWN

St. Magnus Cathedral
Kirkwall, Orkney, Scotland
Begun in 1137 by Earl Rognvald Kolson, cousin of the martyred Saint Magnus, this is an impressive cathedral. Within the pink sandstone interior lie the bones of Saint Magnus. The cathedral is also one of the venues of the annual St. Magnus Festival, held throughout the islands every June.

St. Magnus Church
Egilsay, Orkney, Scotland
Magnus was murdered in 1117 by his cousin, just southeast of the church. The site is marked by a memorial. Construction of this striking church, with its truncated round tower, began in 1137.

FOR FURTHER READING

George Mackay Brown. *For the Islands I Sing: An Autobiography* (London: John Murray Publishers, 1997).

____.*Magnus* (Glasgow: Richard Drew Publishing, 1973).

____.*Portrait of Orkney* (London: John Murray Publishers, 1988).

Iain MacDonald, ed. *Saint Magnus* (Edinburgh: Floris Books, 1993).

Hermann Palsson and Paul Edwards, trans. *Orkneyinga Saga: The History of the Earls of Orkney* (London: Penguin Books, 1981).

RECOMMENDED LISTENING

Sir Peter Maxwell Davies. *Hymn to Saint Magnus.*

____.*The Martyrdom of Saint Magnus.*

Bueno

WELSH SAINT
(circa sixth century)

Glory be to God for dappled things—
For skies of couple-colour as a brinded cow.
GERARD MANLEY HOPKINS

Saint Bueno was the son of elderly parents and of noble lineage. Like a number of early Celtic saints, his birth was deemed a miracle.

When old enough, Bueno received a proper education. He studied the Scriptures and learned the rules and customs of the Church until eventually he was ordained into the priesthood. He became a missionary, devoting his life to the Church and traveling great distances to spread the word of God. He founded monasteries and even performed miracles. The most notable monastery associated with him was at Clynnog Fawr in Wales.

It was here, in this remote northwest corner of Wales, where Bueno died. Just before he passed away, though, he witnessed a remarkable sight of angels at first descending from heaven and then ascending. As he continued to look upward, he saw all the saints climbing up the heavenly staircase, as they sang their songs of praise. And then he was gone.

Bueno was better appreciated in death than in life. His shrine at Clynnog Fawr was, for many years, an important sacred site, as was the chapel of St. Bueno. Eventually, a cult grew around his name, and he became particularly associated with cattle, not surprising given that cattle were such a vital part of the area's economy.

The cult of Saint Bueno continued well into the nineteenth century. Although today, he is one of the lesser-known Celtic saints, Bueno's life and work affected at least one important poet, the Jesuit Gerard Manley Hopkins, who spent some time in the area and was impressed by both its beauty and tranquility.

REFLECTION

Bueno was not particularly known for his piety, and yet, for many centuries, his good deeds and succession of miracles earned the respect of countless ordinary Welsh men and women. Think of the people you know in your life who may not be outwardly spiritual and yet, through individual acts of kindness and goodwill, display sincere Christian charity. Does one need to go to church in order to be deemed spiritual?

Angus Peter Campbell

POET
(1954–)

But the braes of Glenelg,
the steeples of Kintail,
the great pibroch of the Cuillin
are like shrouds covering the dead,
blankets of splendour flung over so much horror,
for the world is not empty without reason.

For men have evicted men,
and men have raped women,
and men have murdered children
to leave such a grave silence,
like a kirkyard on an eternal Sabbath.
ANGUS PETER CAMPBELL ("The Highlands")

ngus Peter Campbell is one of the leading Scots Gaelic poets of his generation, a native Gaelic speaker who composes in both Gaelic and English. The fact that he is little known on this side of the Atlantic is a shame, for his voice is the voice of not only a particular generation, but of an entire group of people. "A post-Presley Gael," lyricist Calum Macdonald of the Gaelic rock band Runrig calls him. "A Gaelic bard of my own generation and geography, for whom English language holds no restriction." Campbell speaks for the voiceless and for those who do not even know that they have a voice with which to speak.

Born and brought up on the Hebridean island of South Uist in Scotland, Campbell studied politics and modern history at Edinburgh University. For several years he worked as a journalist before turning to full-time writing.

Campbell knows all too well the often sad and tumultuous history of his own people, and he gets it down on paper. He is a devout Christian, a socialist, and a Gael—and he is comfortable playing all three roles. He is the author of two books of poetry, including *The Greatest Gift* (1992).

In *The Greatest Gift*, his first collection of poetry, Campbell recalls a Uist upbringing, the memory of his late father, and the indifference wrought by Margaret Thatcher and her governmental policies. The wider world and his own world form the core of his themes. He frequently juxtaposes the present with the past, from soldiers crushing the citizen's revolt at Tiananmen Square in China to a peaceful summer's day in Edinburgh as he anticipates his daughter's first day of school.

Campbell's politics are unabashedly socialist—"I know those who sleep in cardboard boxes," he writes (and one suspects that the Margaret Thatchers of the world know not of which he speaks). His spirituality is fluid: "surrounded by the memory of Abraham and the Celtic thought of Columcille." He composes in a precise and vigorous tongue, creating images that are darkly romantic and yet fiercely realistic, shorn of any sympathy for himself or any patience for displays of false sentimentality. He often plays on words, toying with the popular culture of a seemingly romantic Scottish past, as when he refers to "rowing boats speeding across the bonny sea to Skye."

Campbell's words often refer to the cultural icons of his youth and young adulthood—Robert Burns and the Gaelic poets Rob Donn, Uilleam Ros and, most recently, Sorley Maclean—as well as to the great artists of the world, from Michelangelo to Picasso. His poetry also possesses a strong sense of place.

His themes are many—faith and identity are among his favorites—although oppression and exile are also uppermost in his mind. In "Human Rights," Auschwitz and Strathnaver dwell on a plain of equally unforgivable horror. The Holocaust and the Clearances, the latter being the Scottish equivalent in the poet's eyes, both devastated a people, changed their lives irrevocably, and left behind heartbreaking scenes of death and destruction.

Campbell lists the powerful people who were responsible for the turmoil in the world, from Hitler to the Duchess of Sutherland, and their victims, ordinary men and women who fill row after row of graveyards, headstones silent to their immutable fate. He marvels, too, at how one can share the same land—in his part of the world, at least, referring to the countess and the crofter (farmer)—and yet remain so alien to each other. If the final solution for the Jews in Europe was Hitler's gas chambers, then the "single solution" to the stubborn Highland problem was eviction and exile.

And yet Campbell remains a Christian with a generous Christian heart. Like Robert Burns, Angus Peter Campbell is a great humanitarian and, also like Burns, a great sinner. The world may be at times a terrible place, an unforgiving place, which Campbell unmercifully describes, but it is also a place where grace and kindness and generosity of the spirit live side by side. In a world of Nagasakis, Hiroshimas, and Auschwitzes, he seems to be saying that there *is* salvation, there *is* redemption, there *is* hope, "while the redeemed of the Lord sing a new song of glorious triumph."

REFLECTION

Angus Peter Campbell once referred to the "sound of our memories," and, indeed, memory is a major theme. Individuals matter, the past matters.

You and I are important—just as important as the historic figures in our history books, just as significant as the names that appear in our daily newspapers. Do you believe that everyone on this earth fills a particular purpose? Does everyone matter?

FOR FURTHER READING

Angus Peter Campbell. *The Greatest Gift* (Teangue, Sleat, Isle of Skye: Fountain Publishing, 1992).

Thomas Rain Crowe, ed. with Gwendal Denez and Tom Hubbard. *Writing the Wind: A Celtic Resurgence* (Cullowhee, NC: New Native Press, 1997).

Alexander Carmichael

FOLKLORIST AND COLLECTOR
(1832–1912)

> *As it was*
> *As it is,*
> *As it shall be*
> *Evermore,*
> *O Thou Triune*
> *Of grace!*
> *With the ebb*
> *With the flow,*
> *O Thou Triune*
> *Of grace!*
> *With the ebb*
> *With the flow.*
> JOHN STEWART "Fragment"

lexander Carmichael was an official in the Department of Customs and Excise, which allowed him a tremendous amount of flexibility. That is fortunate, since it enabled him to travel extensively throughout the Hebrides, where he collected poems, songs, prayers, and blessings of the Gaelic people at a time when the indigenous traditions seemed under threat of extinction. Indeed, some felt they were heading inexorably down the long road to oblivion.

Carmichael compiled the monumental five-volume *Carmina Gadelica*, a compendium of Gaelic lore, between 1855 and 1899. He had a lifelong interest in traditional folklore and became determined to record the Gaelic poetry and customs for posterity before it was too late. Methodically and dutifully, he jotted down the words spoken to him by countless "men and women throughout the Highlands and Islands of Scotland, from Arran to Caithness, from Perth to St. Kilda."

Born on December 1, 1832, on the island of Lismore in the Scottish Highlands, Carmichael was educated at the Edinburgh University before becoming a civil servant. His work also took him to other Celtic lands, including Dublin and Cornwall, but it was in his own country where he devoted most of his time and effort. A tall and stately gentleman with a full white beard, he possessed a kindly demeanor—a gentle giant cloaked in an imposing frame, who got along readily with almost every class and level of society.

Historians believe that much of the material contained in the *Carmina Gadelica* is of literary rather than folk origin, and was probably composed outside the Western Isles. It includes invocations (prayers for protection and blessings); seasonal hymns and prayers; praises to the saints; blessings for common tasks (from "smooring" the fire to milking and weaving); incantations or charms; all types of prayers (baptism prayers, morning prayers, journeying prayers); rhymes; and common labor songs (such as milking songs). Simple and sincere, the selections are marked by an intense piety and respect for nature, as well as a strong celebratory embracing of the spiritual and communal life. Some are of pagan origin, but are given a Christian flavor.

> I will kindle my fire this morning
> > In presence of the holy angels of heaven.

The prayers of these Highlanders and Islanders were very much Christ-based and formed in the image of the Trinity. What

concerned them were the mysteries of creation, the death and res-
urrection of Christ, and the overall presence of God in their daily
lives. For example, to begin the day an islander may have sung the
following hymn:

> I am bending my knee
> In the eye of the Father who created me,
> In the eye of the Son who purchased me,
> In the eye of the Spirit who cleansed me,
>   In friendship and affection.

Ritual was always an important part of Highland life.
During baptism, for example, three drops of water were dropped
on the infant's forehead: the first drop in the name of the
Father, representing wisdom; the second in the name of the Son,
representing peace; and the third drop in the name of the
Spirit, representing purity.

The poems were handed down through the oral tradition.
Many, if not most, were quite ancient, although how old, we can't
actually say. According to Carmichael:

> It is the product of far-away thinking come down
> on the long stream of time. Who the thinkers and
> whence the stream, who can tell? Some of the
> hymns may have been composed within the clois-
> tered cells of Derry and Iona, and some of the
> incantations among the cromlechs of Stonehenge
> and the standing stones of Callarnis [Callanish].
> These poems were composed by the learned, but
> they have not come down through the learned,
> but through the unlearned.

The Highlanders and Islanders felt that they owned the
poetry and hymns, and that by conversing with Dr. Carmichael,
they were sharing their heritage with the rest of the world. And,
to his great credit, Carmichael did not betray their trust. A native

Gaelic speaker himself, he would go to extreme lengths to uncover examples of traditional poetry, whether wading in bone-chilling waters from island to island or sleeping in the great outdoors by the fireside in a shepherd or crofter's humble dwelling.

This most ancient of poetry expressed universal emotions. And more often than not, the message was basic and fundamental: everything good comes from God. The ancient Gaels took their religion personally; they addressed angels or saints by name, and nothing separated them from these spiritual messengers. In fact, the angels and saints were welcomed as though they were members of the household, a part of daily life. Favorite saints included Mary, Brigid, and Columba.

The poetry addressed all aspects of the soul, of course, but it also honored crops and animals. After all, in the Gaelic pantheon, cows and hens were also in need of daily blessings. It has been said, for example, that Hebridean cows had grown so accustomed to hearing milking blessings that they would not produce milk without them. Thus, the universe worked in a mysterious harmony and everything was an integral part of it—whether human or animal, visible or invisible.

> God, kindle Thou in my heart within
> A flame of love to my neighbour,
> To my foe, to my friend, to my kindred all,
> To the brave, to the knave, to the thrall,
> O Son of the loveliest Mary,
> From the lowliest thing that liveth,
> To the Name that is highest of all.
>
> BLESSING OF THE KINDLING

Blessings were offered for any and all occasions. There were blessings for baptism, reaping, milking, but also sea prayers, blessings of house, and journey blessings. For the Highlanders and Islanders, life was one long journey from birth to death. So when Carmichael was ready to leave the islands, the islanders sent him off with the soft and soothing words of a journey prayer echoing hypnotically in his ears:

> . . . whole may you be, and well may it go with you, every way you go and every step you travel. And my own blessing go with you. And the blessing of God go with you, and the blessing of the Mary Mother go with you, every time you rise up and every time you lie down, until you lie down in sleep upon the arm of Jesus Christ of the virtues and of the blessings.

Only a portion of what Dr. Carmichael had recorded was published before his death in 1912. In recent years, however, various editions of the *Carmina Gadelica* have become available for all to enjoy.

REFLECTION

To the ancient Celts the reciting of blessings and prayers was all part of their daily ritual. How important is prayer to you? Is it an aspect of your regular routine?

FOR FURTHER READING

Alexander Carmichael, ed. *Carmina Gadelica*. With a preface by John MacInnes (Edinburgh: Floris Books, 1992).

Alexander Carmichael, ed. Introduction by Adam Bittleston. *The Sun Dances: Prayers and Blessings from the Gaelic* (Edinburgh: Floris Books, 1993).

James "Guadalupe" Carney

JESUIT PRIEST AND MARTYR
(1924-1983)

To be a Christian is to be revolutionary.

Men are suffering because they spoke the truth.
JAMES CARNEY

James Carney was a good man with a kind heart who made a lot of enemies. He had spent a good portion of his adult life in Honduras—some twenty years—when he was forcibly expelled and denounced as a revolutionary. But Carney was not the kind of person who would take no for an answer, not when he believed with all his heart that what he was doing was right and just. He took the gospel seriously and dedicated his life to living it to the fullest. So when he asked his siblings to meet him in nearby Nicaragua and from there he would cross the perilous border into Honduras, he must have known that he was virtually signing his own death warrant.

Carney was not born a revolutionary. On the contrary, he enjoyed a typical Midwestern Irish Catholic upbringing. Born in Chicago on October 28, 1924, he was the prototypical good Catholic: altar boy, hero on the high school gridiron, popular college student. He served his country in World War II, as a member of the Army Corps of Engineers during the invasion of France.

Carney was a rebel and a nonconformist, but not in the usual sense that we tend to think of those words. During his army years, for example, he tried to carry out his daily prayers and attend Mass every Sunday. Because he dared to be different, he was often the object of jokes. He wrote in his autobiography:

> Little by little I have come to realize that most people follow the customs of the group they belong to, without critical reflection. The environment in which they live is what most determines the attitudes and actions of almost all men and women. Only a very few have enough moral courage to go against the stream, to be different, to live according to moral principles, even though others make fun of them for it.

After the war Carney entered the University of Detroit, where he studied engineering. It was here, at this Jesuit school, that he heeded the inner voice urging him to do more than just master a particular vocation. Perhaps his stint in the armed services changed his attitude, but the former fun-loving college student was now searching for something more, some kind of purpose in his life. And so he joined the Jesuits.

Although he was not a scholar by inclination, Carney was determined to become a missionary and serve those who needed help the most. Ordained in 1961, he yearned in particular to serve the poor of Honduras—and he got his wish. Because he felt a strong attachment to Our Lady of Guadalupe, he asked that he be referred to as Padre Guadalupe.

Initially, Carney performed the traditional and sacramental duties expected of a priest, such as saying Mass on Sundays or celebrating the sacraments. But the longer he stayed, the more he became aware of the poverty of the people, especially within the rural population. Gradually he became radicalized and believed that nothing less than the empowerment of the poor and the complete transformation of the social infrastructure were required for justice to be realized.

Appalled by the hypocrisy of the *status quo*, Carney became involved in the peasant struggle for possession of the land. Those in power were ostensibly Catholic and yet the vast majority of the rural population was reduced to living in makeshift shacks, illiterate, as they watched their children die of hunger and disease. Any talk of social justice made the powers that be uncomfortable and so, when pushed, they leveled charges of betrayal against anyone who disagreed with them.

Carney made no effort to hide his feelings. He was a highly public and visible figure and a thorn in the side of authority. He worked tirelessly and without the least regard for his own well-being and safety in order to improve the living conditions of the peasantry, instilling in them a sense of dignity and self-worth. He traveled throughout the countryside, leaving his message of love and justice on their earthen floors.

Eventually he felt compelled to surrender his American citizenship to become a Honduran citizen and, in effect, a self-proclaimed revolutionary. His message was Christian love in its purist and most Christ-like form—his method, Marxism. He believed that only by completely transforming Honduran society would the Honduran people be free. "If I love the Honduran poor I have to share their life as much as possible," he wrote.

The new Honduran society he envisioned would be neither capitalist nor communist, but rather egalitarian. He sought to serve the Lord, to seek adventure, and to never surrender. Hating injustice and despising the double standard, he did whatever was in his power to combat both. In his view, capitalism used the most selfish motivations of humanity as the basis of an economic system that exploited others, "transforming Christians into materialists, into agnostics, in practice if not in theory, who in their daily lives do not take God and his commandments into account."

To the Honduran government, Carney was simply a dangerous radical, someone who needed to be disposed of. In 1980 the authorities placed him under arrest, stripped him of his Honduran citizenship, and deported him from the country. For the next three years he lived in nearby Nicaragua, all the while planning to return to his beloved Honduras.

In 1983 Carney snuck across the border with a band of Honduran guerrillas. Their goal was to help the Honduran workers fight for social justice. But the little ragtag "army" didn't last long, and it was disbanded before it could do any real good. And Carney was never heard from again. He simply "disappeared" in Honduras in September 1983. The official story claims that he had starved to death in the jungle. The more plausible explanation, though, is that he was captured, interrogated, and ultimately tortured, his body tossed from a military helicopter to the mountainside below, where he was left to die. But we don't know for sure.

Carney had no illusions about the danger of his mission; he was more than willing to become a martyr for justice. And more than likely, that is exactly what happened.

REFLECTION

James Carney was a nonconformist. He held strong beliefs and would not veer from them no matter the costs. Do you possess core values and beliefs? Are you affected by peer pressure? Would you allow the opinions of others to change your attitude?

FOR FURTHER READING

Donna Whitson Brett and Edward T. Brett. *Murdered in Central America* (Maryknoll, NY: Orbis Books, 1988).

Padre J. Guadalupe Carney. *To Be a Revolutionary: An Autobiography* (San Francisco: Harper & Row, Publishers, 1987).

Cíaran

Abbot
(c.512-c.549)

"In everything, do to others
as you would have them do to you."
Matthew 7:12

iaran is that rare kind of saint—a saint who wasn't afraid to reveal his flaws to the outside world. Known for his impulsive nature, as much as for his tremendous generosity, Ciaran managed to accomplish much in his short life, including the founding of one of Ireland's great monasteries, Clonmacnoise in County Offaly.

Born in northern Roscommon circa 512, Ciaran was a member of Ireland's privileged class and a disciple of Enda, another important if rather obscure Celtic saint. He grew up with a natural love of learning—his maternal grandfather was a noted bard, poet, and historian. He had many friends within the Church, including Columba, Enda of Aran, and Kevin of Glendalough.

Baptized by a deacon who also served as his foster father, Ciaran spent much of his early years as a cattle herder. He also had a love of the outdoors. One story, in particular, tells us much about his character.

One day while Ciaran was in the forest, a fox came out of its hiding place and approached him. Ciaran treated the animal gently and with great respect. He then asked the fox for a favor:

to carry his Psalter back and forth between him and Justus, one of his teachers. The fox agreed and carried out his chore dutifully, until one day it grew so hungry that it began to devour the book. Just at that point, however, a group of men came toward the animal, accompanied by a pack of greyhounds, and proceeded to hunt the fox. The only refuge the fox could find, ironically, was the shelter under Ciaran's cowl. Hence, the book was inadvertently "saved" by the fox, and the fox had been "saved" from the hounds. Rather than treat the animal harshly for almost destroying his precious tome, Ciaran responded with great restraint and generosity.

Ciaran studied under Finnian of Clonard, with a particular goal in mind: to learn wisdom. Now whether one can actually "learn" wisdom is debatable. At any rate, Ciaran asked his parents for a cow to take with him on one of his journeys but his mother refused. Perhaps she didn't think her son was ready for the responsibility that such a decision would entail. Determined as ever though, he blessed a cow that already belonged to his herd, which was referred to as Ciaran's Dun-Cow. Ciaran then made a wise decision, for he divided the cow's milk among Finnian's protégés, the so-called Twelve Apostles of Ireland, who lived at Finnian's school. Such a simple act of sharing was indicative of Ciaran's generous and charitable nature. It's been said that whoever dies and is placed on the Dun's hide will enjoy eternal life.

Eventually Ciaran left the security of Clonard to travel to the island of Aran to study under Enda. Both were visionaries in their own right and witnessed the same vision, that of an expansive tree—a Celtic tree of life perhaps—blossoming beside a stream in the heart of Ireland. When Ciaran mentioned this remarkable vision to Enda, the mentor reportedly responded:

> The great tree you saw is you, Ciaran, for you are
> great in the eyes of God and of all humankind. All

of Ireland will be sheltered by the grace that is in you, and many people will be fed by your fasting and prayers. Go in the name of God to the center of Ireland, and found your church on the banks of a stream.

With eight companions, Ciaran founded Clonmacnoise in 545 on the banks of the River Shannon. The name itself can be roughly translated as "Meadow of the Sons of Nos." It very quickly became recognized as one of the premier centers in Ireland for literature and art. Indeed, it was considered such an august site that many Irish high kings were buried there.

Unfortunately, Ciaran died, possibly of yellow plague, only a scant seven months after the building of a church at the monastery site. He was thirty-three years old.

REFLECTION

Ciaran felt he could learn how to be wise. Can one actually learn wisdom? Or does wisdom accumulate after years of experience? Do you consider yourself wise? If so, how have you earned it?

SITES ASSOCIATED WITH CIARAN

Clonmacnoise
County Offaly, Ireland
A medieval monastery founded by Saint Cairan circa 545, Clonmacnoise flourished between the seventh and twelfth centuries, becoming renowned as one of Ireland's most important monastic settlements and learning centers. Many Irish kings were buried here. Today all that remains are a group of stone churches, a cathedral, two round towers, and three high crosses. A visitors' center, housed in three buildings, resembles the beehive huts of the ancient Celts.

CoLumba

ABBOT OF IONA
(521–597)

When Christ, the most high Lord, comes down from the heavens,
the brightest sign and standard of the Cross will shine forth.
FROM *Altus prosator*

he was a scholar and a poet, a soldier and a saint. He was also one of the few Celtic holy men who left behind a considerable body of work, or at least work that is partly attributed to him. Columba was a mass of contradictions: a worldly man who loved solitude; a soldier of peace who may have been partially responsible for the death of thousands of men. He was a saint—but he was not always saintly.

A son of the aristocracy and a dutiful son of Ireland, Columba, ironically, did not really belong to any one place—although he remained loyal to Derry in his heart—nor to one overriding authority. Like many monks of his day, he felt a calling that lay beyond his control. He belonged to the universal Church, his spirit transcending time and place, as if his purpose on this earth was beyond all human ken.

Very little is known about Columba's early life. He was born to a royal family in County Donegal and could trace his lineage back generations to Niall of the Nine Hostages, founder of the O'Neill Dynasty. It was common in those days for young boys from privileged families to receive the attention of a mentor, usually a priest. Columba studied for ordination, first in Leinster and then, most famously, with Finnian in Clonard. Already a charismatic figure—he also had a sharp tongue and fiery temper—Columba rose rapidly up the monastic ladder, becoming an abbot at a relatively young age. He would eventually establish several important monasteries, including Derry, Durrow, Swords, and Kells.

Columba's life changed forever, though, when Finnian returned from a trip to Rome with a copy of the Psalms (or Jerome's Psalter). When Finnian discovered that Columba had made a copy of the book essentially behind his back, he was understandably upset. In what some consider the first copyright case, Columba became embroiled in a rights dispute with his former mentor. Finnian told Columba that the copy belonged to him since he did not give permission for a copy to be made. (Prior to the invention of the printing press in the fifteenth century, each book had to be meticulously copied by hand.) The case was brought before Diarmid, the high king of Tara, who ultimately ruled in Finnian's favor and uttered the famous judgment: "To every cow its calf, to every book its copy."

Columba vowed revenge for what he considered an unjust call. The already tense atmosphere escalated, however, when a fellow clansman—a cleric—sought by Diarmid, fled to Columba for safety on an unrelated matter. After all, Columba was still a powerful man. Violating the protective custody agreement typically granted monks, Diarmid seized the hapless cleric and executed him right then and there, which led to open conflict between Columba's men and the followers of Diarmaid. Ultimately, some three thousand soldiers fell in battle, and the Church held Columba responsible for the outbreak of violence. Chastised and shaken by the bloodshed, a humbled Columba accepted moral responsibility.

As part of his self-imposed punishment, Columba left Ireland altogether, sailing from Derry with his companions in

563, and established a monastery on Iona. Calling himself "a pilgrim for Christ," he traveled through the Highlands and Islands, earning a reputation as a wise and holy man—and someone whose famous temper had mellowed over the years.

Columba's Irish name, *colm cille*, means "dove of the church," which does ample justice to his core personality traits: compassion, empathy, and persistence. Those who met him knew they were in the presence of someone special.

Columba was said to have established an excellent library in Iona. Indeed, the tradition of copying biblical texts was influenced largely by Columba's interest. It is possible that he wrote the Cathach (the Psalter) there, also known as "the battler," which dates from the later medieval period when it was encased in a gilded-silver shrine and carried into battle to ensure victory.

But the most famous manuscript associated with Iona is the Book of Kells, a decorated copy of the four Gospels and a masterpiece of medieval art. It was probably written on Iona some two centuries after Columba's death. Later it was taken to Kells, in County Meath, Ireland, to escape the Viking raiders.

Iona, located less than a mile off the island of Mull along Scotland's western shore, is only three miles in length and one and a half miles at its widest point. The windswept west side of the island is exposed to the full brunt of the fierce Atlantic winds; the east, sheltered by a gentle ridge of hills. It is a mostly rocky terrain and, at first glance, may not seem like much of a place at all. But to Columba it was the center of his spiritual universe.

In Columba's day the little community would have consisted of a cluster of small wooden buildings, a church, a communal building, a guesthouse, and huts where the monks worked and slept. Columba had two huts: one for sleeping and one for writing. The monks at Iona grew wheat, oats, and barley, as well as peas, beans, and leeks. In addition, they reared cattle and even kept bees.

Columba died on June 9, 597, reportedly while copying yet another Psalter. It is believed that he stopped at Psalm 34:10 ("those who seek the LORD lack no good thing") before breathing his last.

For several centuries after Columba's death, a small band of his disciples maintained, as best they could, the Columban tradition. But faced with the overwhelming reach and power of Rome, they could not hold on. In the early thirteenth century, a Benedictine monastery and Augustinian nunnery were founded on the island of Iona, under the tutelage of Reginald, Lord of the Isles. The onset of the Reformation led to further erosion of the community until gradually the abbey itself fell into ruin. Even so, Iona continued to inspire others. A romantic interest and the growth of antiquarianism led many pilgrims—both secular and sacred—to the island.

In 1899 the eighth Duke of Argyll, who had started the restoration process twenty years or so earlier, granted the ecclesiastical sites to the Iona Cathedral Trust, with the stipulation that the restoration work continue and a place of ecumenical worship be established. In 1938 the Rev. George MacLeod of Glasgow founded the ecumenical Iona Community, which remains an integral part of the island's enduring appeal. Today all that remains of Columba's monastery are sections of the ramparts that surrounded it on three sides.

A number of works have either been attributed to Columba, or at least inspired by him. *Altus prosator* ("Father most high") is about judgment day and the nature of God. *Adiutor laborantium* ("O helper of workers") is a combination of medieval church litany and Irish praise poetry.

In June 1963 a thirteen-man crew consisting of clergy and laymen of the Church of Ireland sailed from Derry in Northern Ireland to Martyr's Bay in Iona in a thirty-foot currach (Irish sailing vessel) to mark the 1400th anniversary of Columba's pilgrimage.

And in 1997 festivities held throughout the year commemorated the 1400th anniversary of the saint's death.

One wonders what Columba would make of all the day-trippers and latter-day pilgrims that flood the isle's narrow shores. Each day the little ferry from Mull deposits more and more people. Some are inspired by the spirit of Columba; others probably have never even heard of him. And yet they come.

REFLECTION

Starting over again is never easy. Columba made a grievous mistake. Some think he spent the remainder of his life trying to atone for his egregious error in judgment. How hard is it for you to admit mistakes? Are you able to learn from them and move on?

SITES ASSOCIATED WITH COLUMBA

Iona Abbey
Isle of Iona, Scotland
Houses the Iona Community, the ecumenical Christian community founded in 1938 by the late Rev. George MacLeod.

Kells Monastery
Kells County Meath, Ireland
Established by Columba in the sixth century, little remains of the original monastic site, although the eighteenth-century church features an exhibit on Kells. There is also a truncated round tower, and several ninth-century high crosses.

Columba Centre
Fionnphort, Mull, Scotland
This fairly new museum displays exhibits on Columba's life and times and offers a fine introduction to the saint and his achievements.

Columcille Heritage Centre
Gartan, County Donegal, Ireland
Exhibition devoted to Columba's life and times, as well as a display on illuminated manuscripts.

Trinity College
College Green, Dublin, Ireland
Houses the famous Book of Kells.

FOR FURTHER READING

Adomnan of Iona. *Life of St. Columba*. Richard Sharpe, trans. (London: Penguin Books, 1995).

Ian Bradley. *Columba: Pilgrim and Penitent* (Glasgow: Wild Goose Publications, 1996).

Thomas Clancy and Gilbert Markus. *Iona: The Earliest Poetry of a Celtic Monastery* (Edinburgh: Edinburgh University Press, 1994).

Brian Lacey. *Colum Cille and the Columban Tradition* (Dublin: Four Courts Press, 1997).

Bernard Meehan. *The Book of Kells* (London: Thames and Hudson, 1996).

Lesley Whiteside. *In Search of Columba* (Dublin: The Columba Press, 1997).

RECOMMENDED LISTENING

Cappella Nova. *Columba, Most Holy of Saints* (Gaudeamus). A musical celebration of the life of Columba.

William Jackson. *Inchcolm* (Linn Records). Features several selections inspired by Columba.

Savourna Stevenson. *Calman the Dove* (Cooking Vinyl). Celebrates the spirit of Columba.

Columbanus

Abbot
(c.530-615)

*The God we are seeking is not one who dwells far away from us;
we have him within us, if we are worthy.*
COLUMBANUS

In sixth-century Ireland, being a monk was considered the noblest possible calling. Throngs of young men flocked to the monasteries in search of peace and a sense of purpose. Columbanus, or Columban, was one of those young men.

He was born in Leinster and brought up in a prominent family. Poet, scholar, abbot, prophet, and saint, he is considered the cofounder of Western monasticism. Columbanus is credited with popularizing the monastic movement in Europe and creating an influential monastic rule. In short, he was a giant within the pantheon of Celtic saints.

Columbanus studied grammar, rhetoric, geometry, and Scripture—a typical curriculum of the Irish monastic education—under a disciple of Finnian of Clonard, with a goal of entering the monastic life. He chose the monastery of Cleenish on Lough Erne, founded only a few years earlier by a monk named Sinell, who himself had paid his dues with the well-known and respected Finnian. Clonard emphasized study and intellectual growth: habits that met with the young Columbanus's approval.

Considered a good-looking young man, Columbanus had his share of temptations. Eventually, though, he came to realize what his life's path would be, turning his back on all earthly pleasures and dedicating himself to a life of faith and self-sacrifice, no matter who it hurt.

Thus, when he told his mother he was leaving home to study under a monk in Lough Erne, she was so devastated that she begged and pleaded with him not to go, even to the point of throwing herself at the door to block his exit. Asking his mother not to grieve, he simply went on his way, determined as ever to follow the sacred path. Ironically, to modern sensitivities, Columbanus's behavior appears unbearably cruel and harsh. He had made up his mind, though, and there was no turning back.

Columbanus fled to a remote monastery in Bangor, one of the most austere of Irish settlements, which consisted of a collection of circular wooden huts built around a small church. The daily menu at Bangor consisted of simple items, namely, bread, vegetables, and water, and the monks wore sandals and long white tunics. A typical day involved prayer, labor, and study, as well as fasting, genuflecting, and prolonged periods of silence. The monastery was entirely self-sufficient.

Columbanus lived at Bangor for many years. Although generally happy with his situation, he still felt restless and thus asked permission from the abbot if he could go abroad. At first denying the request, Comgall, the abbot, finally relented after sensing how important it was to the young man. Comgall allowed twelve brethren to accompany Columbanus on his journey, including Gall, Domoal, and Aedh.

The voyage to the continent was uneventful. According to tradition, Columbanus arrived in Gaul, a spiritually desolate place at a time when heathen Frankish kings ruled most of the land. It didn't take long before his skill as a preacher was acknowledged, though, and he was invited to attend the royal court.

Columbanus was well received. In fact, so impressed were the people with this determined young man and his equally passionate companions that he could have asked for anything and it would have been granted. But Columbanus simply requested that the Gauls follow the teaching of the gospel. "If any want to become my followers, let them deny themselves and take up their cross and follow me" (Matthew 16:24). The king, perhaps taken aback by the simplicity of the request, suggested that Columbanus and his party might be better off looking for a secluded spot, far from the tumult of the towns.

After much searching, the group decided to settle in the valley of the Breuchin, which today is the modern French village of Annegray. They cleared a portion of the forest, built their modest cells, and lived on a diet of herbs, roots, and the barks of trees. The small community, often on the verge of starvation, prayed for assistance.

One story may help shed light on Columbanus's idiosyncratic and determined personality. At one point he mused whether it was better to be attacked by wild animals or set upon by a gang of thugs. Granted, either would be extremely unpleasant, but Columbanus tended to think in extremes. Suddenly, as he pondered this theoretical dilemma, Columbanus found himself surrounded by a pack of wolves. Remaining calm, he recited one of the psalms, and the wolves roamed off. Then a party of troublemakers arrived on the scene. But they too left him alone. Then Columbanus came across an isolated cave in which he found a bear. "Leave this place, never to return," he said to the bear, and the bear obeyed. And there, in the bear's den, Columbanus found his own retreat, his own personal refuge from the outside world.

Columbanus attracted so many followers to his monastery that he built another one at nearby Luxeuil, which would eventually become the mother house and largest of his settlements. He imposed a severe discipline; the Columban rule consisted of obedience, poverty, constant fasting, and a confession of sins followed by penances. During the next century more than one hundred monasteries were founded under these very strict rules, until they eventually gave way to the more lenient Benedictine rules.

And yet, Columbanus had his share of enemies. Local bishops, in particular, criticized his severe band of Celtic asceticism. Worse, he offended the royal family when he refused to bless the illegitimate offspring of the region's young king. As a result, orders were given to boycott all of Columbanus's monasteries. When that didn't work, and Columbanus refused to leave as ordered, the king and his followers rode to Columbanus's dwelling to confront the wayward monk. The king demanded free entry to all who wished to visit the monastery—outsiders were not allowed to enter the living quarters of monks—if Columbanus wished to continue to receive his support. But Columbanus stood his ground and, at one point, even prophesied that closing the monasteries would bring destruction and chaos to the king and his kingdom.

Outraged at the man's insouciance, the king ordered those who wished seclusion to leave and return to their homeland. When Columbanus said he wouldn't leave unless forced, one of the king's men took up the challenge and sent him on his way. And, when the saint returned surreptitiously to the shelter of the cloister a week later, the queen found out and convinced her husband, the king, to send an armed contingent to remove him once and for all. At this point, Columbanus gave himself up without a struggle, raising his hand in a signal of blessing.

After leaving the valley of Breuchin, Columbanus and his party made their way across central France. At Tours he spent a night in deep prayer at the tomb of Saint Martin. Finally, as he and his companions prepared to leave the continent and set sail for Ireland, he requested that the authorities allow his companions to travel separately while he would take a small boat on the open sea. While waiting to set sail, however, a storm erupted and the ship that was scheduled to carry his party ran aground on a sandbar. When the ship didn't arrive, the captain of the stalled ship took it as a sign from the heavens that perhaps the saint should not leave Gaul after all, that God wished for him to stay.

Columbanus and his companions then journeyed to the court of Theudebert, a king who was sympathetic to the Columban mission. He invited the monks to establish a settlement in what is now northern Switzerland, where they would be free to preach the gospel to the pagan population.

The next part of the journey involved a trip up the Rhine, where Columbanus may have been inspired to write the famous rowing song, "Carmen Navale," that has been attributed to him:

> Lo, little bark on twin-horned Rhine
> From forests hewn to skim the brine,
> Heave, lads, and let the echoes ring.

The death of his friend and protector, Theudebert, meant Columbanus once again fell under the rule of his enemy, Theuderich. This time, however, Columbanus made no attempt to fight back. A vision called him to go to Italy which, for reasons still unclear, was not universally accepted by members of his community, including his long-standing ally, Gall. (Some accounts indicate that Gall may have been too ill to continue the journey.)

So at the age of seventy, Columbanus made a difficult and strenuous crossing of the Alps. For a short time he settled in Milan, until he became embroiled in another controversy—the Arian controversy. (The Lombards, the Germanic people who lived there, had been converted not to the Roman form of Christianity but to the Arian form; that is, they did not acknowledge the divinity of Christ.) As a firm believer in the Roman Catholic doctrine of the Trinity, the monk was sure to make enemies.

By then, Columbanus had turned his eyes toward a ruined church called St. Peter in the hill country of northern Italy—a wild and remote terrain near the Bobbio River. The king offered Columbanus the land, and the monk gladly accepted. By the winter of 614, a new Irish monastery had been established here, in the foothills of the Apennines. It was here, in this home away from home, that Columbanus passed on. Typically, he did not die within the comforts of the monastery but in one of the remote hollows that he retreated to when he wanted to be closer to God.

Columbanus lived a long and eventful life, one marked by controversy and turmoil. He is a complex figure—not always likeable— and yet someone you can't help but admire. He was known for his austerity, persistence, honesty, discipline, integrity, and humility. The sick and the poor found in him a sympathetic ally. He was a missionary, a monk, but above all, he was a contemplative. And it was as a contemplative that he was most at peace.

REFLECTION

Columbanus wouldn't compromise when it came to his beliefs. Under what circumstances would you compromise in order to do what needs to be done? When would you stand your ground?

FOR FURTHER READING

Tomás Ó Fiaich. *Columbanus in His Own Words* (Dublin: Veritas, 1990).

Cuthbert

BISHOP AND MONK
(c.634–687)

Live in harmony with all other servants of Christ.
CUTHBERT

orn into an aristocratic Northumbrian family near the River Tweed in southern Scotland, Cuthbert, like many children of his day, was placed with a foster mother at a young age.

As a child, Cuthbert, or so the story goes, had the good fortune of meeting a special angel. One day his knee swelled to tremendous proportions. Indeed, a large tumor had developed, which caused the young boy much pain and discomfort, allowing him to hop on only one foot at a time. His condition gradually worsened, until he could hardly walk at all. Servants had to carry him outside so that he could enjoy the fresh air.

One afternoon, Cuthbert witnessed the marvelous sight of a man on horseback, all dressed in white, approaching from what seemed to be a great distance. As the man drew near, he greeted young Cuthbert in a friendly manner. Overjoyed, the lad saluted the man in return. When the stranger asked Cuthbert if he would be willing to offer some modicum of hospitality, the young boy explained that he could not act the part of the proper host because of the nature of his physical ailments. The horseman then examined the damaged knee and ordered, "Boil some wheat flour in milk and bathe the tumor with it hot, and you will be healed." With that, the "angel" on horseback rode off and disappeared just as quickly and mysteriously as he had arrived.

Cuthbert did what he was told, and within a few days his leg had improved. From that day forward, he became determined to devote his life to God.

One night while his companions were sleeping, Cuthbert, as was his wont, maintained a vigilant watch and prayed while tending a flock of sheep in the Lammermuir hills in the Scottish Lowlands. As he looked up, he saw a powerful light emanating from the night sky or, as he put it, "choirs of angels" coming down to earth. Experiencing the sight as a revelation, he knew something both terrible and wonderful had occurred. As it turned out, the great and gentle Aidan, Bishop and Abbot of Lindisfarne, had left this earth at that exact moment. Once Cuthbert realized this, he decided to enter the monastery at Melrose, the first and most famous of the numerous monasteries that Aidan had founded.

Cuthbert's mentor at Melrose was a priest by the name of Boisil, renowned throughout the land for his virtue. Boisil welcomed Cuthbert to the monastery, for he felt a sense of holiness resided within the boy. A zealous and highly disciplined worker, Cuthbert studied and prayed harder than almost anyone within the monastery walls.

After Boisil's death in 661, Cuthbert became prior at Melrose. At that time, the countryside was in the throes of the yellow plague, which Cuthbert himself had caught earlier but survived. Concerned for the welfare of his people, he ventured into the hill country, caring for the sick and preaching the words of the gospel.

Cuthbert was a popular figure, and one who maintained high standards within the confines of the monastery, but he also tried to convert people on the outside as well. Whether on horseback or on foot, he made the rounds of the villages, always preaching, always spreading the word of God. As a result, his reputation as a loving and caring man increased both inside and outside the monastery.

It was Cuthbert's custom to rise in the dark of night, while everyone else was sleeping, to pray without any distraction. He would always return in time for morning prayers, however. One night, while visiting a monastery on the North Sea, he went down to the beach and walked into the ocean until he was up to his arms and neck in bone-chilling water. There he spent the night in vigil, with his arms outstretched in the form of the cross. Over time, this became a frequent form of worship and prayer for Cuthbert.

Bede writes of the time when, after emerging from the sea at dawn, Cuthbert was followed by two otters. So taken were they with the man's saintly character that the frisky creatures rubbed themselves against his feet and refused to budge until he blessed them. Such was the hypnotic power that Cuthbert held over both humans and animals.

After many years at Melrose, Cuthbert was transferred to the monastery at Lindisfarne to teach the rule of monastic living. He was, after all, considered an exemplar of the religious life. At Lindisfarne he became famous for his miracles; it was said that he could heal diseases and afflictions.

Despite his affable personality and general good-naturedness, however, Cuthbert truly preferred a life of contemplation. When he was finally granted permission to pursue his heart's desire, he decided to settle on the island of Farne, a few miles to the east of Lindisfarne. He chose to live there alone, even though it was said to be haunted by devils. He built his own dwelling place, a circular wall of stones, and lived the hermit's life of prayer and fasting.

Despite the distance from Lindisfarne, many people came to visit Cuthbert on Farne. Some came to confess their sins, others simply to seek his counsel. Cuthbert welcomed them all.

But the day came, in 684, when he was elected Bishop of Lindisfarne, against his wishes. Cuthbert ignored the call to service, uncharacteristic perhaps but understandable, given his deep need for solitude. Although letters were sent to him and messengers traveled to the lonely island to bring him back to Lindisfarne, he refused to acquiesce, until one day the king himself, accompanied by his comrades, arrived on Farne. The little party knelt before Cuthbert and begged him to return to Lindisfarne. Only then did he reluctantly agree—and only after much prodding, pleading, and tears.

After only two years as bishop, however, Cuthbert sensed that the end was near, and so he once again returned to his beloved Farne to spend his last days. When the end finally came, his eyes searched the skies, and he stretched his arms upward, as if inviting himself to the heavens.

Cuthbert died on Inner Farne on March 20, 687, and was buried at Lindisfarne. His body was moved several times, however, as a precautionary measure against rampaging Viking raiders. In 995 it was moved to Durham and, in 1104, the shrine there was rededicated in Durham Cathedral, where Cuthbert's body remains to this day.

The famous Lindisfarne Gospels were written by Eadfrith, Bishop of Lindisfarne, in honor of Saint Cuthbert. Written mostly in Latin on vellum sheets and containing the texts of the four Gospels according to the evangelists Matthew, Mark, Luke, and John, the Lindisfarne Gospels is considered one of the most beautiful examples of Celtic art.

REFLECTION

Cuthbert was a loyal and devout servant. What would you do if you were asked by someone you trusted and admired to do something you didn't particularly want to do?

SITES ASSOCIATED WITH CUTHBERT

Durham Cathedral
Durham, England
Contains the tomb of Cuthbert and Cuthbert's relics.

Inner Farne
Farne Islands, Northumberland
Site of Cuthbert's remote retreat.

Melrose
Old Melrose, Borders, Scotland
Site of St. Aidan's monastery that was established in the seventh
century on the Banks of the Tweed. Best seen from Scott's View
on the B6356 to the east of Melrose.

St. Cuthbert's Way
A 62.5-mile walking route inspired by Saint Cuthbert and linking
the Southern Upland Way and the Pennine Way with the
Northumberland Coast. The route incorporates Melrose Abbey,
the Eildon Hills, the River Tweed, the Cheviot Hills, and
Lindisfarne National Nature Reserve. The walk starts at the
twelfth-century Melrose Abbey in the Scottish Borders and ends
at Lindisfarne.

Pilgrims Way
Posts mark the routes for the benefit of pilgrims, visitors, and residents. The causeway opened in 1954 and was extended in 1965,
so it is now possible to drive to the island at low tide.

MUSEUMS

Lindisfarne Priory and Museum
Lindisfarne, England
History of Lindisfarne from early times to the present day.

British Library
London, England
The Lindisfarne Gospels are housed here.

FOR FURTHER READING

David Adam. *Holy Island: Pilgrim Guide* (Norwich: Canterbury Press, 1997).

Janet Backhouse. *The Lindisfarne Gospels: A Masterpiece of Book Painting* (London: The British Library, 1995).

Jane Hawkes. *The Golden Age of Northumbria* (Morpeth, Northumberland: Sandhill Press, 1996).

Iain Macdonald, ed. *Saints of Northumbria: Cuthbert, Aidan, Oswald, Hilda* (Edinburgh: Floris Books, 1997).

David

PATRON SAINT OF WALES
(c.520–c.589)

Brothers and sisters, be cheerful and keep your faith and belief,
and do the little things that you have heard and seen through me.
DAVID

avid was the son of a Welsh chieftain named Sant (or Sanctus), and Non, a female saint of the early Celtic Church in both Cornwall and Brittany. Affectionately called "Dewi" by his flock, he was said to have been endowed with magical powers, and was known for his wisdom and abstinence.

Legend tells us that an angel appeared to his aging father one day, predicting the child's birth and telling him to prepare gifts for this special infant: a honeycomb, a fish, and a stag. A honeycomb symbolized wisdom; a fish symbolized bread and water; a stag symbolized the power to eradicate the land of devils or, more accurately, pagans.

Before David was born, however, Sant abandoned Non, leaving the woman on her own, with little in the way of emotional or physical support. She went into labor during a raging storm, but at the moment of birth, the fierce weather suddenly subsided, everything turned still and, it was said, a great light shone from above. Prophecies indicated that the newborn would be great, a singular leader of men. Clearly, David's birth has strong Christian overtones.

David was baptized by a bishop from Munster in Ireland. There's the story of how the newborn restored sight to a blind cleric, who cradled him in his arms, after drops of baptismal water splashed into the man's eyes.

As a young boy, David was taught the rituals of the Church. After studying under Saint Illtyd, he was eventually ordained a priest and spent a decade or so with his mentor, Paulinus, a Welsh saint. One of the legends circulating around David tells of how Paulinus reportedly became blind but David restored his eyesight, too.

David is credited with establishing nearly a dozen monasteries, including Glastonbury. At one point he even traveled to Bath, where he blessed the polluted waters, thereby cleansing them and making them warm enough for bathing.

One day an angel appeared to David and told him to found a monastery at what is now St. David's in southwest Wales. Emulating the Desert Fathers, he practiced a severe brand of asceticism, drawing to his monastery other monks who were just as committed as he was to a sparse lifestyle. Although the monks spoke only when necessary, they prayed constantly, even while working. After toiling in the fields—they plowed with yokes rather than using cattle or oxen—they would return to the monastery to read, write, or pray and in the evening, they would chant the psalms. Even their meals were simple. A typical supper consisted of not much more than bread and herbs.

David earned the nickname of "the Waterman" for his habit of immersing himself in bitterly cold water to ward off any temptation. He celebrated the Eucharist daily and spent the rest of his day teaching, praying, and genuflecting. His eloquence earned him the primacy of the Welsh church.

David became known throughout the land for his good deeds. He cared for the sick, for the needy, for pilgrims. One evening an angel appeared and beckoned him to travel to the Holy Land, to Jerusalem itself. Accompanied by two disciples, he sailed across the English Channel and arrived in Gaul, proceeding from there to Jerusalem. The patriach of Jerasulem welcomed the three Christians warmly and ordained David an archbishop. Aglow with the warmth of welcome, they returned home, satisfied and happy.

One day in late February an angel spoke to David, declaring that the day he had patiently awaited was about to arrive. For eight days he remained in the church, preaching and praying, until the first of March. It's been said that his soul was transported to heaven by a choir of angels on that very day.

Years after David's death, his body and relics were transferred from a rural monastery church in Wales to St. David's Cathedral. Canonized by Pope Callistus II in 1120, David has remained a popular figure over the centuries. Kings William I, Henry II, and Edward I reportedly made pilgrimages to his shrine in Pembrokeshire, Wales, and today St. David's Cathedral is an important stop for many latter-day pilgrims.

REFLECTION

David was an ascetic. He took his vows seriously and devoted his entire life to serving the Church. Have you ever felt this strongly about something? about someone?

SITES ASSOCIATED WITH DAVID

St. David's Cathedral
St. David's, Pembrokeshire, Wales
The cathedral stands on the site where Saint David founded his monastery in the sixth century. The present cathedral, however, was erected in the twelfth century.

fursey

MONK AND MISSIONARY
(c.575–648)

I will go on to visions and revelations of the Lord.
PAUL (2 Corinthians 12:1)

ursey (sometimes spelled Fursa) was born in Galway during the latter half of the sixth century, circa 575. According to tradition, Fursey was baptized by Saint Brendan, and so he came across his inherent saintliness quite naturally. As a child he loved to read the Scriptures, and later studied under a well-known Irish abbot by the name of Meldan. He was considered a fine student, performing so well and learning so fast that he began traveling throughout the land, spreading the word of Christ. Wherever he went, his passion and commitment attracted large crowds.

Then, Fursey fell ill. During his illness he experienced a series of remarkable visions. He heard choirs of angels participating in rapturous song and witnessed the souls of the departed ascending to heaven. At the same time, evil spirits tormented him shamelessly. Finally, approaching the doorway to heaven, he was accosted by two Irishmen who told him he must return to earth to preach the joys of heaven and save men and women from their wicked paths of sin.

For a dozen years Fursey preached the gospel throughout Ireland. Unfortunately, the more people who gathered around him, the more anxious he became. Finally, when the pressure overwhelmed him, he fled to the safety of a remote island off the west coast of Ireland to pray for guidance.

It was here, in glorious solitude and far away from the crowds, that Fursey felt refreshed and renewed. Feeling the time was right, with his two siblings and a cadre of friends, he set sail in the direction of England, as a pilgrim for Christ. Now whether he knew he was going to East Anglia or, like Brendan and other Celtic saints, trusted his fate to the good Lord, we cannot be certain.

Either way, the small party arrived on the east coast of England in 633, where they were welcomed by the local king, Sigebert, who had already converted to Christianity and who offered them an abandoned fort. Fursey soon converted the fort into a monastery and thus established a base in this corner of England, catering to the spiritual needs of the Angles.

Eventually, Fursey grew tired of the physical and spiritual upkeep of the monastery and, once again sought solitude in the English fens as a hermit. Fearful of attack from the pagan Mercians under King Penda (who would eventually kill Sigebert and lay siege to Anglia), Fursey decided to leave England altogether. With a band of like-minded pilgrims, he set out for Rome to see where fate would take him.

The party first landed in Brittany, where Fursey preached for a while before traveling onward. He paused momentarily at a castle near the Sommes, where he revived the son of the region's duke. Impressed by this miraculous turn of events, the mayor of the royal palace at nearby Peronne invited Fursey to stay. Fursey graciously declined, however, to complete his pilgrimage to Rome. In 644 he established another monastery, outside Paris.

Fursey died in Mezerolles in 648 and was buried at Peronne. As Fursey's tomb became a notable place of pilgrimage, the town in turn, flourished and attracted many pilgrims, especially the Irish.

Throughout his life, Fursey would occasionally fall into trance-like states. These visions were said to ignite the religious imagination of Western Europe in the later Middle Ages. One particular vision is worth describing.

Looking down upon the earth, Fursey saw a valley consumed by fire. The angels told him that these deadly conflagrations represented the various evils in the world, specifically the pursuit of wealth at the expense of God, the disruption of human relationships, and the injustices directed toward the weak and the poor. Wracked by terror, he witnessed violent battles between angels and demons.

These prophetic visions affected Fursey profoundly. The Venerable Bede described them nearly a hundred years later in his writings, and added that Fursey was "renowned for his words and works, outstanding in goodness." His visions entered the popular imagination of the Middle Ages and were translated into several languages, reportedly influencing Dante's *Divine Comedy*.

Fursey is the patron saint of Northampton, England, as well as one of the most popular saints in France.

REFLECTION

The visions that Fursey described in great detail—the so-called fires of falsehood, covetousness, discord, and injustice—continue to plague humankind. In your estimation, has the world improved over the years? Do you see humanity turning kinder and gentler in the future? Do you have hope in the future?

Seamus Heaney

POET
(1939–)

Everywhere being nowhere,
who can prove
one place more than another?
SEAMUS HEANEY ("The Birthplace")

I t can be said, without much disagreement, that Nobel-prize
winning poet Seamus Heaney is probably today's best-known
living poet; certainly the best-known Irish poet. His work is
both immediate and profoundly appealing, his themes universal
yet couched in the language of the Celt. His concerns, often of a
provincial Irish nature, transcend ethnicity and national boundaries to speak to the collective soul, to the transcendent human
spirit. In short, his poetry addresses immemorial themes: Who
am I? Why am I here? What is my purpose on this earth?

Born in 1939 in County Derry, Northern Ireland, the eldest
of nine children, Heaney published his first poems in the late
1950s. In the early 1960s he taught in Belfast before becoming a
lecturer at the city's prestigious Queen's University in 1966. Half
a dozen years later, Heaney and his family moved "south of the
border," to County Wicklow in the Republic of Ireland, settling
in a former gatekeeper's cottage on the estate of the late playwright John Millington Synge. After a short stay there, the family
moved once again, this time to Dublin. Off and on, Heaney

served as a visiting professor at several American universities, including the University of California at Berkeley, 1970–1971, and at Harvard University in 1979 (later accepting a full-time professorship at Harvard).

Among Heaney's many works include *Death of a Naturalist* (1966); *Door into the Dark* (1969); *Wintering Out* (1972); *North* (1975); *Field Work* (1979); *Sweeney Astray* (1983), a translation of the medieval Irish poem *Buile Suibhne*; *Station Island* (1984, for which he won the Nobel Prize in Literature); *Haw Lantern* (1987); and *The Spirit Level* (1996). In January 2000 Heaney's verse translation of *Beowulf* was awarded the Whitbread Award as best book of 1999.

As a poet, Heaney often spoke for the unsung heroes of Ireland, of the forgotten figures of the past—the farmers, the laborers, the freedom fighters—who made Ireland what it is today. He writes frequently, too, of the ancient past, of murder victims preserved in the peat bogs of Denmark, of the megalithic tombs in prehistoric Ireland, of the Viking warriors who came in their longships first to raid and wreak havoc and then to settle down, eventually founding the city of Dublin.

But it is the family and all that the family represents that Heaney writes most eloquently about. Heaney composes from a number of perspectives: as a child; as a member of the Heaney clan; as a son, brother, husband, and father; as a Catholic; as an Irishman; as a poet living in the wider world. "If we understand our own minds, and the things that we are striving to utter themselves through our own minds," he once wrote, "we move others, not because we have understood or thought about those others, but because all life has the same root."

And yet Heaney is not a particularly religious poet—religion is not a common theme in his writing—but he is a profoundly spiritual one, if only because the past and the present, the natural order and the practical world, come together in his works.

Sometimes the old Christian legends make their way into his poetry. In *Death of a Naturalist*, for example, he retells the story of Saint Francis's sermon to the birds. He also uses, on occasion, Greek and Latin myth, such as the tale of Romulus and Remus or Mycenae in *The Spirit Level*.

Heaney's most ostensibly spiritual work, *Station Island*, takes place on the island of the same name in Lough Derg, County Donegal, an Irish pilgrimage site for more than a thousand years. Also known as St. Patrick's Purgatory, it's been said that Station Island was the place where Patrick spent forty days praying in an attempt to rid Ireland of evil spirits. As part of the three-day vigil of fasting and prayer, latter-day pilgrims walk barefoot around the Stations of the Cross and consume just one meal of dry bread and one cup of black tea per day.

In *Station Island*, the narrator embarks on an inner journey where he encounters a number of long-departed figures—ghosts of Heaney's near-forgotten past—who eventually lead him back to the present. It's been called by at least one critic "an anthropology of the dead."

> A stream of pilgrims answering the bell
> Trailed up the steps as I went down them
> Towards the bottle-green, still
> Shade of an oak. Shades of the Sabine farm
> On the beds of Saint Patrick's Purgatory.

In *Sweeney Astray*, the narrator reinvents himself as a bird, the mad King Sweeney of Irish legend. And in *St. Kevin and the Blackbird*, Heaney recalls the poignant relationship that the Irish saint had with a small bird. It is a simple poem commemorating the legendary patience and stoicism of Kevin and, in Heaney's sympathetic portrait, the saint becomes an object of selfless devotion.

Donnie Munro. "Dreams from Hard Places: A Lecture" (Glasgow: Sabhal Mor Ostaig and Scottish Television, 1996).

John Prebble. *The Highland Clearances* (London: Penguin Books, 1963).

Eric Richards. *The Highland Clearances: People, Landlords and Rural Turmoil* (Edinburgh: Birlinn, 2000).

___. *Patrick Sellar and the Highland Clearances* (Edinburgh: Polygon, 1999).

Iain Crichton Smith. *Consider the Lilies* (Edinburgh: Canongate Publishing, 1987).

RECOMMENDED LISTENING

Steve McDonald. *Highland Farewell* (Strathan Music). The Clearances as seen through a New Zealand-born grandchild of the victims.

Angus Macleod. *The Silent Ones: A Legacy of the Highland Clearances* (Torquil Productions). The story of the evicted crofters (farmers) from Lewis. Recorded at the site of Macleod's great-grandfather's original homestead.

Runrig. *Recovery* (Ridge). The Clearances and their ongoing legacy by Scotland's most famous rock band. A hopeful record despite the somber subject matter, the title song commemorates one of the heroes of the period, John Macpherson of Glendale in Skye.

hilda

ABBESS OF WHITBY
(614–680)

All that knew her called her Mother.
BEDE

lthough Hilda was Anglo-Saxon, she was also a protégée of Aidan of Lindisfarne, who encouraged her to establish monasteries in Northumbria. Hilda is best known for founding a double monastery—that is, a monastery that accepted both men and women—at Whitby in the north of England. In addition to earning a reputation for its overall excellence, Whitby was also the home of the first English poet, Caedmon.

Of noble birth, Hilda was a member of the Northumbrian royal family and the daughter of Hereric, nephew of King Edwin. She was born while her parents were in exile and was baptized by Paulinus of York in 627. She spent her early years in East Anglia before entering the double monastery in Gaul, at Chelles near Paris.

When Bishop Aidan called, she was ready to take the land she was given, near the river Wear, to establish a monastery. Here she lived the monastic life, with like-minded companions, for a year. Then, in 649, she was made abbess at a monastery at what is now Hartlepool, England, after the previous abbess retired. Hilda initiated a rule that emphasized discipline and order.

After several years, Hilda was able to establish her own monastery at Whitby. Here amply representing the virtues of justice, devotion, and chastity, the inhabitants of Whitby lived an egalitarian existence where all things were held in common. Hilda earned a reputation as a wise and prudent administrator and spiritual leader whose primary concern was the ongoing performance of good works. She had a reassuring and motherly presence, and for this and other reasons, her disciples called her "Mother," for her grace, her wisdom, and her devotion to the faith. Hilda also served as a spiritual director for not only the members of the monastery, but for the larger community as well. Everyday men and women as well as kings and queens sought her sage advice.

After Aidan died, a long-simmering controversy involving several unresolved issues came to a head. From a twenty-first-century perspective, it seems like much ado about nothing. But to medieval minds, the issues were very important, indeed; namely, the correct date for observing Easter, tonsure (referring to the distinctive way in which Celtic monks wore their hair), and administration.

Whereas the Irish shaved the front of their heads while keeping their hair long in the back in the fashion of the druids, the old Celtic priests, the Romans shaved their heads entirely, with short tufts sprouting around the sides of the head. Administratively, the Romans favored a highly structured model, while the Celts preferred a more informal, monastic approach.

But by far the most important issue concerned Easter. Outsiders claimed that the Celtic observance of Easter Sunday was contrary to that of the universal Church—namely, the Church in Rome. The discrepancy was tolerated as long as Aidan was alive—he was so loved that no one wished to confront him on this issue. But after his death, the problem could no longer be avoided.

The powers that be decided to hold a council to settle the matter once and for all. Because of Hilda's influence, King Oswy chose the monastery at Whitby as the preferred site for a synod in the year 664. Among those in attendance were kings and bishops and members of the Irish clergy. While Hilda and her followers sided with the Irish, King Oswy countered that those who served one God should also observe the heavenly sacraments in the same way. The purpose of the council, then, was to establish the one and true tradition.

In defense of the Irish, Bishop Colman, an Irish monk, explained that he followed in the tradition of Aidan who believed that John the Evangelist celebrated Easter in the same way. Wilfred, a priest, represented the other side. "The Easter we celebrate is the same as that universally celebrated in Rome, where the apostles Saint Paul and Saint Peter lived, taught, suffered, and were buried." He also mentioned that he found the Roman model celebrated throughout his travels on the continent, as well as in Africa, Asia, Egypt, Greece, and elsewhere. The only exceptions were Britain and Ireland.

Ultimately, the king decided to follow the tradition of Peter and the Roman way. Colman and his disciples, feeling defeated, returned to Ireland to continue the tradition of the Celtic church. Thus, the Celtic church would retain its Celtic character for many more centuries after Whitby, and yet a precedent had been established—the supremacy of Rome—that would eventually be accepted even among the Celts.

Hilda died in 680. She remains among the most respected of saints, Celtic and Anglo-Saxon alike.

REFLECTION

Despite her considerable influence, Hilda could not persuade the members of the Synod of Whitby to vote in her favor. And yet, she retained a considerable moral presence at the council. In other words, the participants agreed to disagree. What lessons can one learn from Hilda's experience?

FOR FURTHER READING

Iain Macdonald, ed. *Saints of Northumbria: Cuthbert, Aidan, Oswald, Hilda* (Edinburgh: Floris Books, 1997).

Victims of
the Irish Famine

(1845–1849)

Oh, son! I loved my native land with energy and pride,
Till a blight came o'er my crops—my sheep, my cattle died;
My rent and taxes were too high, I could not them redeem,
And that's the cruel reason that I left old Skibbereen.
ANONYMOUS ("Skibbereen")

t first there was the wailing. Then silence.

Of all the many tragedies and misfortunes to befall the Irish people, the most devastating must surely be the Great Famine of the 1840s. Consider the grim statistics: a population reduced from 8.1 million in 1840 to 6.5 million a decade later. In total, some one million people perished and more than a million left Irish shores forever.

Consider, too, the dangerous fact was that some three million people relied solely on the potato for food. If the crop failed, people died. It was as simple and as terrifying as that.

An elderly Irish farmer described the eerie mood that settled over Ireland at the beginning of the Famine:

> A mist rose up out of the sea, and you could hear
> a voice talking near a mile off across the stillness
> of the earth. It was the same for three days or
> more, and then when the fog lifted, you could

> begin to see the tops of the potato stalks lying over
> as if the life was gone out of them.

It all began in the summer of 1845 when a mysterious blight laid waste to the land, a blight that turned the potatoes black and rancid and thus inedible. The culprit was actually a type of fungus. But whatever the name or whatever the cause, the end result was the same: death and devastation quickly spread throughout the Irish countryside. The once-green fields were transformed into a mass grave, especially in the west where certain regions, like Connemara, were studded with derelict cottages and ruined villages.

The village of Skibbereen in County Cork was one of the worst hit. Skeletal, hollow-eyed men and women, on the brink of starvation, roamed the countryside in a futile search for one last scrap of food. Orphaned children, their cries of sorrow indistinguishable from the ongoing chaos, stood and wailed under gray, leaden skies. "Nothing can exceed the deplorable state of this place," wrote one exasperated official.

And so the same stories were told over and over again, and the suffering continued. The London government, under the direction of Prime Minister John Russell, did little to help (the previous minister, Robert Peel, was forced to resign because he had the gall to want to do something about the desperate situation). Indeed, the head of relief operations in Ireland, Charles Trevelyan, interpreted the Famine as an act of God, as the Maker's attempt to reorder Irish society. Employing a combination of Darwinian fate and laissez-faire nonintervention, he allowed the future of the Irish to fall prey to natural forces. The country would have to fend for itself and the devil take the hindmost.

Of course, some helped. The Quakers, for example, set up soup kitchens throughout Ireland. Physicians and members of the clergy did their best, and risked their own lives, to relieve the perilous state of affairs.

The year 1847 was the worst year of the Famine and so became known as Black '47. Years later, in honor of the victims of the Famine, an Irish American rock band would call themselves Black '47.

But the government couldn't turn a blind eye forever. Eventually, they had to do something. Finally realizing the severity of the situation, in 1847 the authorities began to give food away. Soup kitchens were opened throughout the land, which involved a massive effort of government intervention. Some three million starving people lined up every day for a small token of nourishment. From America came relief supplies, boatload after boatload.

Most of those who were able to emigrate went to America, but the Famine Irish who arrived on American shores were uniformly unskilled and, of course, destitute. Thus, being both poor and Catholic, they were unwanted. And yet they came, for America would be their only—their last?—hope. Nowhere else could they turn. And so they left their country of birth to find, in the words of Elvis Costello, a famous child of Irish immigrants himself, "a better life than I left behind." By living in perpetual exile, they, like the wandering Celtic saints of old, hoped to reach home.

Years later, the children, grandchildren, and great-grandchildren of the Irish Famine would have their day in the sun. Some would turn to politics, others to the arts. The Kennedy clan, Eugene O'Neill, and so many countless unnamed and unsung others like them would contribute to the great Irish American experience. Whether politician, poet, priest, actor, accountant, police officer or, indeed, whatever occupation one happened to choose, the story continues today, a never-ending stream of Irish consciousness that courses through the national bloodstream.

REFLECTION

If there is any lesson to be gained from the Famine it may well be a simple yet profound one: from tragedy and sorrow can come hope and joy. For the sacrifice of the Famine Irish was not in vain. Their descendants have achieved remarkable success in their "new" homes across the ocean. Do you know your own ancestors and where they came from? Are you aware of the struggle and hardship they endured and the obstacles they had to overcome to reach the New World? Are your children and grandchildren aware of their heritage?

SITES ASSOCIATED WITH THE FAMINE

Famine Museum, Strokestown House
Strokestown, County Roscommon, Ireland
Housed in Strokestown Park House and built in the 1730s, the Famine Museum is situated on the grounds of the old stable yards. It tells the story of both the tenants and the landlords during that terrible time.

Cobh Heritage Centre
Cobh, County Cork, Ireland
Cobh served as Cork's harbor. The center features displays on the mass emigrations in the wake of the Great Famine and depicts life below decks on one of the notorious coffin ships. A statue of fifteen-year-old Annie Moore, the first of seventeen million emigrants to pass through Ellis Island in New York, stands in front of the museum. She is accompanied by her two brothers.

Grosse Ile
Near Montreal, Quebec, Canada
Grosse Ile was a quarantine camp for victims of the Irish Famine, most of whom were trying to make their way to America via Canada. About 5400 Irish men, women, and children died on this island (although estimates range as high as 15,000). A five-story Celtic cross commemorates the spot where the victims were buried.

FOR FURTHER READING

Michael Coffey and Terry Golway, eds. "The Great Famine: Between Hunger and the White House" in *The Irish in America* (New York: Hyperion, 1997).

Edward Laxton. *The Famine Ships: The Irish Exodus to America* (New York: Henry Holt, 1996).

Kerby Miller and Paul Wagner. *Out of Ireland: The Story of Irish Emigration to America* (Washington, D.C.: Elliott & Clark, 1994).

Liam O'Flaherty. *Famine* (New York: The Literary Guild, 1937).

Cormac Ó Gráda. *Black '47 and Beyond: The Great Irish Famine* (Princeton: Princeton University Press, 1999).

Cecil Woodham-Smith. *The Great Hunger: Ireland 1845–1849* (New York: Penguin Books, 1991).

RECOMMENDED LISTENING

Black 47. *Fire of Freedom* (EMI). Traditional, reggae, hip-hop, and rock—all filtered through the eyes of playwright, poet, and Irish emigrant, Larry Kirwan.

Patrick Cassidy. *Famine Remembrance* (Windham Hill). A poignant musical commemoration.

Charlie Lennon. *Flight from the Hungry Land.* (Worldmusic). Suite for orchestra and traditional instruments written to honor the victims of the Great Famine. It is set in three parts: in rural Ireland prior to the Famine, the period from 1845 to 1849 during the height of the Famine, and in the New World.

Long Journey Home (BMG). Various artists. Companion CD to *The Irish in America*. Contains Sinead O'Connor's chilling version of "Skibbereen."

Ílltyd

ABBOT
(c.450–c.525)

Hast thou heard the saying of Illtyd,
The studious, golden-torced knight;
"Whoso doeth evil, evil betide him."
THE SAYINGS OF THE WISE

The story of Illtyd, one of the founders of the Welsh church, is a classic tale of a warrior turned devout peacemaker.

Illtyd was the son of a British nobleman, a military official, while his aunt was the legendary King Arthur's mother. Illtyd served as a knight under Arthur and then under the Welsh king of Glamorgan. One day, while out hunting on a military expedition, the earth transformed into a gaping maw and swallowed wholesale all of his companions, all, that is, save Illtyd.

Shocked and humbled by this totally unexpected act of grace, Illtyd sought out Cadoc, a gentle man known for his wise counsel, who told him that God had intentionally rescued him from certain death. Right then and there, Illtyd abandoned both the military and his own wife to live as a monk along a lonely Welsh river. He adopted an ascetic life, fasting and offering penance to the Lord. Each night he would bathe naked in the icy waters of a cold spring.

By giving up everything and adhering to such harsh living conditions, Illtyd hoped to redeem his past violent life in the eyes of God. He hoped, too, to be a role model for other members of the military profession and for the politicians of his day.

Illtyd was also a scholar in his own right. He was very knowledgeable, for example, of the Scriptures, and was well versed in philosophy, geometry, rhetoric, grammar, and arithmetic. It was also said that he turned into quite a prophet who, by the grace of God, was able to see what lurked behind the corners of life.

After his conversion, Illtyd traveled to several other Celtic lands, particularly Brittany and Cornwall, setting up monasteries and churches whenever and wherever he could. His most important monastery, though, was located at Llantwit Major in south Wales, which became known as an important educational center. Founded around 500, it was reportedly the earliest, or at least one of the earliest, centers of learning in Britain. Saint David and even Saint Patrick were said to be among his students. Later, Llantwit Major also was supposed to be the burial place of the kings of Glamorgan.

The parish church at Llantwit Major houses a collection of decorative Celtic crosses and stones, including an eighth-century boulder on which several letters of Illtyd's name are still clearly visible. Clearly Illtyd's legacy lives on in this obscure corner of south Wales.

REFLECTION

Illtyd's life changed drastically after his conversion, from that of worldly warrior to ascetic monk. Do you think it's possible for someone to change his or her life virtually overnight?

Íta

ABBESS
(c.480–c.570)

Three things that please God most are true faith in God
with a pure heart,
a simple life with a grateful spirit, and generosity inspired by charity.
The three things that most displease God
are a mouth that hates people,
a heart harboring resentments, and confidence in wealth.
SAINT ITA

Ita is known as "a second Brigid" and the "foster mother of the saints of Erin." This sixth-century abbess established a religious community and school on the site of what is now the ruins of the Romanesque church of Killeedy in County Limerick.

Ita was born near Waterford to a royal family. Baptized Deirdre, she later was given the name Ita, which means, "thirst for divine love." As Ita was growing up, miraculous things happened around her. For example, one day while she was asleep, her room caught fire yet, when alarmed neighbors came to her rescue, they found that the blaze had fizzled out. Through all the commotion, young Ita remained asleep. When she woke up, she appeared aglow, as if an inner light radiated from within.

Known for her generosity, chastity, grace, and charity, Ita experienced visions throughout her life. Yet, despite her apparent spiritual characteristics, her family still wished for her to marry a suitable partner, preferably a man of noble birth. In response, Ita fasted in protest. Then one day an angel appeared to her, prophesying that she, and the people around her, would be better if she were to serve God rather than live the ordinary life of a wife and mother. (Understandably, such a statement today might be deeply offensive to many readers.) Hence, Ita's family reluctantly agreed to permit her to leave her native village to settle near the foot of Sliabh Luachra. Some like-minded women soon joined her there, while other people, attracted by her obvious goodness, offered her land, gifts, and alms.

Ita lived an ascetic life, very demanding and very rigorous. She also spent many hours in prayer and meditation, finding silence to be a bracing antidote for the demands of communal living. It was said that she possessed gifts of prophecy and healing, and was in great demand for her wise counsel. A nearby holy well, because of its near proximity to Ita, was said to cure smallpox and other deadly diseases.

As part of self-imposed educational mission, Ita established a school for boys, where she encouraged her students to adopt the saints as their own special "soul friends." According to tradition, Saint Brendan was one of her pupils. When asked what three things are most pleasing to God, Ita replied, "faith, simplicity, and generosity."

Ita was buried in the monastery she had founded, and her remains lie there to this day. She is popular in Cornwall as well as on the Continent.

REFLECTION

Faith, simplicity, and generosity formed the cornerstones of Ita's life, core values that transcend time and place. What values do you hold most dear?

Kentígern

BISHOP
(c.518–c.603)

Good Bishop Kentigern, worthy to receive exultant praise,
when you brought light to the people who were in darkness,
you shone out with many a bright jet of flame
as a light set on a candlestick.
Into the presence of the Lord bring us who sing your praises.
FROM *The Ceremonies of St. Kentigern*

Kentigern, or Saint Mungo, as he was affectionately known, lived during a time of great turmoil and uncertainty. He himself had to endure considerable pain growing up as the illegitimate son of a Scottish princess. A contemporary of Columba—it's even been said that Columba visited him in Glasgow—Kentigern was considered one of the shining lights of the northern lands. He even inspired a Glasgow children's rhyme.

Kentigern was the child of a princess named Thenew, who was the daughter of a local king (the name survives to this day as St. Enoch's Square, a former railway station and now a major shopping district in central Glasgow). Thenew was a headstrong and bitterly independent woman who refused to marry the suitor her father had chosen for her, a prince by the name of Owen. Banished from her father's house for her disobedience, Thenew became a swineherd. The determined suitor, though, chased after her and, when he found her, he raped her. Having no where else to go,

Thenew returned home, but when she could no longer hide her pregnancy, her outraged father ordered her stoned to death. Thrown from the top of a mountain, she miraculously survived.

Thenew's angry father again ordered her death. But when the executioners who were hired to do the job didn't have the heart to finish it, the young woman was cast off in a boat that veered toward the Firth of Forth, on Scotland's east coast. Managing to reach dry land, Thenew gave birth to Kentigern at Culross in Fife, where Serf, the head of the monastic community there, took the infant under his wings and watched him grow to young manhood. It was Serf who gave him the name of Mungo, which means "dear fellow."

As a young man, Kentigern revealed his compassionate side. A local queen had given her lover a gift, a ring that she had received from her husband. When the king found out about this, he took the ring from the sleeping lover, threw it in the River Clyde, and then demanded that his wife produce the gift. The distraught queen, knowing that such a feat was impossible, approached Kentigern, who answered her prayers when he found the ring in the belly of a salmon.

Eventually Kentigern left Culross and went to Stirlingshire accompanied, according to legend, by the corpse of a holy man named Fergus, which was carried along on a cart drawn by two wild oxen. By this time, Kentigern had earned a reputation as quite a spiritual figure himself. The king, members of the clergy, and people of what was later to become the city of Glasgow wanted this humble servant of God to be their bishop. So, there, near the banks of the Clyde—actually closer to a small stream called Moledinar—he founded a monastic community and built a church.

But Kentigern had his enemies, too. He was said to be banished from Scotland by a pagan tyrant named Morcant, who was envious of Kentigern's success converting people from their native pagan religion to Christianity. Kentigern took refuge in Wales at what is now St. Asaph's, where he founded a monastery and became its first bishop, before eventually returning to Scotland until his death in 603.

Kentigern—actually, Saint Mungo is the preferred term—is Glasgow's patron saint. Symbols associated with his legend—such as the bell, the bird, the tree, and the fish—form the coat of arms for the city of Glasgow. The bird refers to the pet robin owned by Serf that was accidentally killed by monks who, in turn, blamed Kentigern. By cupping the bird gently in his hands, Kentigern was able to restore it to life, and it flew away to safety.

The tree refers to the time Kentigern was left to watch the holy fire in Serf's monastery. When he fell asleep and then awoke to find that the fire had gone out, he simply broke off some frozen branches from a nearby hazel tree and managed to rekindle it.

The bell is symbolic of a bell that was reportedly given to Kentigern by the pope.

Finally, the fish is a symbol that refers to the story mentioned above, when Kentigern recovered the queen's ring. When he slit open the fish, he found the ring that belonged to the queen who had been suspected of adultery by her husband.

Even a Glasgow children's rhyme recalls Kentigern, or Saint Mungo's legend:

> This is the bird that never flew.
> This is the tree that never grew.
> This is the bell that never rang.
> This is the fish that never swam.

Kentigern's body is enshrined in the lower church of Glasgow Cathedral, where the high altar was dedicated to his name.

In the spring of 1997, Cappella Nova, Scotland's only professional vocal ensemble, offered the fist complete performance in modern times of Scottish medieval plainchant from the fourteenth-century Sprouston Breviary, which celebrated the life and miracles of Saint Kentigern.

REFLECTION

Despite confronting many obstacles as a child and young man, Kentigern grew up to be a kind and compassionate figure and one dearly beloved by the community. How do past troubles affect your own life? Do you allow them to gain control over your emotions or are you, like Kentigern, able to learn from the past and move on?

SITES ASSOCIATED WITH KENTIGERN

Glasgow Cathedral
2 Castle Street, Glasgow, Scotland
Telephone: 0141-334-1010
Dedicated in 1136, the "new" building was consecrated in 1197, although what you see today was built primarily between 1230 and 1330. Glasgow Cathedral is considered one of the finest examples of Gothic architecture in Scotland. It houses the tomb of Saint Kentigern and also contains the St. Kentigern Tapestry, which was designed by Robert Stewart and dedicated in November 1979. The cathedral holds regular services in addition to recitals, concerts, and other events.

St. Mungo Museum of Religious Life and Art
3 Castle Street, Glasgow, Scotland
The only institution of its kind in the world, the St. Mungo Museum reflects the significance of religion in human life. Of course, the story of Saint Mungo, or, if you wish, Kentigern, himself is featured prominently.

RECOMMENDED LISTENING

Cappella Nova. *Scottish Medieval Plainchant: The Miracles of St. Kentigern* (Gaudeamus). Dedicated to Glasgow's patron saint.
William Jackson. *St. Mungo: A Celtic Suite for Glasgow* (Greentrax). Recorded live in Glasgow in 1990 with the Scottish Orchestra for New Music. Led by harpist William Jackson, this lovely recording consists of contemporary orchestral

music punctuated by traditional flourishes. Features the glorious Gaelic vocals of Mae McKenna.

Kevin

ABBOT
(c.498–618)

A soldier of Christ into the land of Ireland
A high name over land and sea
Coemgen [Kevin], the holy fair warrior
In the valley of the two broad lakes
ANONYMOUS

It's been said that Kevin, also known by the name Coemgen, which means, "beautiful shining light," first came to Glendalough from over the mountains. He then crossed the summits with an angel and built a monastery among the glens. He was a hermit, most certainly, but also something of a Christian mystic. A gentle soul with a special affinity for animals and nature, he lived an admittedly austere lifestyle, the bleakest of the bleak. His great strength and determination, matched by equal doses of bullheadedness and resiliency, emerged from his astounding faith and a dogged commitment to living the life of a monastic. Kevin looked to the Desert Fathers—to Antony and his disciples—for inspiration, for sustenance.

Kevin's was no ordinary birth. His mother experienced no labor pains, no indication that she was about to bear a special child. Born in Leinster of royal blood, he was sent by his parents at the age of seven to be educated by monks, a common occurrence at the time for someone of his social class.

Kevin spent many years among the monks, until he was mature enough to become a priest. Following his ordination, an angel encouraged him to go to "the desert glen," which led him ultimately to Glendalough, "the valley of the two lakes." Sheltered in a remote area called the Upper Lake, he made his home within a cave, now known as "St. Kevin's Bed," where he would pray for many hours or spend a considerable amount of time wading in waist-high water, reciting the divine hours. Here, in this remote part of Ireland, Kevin lived as a hermit for seven years, "clad only in animal skins," according to Edward Sellner, "sleeping on stones at the water's edge," and surviving on a rudimentary diet of nuts, herbs, and fresh water from the two lakes.

Kevin was the very model of the ascetic life. He spent every Lent in a hut with a gray flagstone as his bed. One Lent, a blackbird came to his hut and perched herself on the palm of his hand as he lay on the flagstone, his hand outstretched, as if to welcome the little creature to his home. Kevin kept his hand in that position to allow the blackbird to build her nest in it, and there he remained until she had hatched her offspring.

When an angel appeared to Kevin and ordered him to return to society to teach, he protested but eventually left the solitary life behind. Indeed, a prophecy stated that an honorable and noble priest would one day arrive at Glendalough, the lush valley located just south of Dublin. This priest would raise the dead, admonish the mighty, uplift the poor, and heal the blind, the deaf, and the lame. What's more, this very same priest would establish a great monastic city in the glen for natives and strangers alike, for spiritual pilgrims, and for those just passing through en route to their next destination.

Despite his reluctance to participate in the daily affairs of the outside world, Kevin stayed true to the course. It was he who founded a great monastic city and school at Glendalough, which was soon to become one of the most sacred pilgrimage sites in Ireland. So important was this site that people came to believe that anyone who made seven pilgrimages to Glendalough would be allowed to take one pilgrimage to Rome.

Kevin passed away soon after the founding of Glendalough. Some accounts say he died in 611 or 612; others say he died in 618. Regardless, beloved and honored Kevin lived to be an impressive 120-some years of age, or so the story goes.

REFLECTION

Kevin was known as a patient and gentle man and yet, like most of us, he struggled with conflict and paradox. If you wanted to accomplish something badly enough, would you be willing to do whatever it takes to get it done? What sacrifices would you make to reach a particularly vaunted goal?

SITES ASSOCIATED WITH KEVIN

Glendalough Visitor Centre
Glendalough, County Wicklow, Ireland
Remains of the monastery founded by Kevin in the sixth century, although most of the buildings date from the eighth to twelfth centuries. Includes a well-preserved round tower, some fine stone churches, and various stone crosses. Exhibits, audiovisual presentation, and guided tours available.

FOR FURTHER READING

Michael Rodgers and Marcus Losack. With a Foreword by Esther de Waal. *Glendalough: A Celtic Pilgrimage* (Harrisburg, PA: Morehouse Publishing, 1996).

thomas Lynch

POET AND ESSAYIST
(1948–)

The facts of life and death remain the same.
We live and die, we love and grieve,
we breed and disappear.
And between these existential gravities,
we search for meaning, save our memories,
leave a record for those who will remember us.
THOMAS LYNCH (*Bodies in Motion and At Rest*)

homas Lynch is truly a rare bird, a breed apart: an undertaker who is also a fine essayist and eloquent poet. Lynch has been making his living as an undertaker in the town of Milford, Michigan, for more than twenty-five years. But in between wakes and burials, he has managed to publish some of the most effective writing on death and dying—and on living—with grace, sensitivity, and large doses of wickedly good humor. "There is much joy in grief," is an old Celtic saying, and Lynch, more than anyone writing today, epitomizes the gray area between those two extremes. Indeed, the *New York Times* has described him as being an unlikely cross "between Garrison Keillor and William Butler Yeats."

As would be expected of a good Irish Catholic, Lynch received a proper Catholic school upbringing at a time when the Mass was still celebrated in Latin. He confesses to loving rituals:

the dark wine and water and bread of his youthful churchly duties; the lit candles; the scent of incense; the bells, books, bowls, and vestments; the mystery of foreign-sounding prayers and ancient hymns sweetly sung. "My Catholicism is impressed, embedded, inexorably a part of my being," he admits in *Bodies in Motion and At Rest.* "It is instinct and intuition. I might cease to believe as one, but I will ever behave and misbehave as one."

And perhaps because of his profession and his cultural heritage, Lynch finds humor in the most dire of situations. As when, one day, waking up on the wrong side of the bed and bemoaning his stock in life, he went to work and looked at the body lying peacefully in the casket and imagined what the fellow would say if given another chance: "So, *you* think *you're* having a bad day?"

In a long poem called *The Moveen Notebook,* Lynch honors the memory of his aunt Nora Lynch, from whom he inherited a cottage in County Clare. By returning to the place where his ancestors had left long before he was born and, indeed, by being the first to return "home" since his people had departed Ireland's shores, he finds solace and a tangible connection to the past and to the people who came before him. He hopes that his children, too, will eventually find an attachment here, in this place that is at once familiar and foreign, a place that belongs to him and yet is not of him—a place that, wherever he travels and no matter how long he is away from it, is ultimately home. This is a particularly Celtic way of looking at the world. History repeats itself. Life goes in cycles. It is rhythmic. It is the Return. It is the final Homecoming.

Lynch's words, subtly and powerfully stated, fight against the inevitable void, the ineffable darkness. What concerns him most is what happens to us between life and death. He reminds us that we look at familiar places differently after people die; the places we associate with them take on deeper meaning. We will never again see them—at least in their physical form—and yet, even in their absence, we look for them in the old haunts, hoping against all hope and all rational thought that their reassuring form will be lurking around the next corner.

Lynch celebrates meaning in the ordinary triumphs, and inevitable failures, of daily life. He accords them the respect that the little acts rarely receive. "[I]f you love, you grieve and there are no exceptions," he writes.

Between the indomitable faith of his mother and the stubborn vigilance of his father, Lynch grew up to find a middle ground of living within both extremes. Faith, fear, and anger are the primary emotions elicited in his work: faith in letting go and surrendering to a greater power; fear of what lies ahead, fear of the unknown; anger at our inability to control our fate, to change the outcome.

And so what are we left with but mysteries: the Mystery. Why? Why are we born? Why must we die? Will it happen to me? When will it happen to me? Why must we all eventually become orphans? These are some of the questions that Lynch's "customers" ask. These are the questions we all ask—eventually.

And the answers are fleeting. In fact, there is no one answer, just variations of answers and sometimes, of course, no answers at all, or at least not satisfying ones.

But in the words of Thomas Lynch, in his humanely lyrical prose-poetry, there is much comfort. Sometimes it comes in the most fleeting of phrases, touchingly poetic:

. . . souls sing behind the reaches of bodies . . .

At other times, stark and direct . . .

. . . time runs out, runs on, with or without us . . .

And quite often it simply arrives in warm words of fatherly advice . . .

Warm to the flesh that warms you still . . .
to always remember, forever and ever.

He tells us of the days when societies used to mourn the death of a loved one for an entire year. The grieved would wear black every day, even the wreaths that hung from the front door were black. No music would escape from the warmth of the dwelling. And the bereaved were allowed to express their grief without guilt, without covering up their inner emotions or pretending that those emotions didn't exist. The wailing and crying and keening were allowed full vent—no discreet drying of tears here. And then the official mourning period would be over and the berieved would resume their normal routines. From "sharp grief" to "glad remembrance," is how Lynch describes it.

Today there is less time for everything, even mourning. Modern society expects us to be back in working order within days after a funeral, permitting little time for reflection, for stillness, for fully remembering. And so we do that "after hours," in the safety of our bed, in the comfort of our memories. And when spoken words fail, we must rely on the strange reassurance of silence, hoping that the pain will eventually leave us, or at least diminish over time. All in good time. All in good time.

Thomas Lynch writes about all these things, of doubt and wonder—of loss and testament, of the pain and uncertainty of not knowing. This modern child of the Irish Diaspora is a poet, an essayist, an elegist, a memoirist, an observer, and a witness to the routines and rituals of ordinary life. Through his words we feel connected to the past. Through his words we anticipate the future. And the cycle of life repeats itself, as it must, caught between time and eternity. Over and over.

REFLECTION

Think of a loved one now departed. How did you mourn that person's passing? In what ways, large and small, do you remember that person today?

FOR FURTHER READING

Thomas Lynch. *Bodies in Motion and At Rest: On Metaphor and Mortality* (New York: W. W. Norton & Co., 2000).

_____. *Still Life in Milford: Poems* (New York: W. W. Norton & Co., 1999).

_____. *The Undertaking: Life Studies from the Dismal Trade* (New York: Penguin, 1998).

Catherine McCauley

IRISH NUN AND MISSIONARY
(1778-1841)

My God, I am yours for all eternity.
CATHERINE MCCAULEY

atherine McCauley, a pioneer in the field of Irish Catholic education, founded the Sisters of Mercy in her native Dublin in 1835. McCauley encouraged her charges to get fully involved in the life of the community, not to hide behind the safety of four walls. Because of the women's ubiquitous street presence, Dubliners gave them the sobriquet of "walking nuns." This can-do spirit was particularly important, and infectious, in frontier outposts, such as early Chicago, where they were the first community of nuns to establish themselves. According to historian Suellen Hoy, the sisters "provided the model and set the pace for social reform in the nineteenth century."

Eventually, the influence of the Sisters of Mercy would stretch worldwide, from the United States and Canada to Australia and New Zealand and South America, a far cry from the congested streets of Dublin where they originated.

McCauley was born into a comfortably well-off family in north Dublin on September 29, 1778, one of the few Catholic families that were able to maintain their wealth despite the odious Penal Code that restricted Catholic business practices. A pious child, she was the daughter of a devout Catholic father and a mother known for her sweetness and courtesy. McCauley lived her life guided by the biblical phrase, "Be merciful, just as your Father is merciful" (Luke 6:36). She possessed a strong sense of justice and compassion for the poor.

After her parents died, McCauley lived with her maternal uncle, Owen Conway, until he could no longer afford to keep her. She then moved into the home of Protestant relatives who, although they were sympathetic, still pressured McCauley to renounce her Catholicism, which of course she refused to do. With the assistance of a kindly Jesuit priest by the name of Thomas Betagh, she studied Scripture and continued her makeshift Catholic education.

For twenty years McCauley lived among the Protestant gentry. Then, in 1822, she inherited the family residence and a considerable amount of money from a childless couple who had taken her in—Catherine was the daughter they never had—and who had themselves converted to Catholicism because of her influence. With the funds she realized from the sale of the family residence, she established a school for poor girls on Baggot Street in Dublin that would profess a practical application of the gospel message. Soon, she was joined by several other like-minded women and, as a community, they taught and cared for the poor.

All along, McCauley's goal had been to establish an institution that would support and prepare young women for life in the real world. Even before the term had been invented, she advocated the idea of technical or vocational education. Eventually, Ireland's archbishop, impressed with her work and unerring sense of commitment, designated Baggot Street House, as it was then called, as the first Convent of Mercy, with Catherine installed as mother superior.

McCauley projected a magnetic and warm personality, as well as a lively sense of humor. Although her devotional tendencies placed her firmly within the mystical and ascetical tradition of Celtic Christianity, her practical nature preached the timeless message of the Christian gospel. She tried and, by all accounts, was successful in balancing between contemplation and action.

God, she felt, was not "something" you could turn off and on like a hot water faucet. Nor was her awareness of the presence of a spiritual being confined to prescribed hours of the day or to formal rituals. Like her fellow Celts, she believed that God was everywhere and at all times.

Possessing a selfless and generous nature, McCauley made sure all the sisters were served first at the dinner table before she would even consider touching a morsel. A woman of prayer, she firmly believed that we should imitate Christ in our daily actions, in our daily practice.

Mother McCauley died in November 1841. By the time of her death she had established ten convents in Ireland and one in London. Today the Sisters of Mercy are one of the largest orders of women religious in the world, known for their commitment to the fields of social work, health care, and education.

Mother McCauley's image graces the Irish five-pound note. In April 1990, Pope John Paul II declared her "Venerable," reportedly the first Irishwoman so honored.

REFLECTION

Catherine McCauley never put herself first. Both deeply religious and practical, she seamlessly combined the spiritual world with the business world. Do you find it hard to separate these two realms? How successful are you in incorporating your spiritual life with the demands of your professional life?

FOR FURTHER READING

M. Angela Bolster, RSM. *Catherine McAuley: Venerable for Mercy* (Dublin: Dominican Publications, 1990).

Suellen Hoy. "Walking Nuns: Chicago's Irish Sisters of Mercy," in *At the Crossroads: Old Saint Patrick's and the Chicago Irish,* Ellen Skerrett, ed. (Chicago: Wild Onion Books, 1997).

Calum and
Rory Macdonald

Songwriters/Musicians
(1949-/1953-)

Travellers on an olden road
With all the baggage of our days and years
We're life's carriers to the next unborn
And I'll carry you
Till this great race is over.
Calum and Rory Macdonald ("Travellers")

think of the great songwriting partnerships of the modern
era: Rodgers and Hammerstein, Simon and Garfunkel,
Lennon and McCartney.

Now, if one were to travel to the Celtic world, the Macdonald
brothers, Calum and Rory, should be added to the list, for these
siblings and sons of Scotland have done what no other modern
musician has ever accomplished: as members of the Gaelic rock
band, Runrig, they have written, and continue to write, rock
songs in the Gaelic language that appeal to a popular audience.
In fact, they are the most successful and one of the most durable
rock groups to emerge from Scotland. Quite a feat in its own
right, grant you.

But what's even more remarkable is that this sibling partner-
ship also happens to write contemporary popular songs from a
Christian perspective, yet they are not Christian artists and have
never been categorized as such. They are simply musicians whose

music is rooted in the Christian tradition but not overwhelmed by that tradition. Anyone can appreciate their music—whether Christian, non-Christian, or nonbeliever.

Calum and Rory Macdonald founded the Scots Gaelic rock band, Runrig, in the 1970s. Unlike most rock groups, the lineup has been fairly steady over the years: lead vocalist Donnie Munro, Malcolm Jones, Peter Wishart, and Iain Bayne have formed the core of the band during its most formative years. It's been only recently that Munro, the voice of Runrig, has been replaced by Bruce Guthro, a native of Cape Breton. Throughout its entire existence, though, the band's vision has remained consistent.

Malcolm Morrison Macdonald (he would later adopt the more Gaelic-sounding Calum) and Rory Macdonald are the sons of Mary Morrison, originally from the island of Scalpay, and Donald John Macdonald, who hailed from North Uist in the Outer Hebrides. Both parents were musical. Their mother knew many religious songs, while Donald John was known to sing more than a few Gaelic songs.

After a short time on the Scottish mainland, the family returned to North Uist, where the Macdonald brothers spent many magical moments during their childhood years. And it is here that they return over and over again in their songs.

But Calum and Rory did not live in a cultural vacuum. Rather, they listened to the Hollies, Bob Dylan, and the Beatles. The English roots band, Fairport Convention, also had a profound effect on the brothers. In fact, it was Fairport's music that encouraged them to seek out their own native traditions, to rediscover their own Gaelic roots.

Calum eventually began to write his own songs, songs that had more in common with poetry than with the typical simple-minded songwriting of the time. Significantly, though, he wrote in English; Gaelic was not yet fashionable. In fact, during his mid to late teens he turned his back on the language entirely.

By this time, the brothers had already formed a dance band back in their native Skye—the family had moved to the famed isle—before the wider world began to take notice. The themes of the band range from the universal longing to return home to more specific Gaelic concerns, such as the recovery of language, the manifestation of culture, and the perpetuation of heritage—from the heartfelt Christian renewal of "Hearts of Olden Glory" to the Gaelic psalm-singing tradition that forms the foundation of the lovely "An Ubhal as Airde" ("The Highest Apple").

The group's first recording was sung entirely in Gaelic and is steeped in Gaelic history and culture. Not surprisingly, it is their most folk-based effort. Over the years, though, their focus shifted from exclusively Gaelic-language material to writing and performing songs in English, albeit with either Gaelic themes or Gaelic sensibilities.

Their lyrics often soar, capturing moments "that make angels lose their wings and make poets lose their wonder." The words stand outside of time and yet the band's time is very much the present. A waking of souls, they gaze out on the road that brought them to where they are at this moment, at this place.

In the morning dawn, as the landscape and the people that they know so well are drenched in a rain of grace, they acknowledge a beauty that few of us can even imagine. And when the winter night is frozen and cold and the years seem to be rapidly moving away, they find solace in a greater power and in a fate that lies outside of their control. With that total surrender comes peace.

> It's coming again
> Gathering the wind
> Returning to claim a harvest

Hunger and thirst may have been the legacy of a large number of their fellow Highlanders over the centuries, but the Macdonald brothers remain forever optimistic. The rains fall on our sins; yet there is still hope. Looking upward, they scan the blue sky in search of angels with the Uist eyes. Sundown on barren words, yet they know that another sun from the light of God will rise again on the morning moor.

The present time is the only time we have as the road reaches out before us. The poet Edwin Muir encourages us to "seek the beginnings, learn from whence you came." For many are the days that are gone; they cannot be brought back. But the big wheel keeps turning, from youth to old age, and back again to the beginning. The ties that bind us always bring us back home. Always.

REFLECTION

Calum and Rory Macdonald often speak of the blood of generations. Their lyrics link the present day back to the mists of bygone ages to a time before time began. They write of memory and connections and the ties that bind us together as members of individual families and as members, too, of the greater human family. How aware are you of your family tree? How far back can you trace your ancestry? How important is it to you to maintain the ties through the generations?

FOR FURTHER READING

Tom Morton. *Going Home: The Runrig Story* (Edinburgh: Mainstream Publishing, 1991).

RECOMMENDED LISTENING

Runrig. *In Search of Angels* (Ridge).
Runrig. *Long Distance: The Best of Runrig* (Chrysalis).

Norman Maclean

Writer
(1902–1990)

*. . . The nearest anyone can come to finding himself at any given age
is to find a story that somehow tells him about himself.*
NORMAN MACLEAN

The essence of Norman Maclean's long life can be summarized in two key words: fly-fishing and Presbyterianism.

Maclean was born in Clarinda, Iowa, on December 23, 1902. In 1909 his family moved to Missoula, Montana, where he and his younger brother, Paul, grew up. Educated at home by his Scots Presbyterian minister father, Maclean has called his youthful years "schizophrenic": the strict Presbyterian atmosphere at home contrasted with the rough, profane streets of Missoula, which, around the turn of the last century, was still very much a wild West kind of town. "A tough choirboy," he once said, describing the dichotomy.

Maclean's father, the Reverend John Norman Maclean, was a Canadian Scot born in Dalhousie, New Brunswick, who enjoyed quoting the poetry of William Wordsworth and Robert Burns. The Reverend Maclean never tired of reminding his children that Christ's disciples were fishermen. "My father was very sure about certain matters pertaining to the universe," wrote Norman. "To him, all good things—trout as well as eternal salvation—come by grace and grace comes by art and art does not come easy."

Maclean worked in logging camps and for the U.S. Forest Service before receiving his B.A. in Latin from Dartmouth in 1924, where he taught briefly. He then did graduate work at the University of Chicago, where he would eventually spend most of his adult working life, teaching from 1931 until his retirement in 1973. A scholar of Shakespeare and the Romantic poets, Maclean earned a reputation as a tough but fair professor, dedicated to his work and to the education of his students. He was a popular figure on campus.

Only after retirement did Maclean begin to write down the stories he used to tell his children. His most famous tale, *A River Runs Through It*, was published in 1976. At its simplest level, it is about fly-fishing in Montana, but it is also about the death of a brother and the quiet love of a family—a love that is not always publicly demonstrated but is nonetheless deep and biding and true. The story, which actually takes place years earlier, is written by a mature Norman Maclean as he looks back on his own life and the life of his family. "The past is everywhere around me," he admits. "Now nearly all those I loved and did not understand when I was young are dead, but I still reach out to them."

The river of this story that made Maclean famous takes on spiritual significance, even at one point becoming the physical manifestation of the Trinity: the fast rapids (the Father), the big turn (the Son), and the shallow water below (the Spirit)—so shallow, in fact, it is said that one could actually wade across to "the other side." The life of the river, its patterns, and the life of the people merge into a single whole: the sharp turn of life, the depth of feeling that one encounters, and the quietness that it eventually leaves us with.

And so the artistry of fly-fishing becomes an apt metaphor for the meaning of life, its cyclical nature, its uncertainty. We never know where the waters of life will lead us. We never know what turns we will take—whether joyful or tragic. "Eventually," writes Maclean, "all things merge into one and a river runs through it."

To the Reverend Maclean, fly-fishing and religion were irretrievably intertwined. In both fly-fishing and religion, one could "attain" grace. It would require constant effort, as all worthwhile things do, but it was possible. Paul, Norman's brother, was the perfect fly fisherman—and he was able to do it effortlessly and gracefully. In fact, the reverend was held in awe by his son's seamless artistry. It was a moment of perfection, but, like all such moments, it could not last.

In 1938, at the age of thirty-three, Paul was beaten to death in an alley in Chicago. The family never discovered the details of his death, only that the muscular Maclean put up a valiant fight. The Macleans were as haunted by the uncertainty of Paul's passing as they were by the contours of his life. The memory of Paul Maclean loomed large in the mythology of the Maclean family.

Norman Maclean died on August 2, 1990, in Chicago, at the age of eighty-eight, two years before the release of the movie version of *A River Runs Through It*. The film remains a visual and oral treat, an elegiac tribute to the reticent man whose slim novella served as the foundation for the story that was brought to the big screen. And yet, despite all the attention he received in his later years, Norman Maclean remained an enigmatic man, a man of his time and culture, who revered privacy and the unspoken language of love.

REFLECTION

It is often said that we hurt those we love the most or, as Norman Maclean's father once said in one of his sermons, "It is those we live with and love and should know who elude us. We can love completely, even without complete understanding." Think of your own family members. Are you close to them? Do you know their hopes and dreams? What can you do to become closer to them?

SITES ASSOCIATED WITH NORMAN MACLEAN

Maclean House
University of Chicago
54th and Ingleside, Chicago, Illinois
Norman Maclean spent many decades walking down the august corridors of the University of Chicago and imparting words of literary wisdom to his many students. Now a residence hall has been named in his honor.

FOR FURTHER READING

Richard Friedenberg, with an introduction by Robert Redford. *A River Runs Through It: Bringing a Classic to the Screen* (Livingston, MT: Clark City Press, 1992).

Ron McFarland and Hugh Nichols, eds. *Norman Maclean* (Lewiston: ID: Confluence Press, 1988).

Norman Maclean. *A River Runs Through It and Other Stories* (Chicago: University of Chicago Press, 1976).

____. *Young Men and Fire* (Chicago: University of Chicago Press, 1992).

Wallace Stegner. "Haunted by Waters" in *Where the Bluebird Sings to the Lemonade Springs: Living and Writing in the West* (New York: Random House, 1992).

RECOMMENDED VIEWING

A River Runs Through It (Columbia Tristar, 1992). A lovely and quiet movie based on Norman Maclean's novella. Director (and narrator) Robert Redford beautifully captures the elusive nature of Maclean's story. With Craig Sheffer as Norman, Brad Pitt as Paul, Tom Skerritt as the Reverend Maclean, Brenda Blethyn as his mother, and Emily Lloyd as Norman's wife, Jessie.

Sorley Maclean

POET
(1911–1996)

Never has such turmoil been put
nor vehement trouble in my flesh
by Christ's suffering on the earth
or by the millions of the sky.
SORLEY MACLEAN
("Never Has Such Turmoil Been Put")

I f anyone represents the spirit of the ancient Celtic bards in modern guise, surely it must be the late Sorley Maclean, probably the greatest poet to emerge from Gaelic-speaking Scotland in the twentieth century. "What Robert Frost and Carl Sandburg are to modern American letters," someone once wrote, "MacLean is to Scotland."

Born on October 26, 1911, on the island of Raasay, Maclean comes from a long tradition of storytellers. After studying English at Edinburgh University in 1929, he became a teacher, until his retirement in 1972. Maclean taught in Portree and Edinburgh and, for most of his career, he served as the headmaster of Plockton High School on the Scottish mainland.

The sins of the past weighed heavily on Maclean's life. Relatives on his father's side, the Mathesons, were cleared from their lands in the Western Highlands as part of the tragic Highland Clearances in the eighteenth century, when poor inhabitants of the Highlands and Islands were evicted to make way for more profitable sheep farms. From Lochalsh on the mainland, they moved to Skye, first in the north of the famed island, then to the area near Portree, and finally to the Braes district, which would prove so historic in Gaelic Highland history. Maclean's paternal grandmother, Mary Matheson, was a singer and storyteller, and carried with her many of the old songs of Lochalsh and Kintail, as well as the old songs of Skye. He recalled her influence: "I think that the first great artistic impact on me was my father's mother singing some of the very greatest of Gaelic songs, and all in her own traditional versions." His father, a tailor by profession, was also a fine singer in his own right.

Maclean was raised within the tradition of the Free Presbyterian Church, a sect known for its severe brand of Protestantism. Much of its rigid character was inspired by the church doctrine of Swiss theologian John Calvin, a far cry from the expansive spirituality of his Celtic ancestors. Perhaps it was this very rigidity that disturbed him for, by the tender age of twelve, he had given up Calvinism altogether for socialism. One of his uncles, Calum Nicolson, had introduced Maclean to the songs of Mary MacPherson (also known as Màiri Mhór nan Oran), the nineteenth-century Skye bard and social agitator who had a major and lasting influence on his life and work.

Thus, suitably armed with a little bit of knowledge and a lot of fire, Maclean thought he could change the world. But rather than march in the streets or enter the political sphere, Maclean chose a quieter mode of expression: his fertile mind and creative imagination. The poetry of John Donne, T. S. Eliot, and Ezra Pound, among others, significantly affected his own work, as did Wordsworth, Shelley, and Blake. He especially admired the lyric as a literary form, with its lilting marriage of poetry and music. Other influences included everything from the seventeenth-century metaphysical poets to Yeats and the nineteenth-century Celtic

Revival. William Ross, the eighteenth-century Gaelic poet, also made an indelible impression.

In the late 1930s and early 1940s Maclean wrote one of his signature pieces, "Songs to Eimhir," which expressed his strong feelings against fascism and the ongoing turmoil during the Spanish Civil War. It also functioned as a commentary on an intense love affair. Indeed, this series of love poems was compared, and quite favorably so, to the love poems of Sappho. Somehow love and struggle for freedom became equally noble ends in his poetry.

Maclean was also an intensely spiritual poet, but he conveyed a subtle spirituality, elegantly stated. What's more, his was a natural spirituality, derived from the blood of his ancestors and the shared experiences of a collective folk memory. In his poems, the spirit of his people—the Macleans and MacLeods of generations ago—live on the printed page. Although the dead populate the glens and woods of places long abandoned, in Maclean's imagination they live on, "with the music of laughter . . . the joyful, sorrowful." They have returned to the rich loam of his beloved island, never to depart. He writes:

> There is no knowledge, no knowledge,
> of the final end of each pursuit,
> nor of the subtlety of the bends
> with which it loses its course.

Maclean's poetry is infused with a grand empathy. Consider, for example, the figure of the once youthful Highland woman ("And every twenty autumns that have gone / she has lost the golden summer of her bloom; / and the black-labour has ploughed the furrow / across the white smoothness of her forehead"), now bent over from a life of drudgery and bitter sweat. Maclean compares her to Jesus, who himself walked among the wretched and the forgotten of the earth, the castaways who few people heeded or even noticed. "Thou hast not seen her, Son of the carpenter," he asks, "who art called the King of Glory, among the rugged western shores in the sweat of her food's creel." In her loneliness and pain, she becomes almost larger than life, as if the whole history of her people—the long sad history of the Highlands—fell on her frail shoulders.

Maclean bridged the gap between traditional and modern poetry. In the last few years prior to his death in 1996, his poetry finally gained the kind of public recognition worthy of someone of his skill and talent. For many years, though, his work was a secret to the outside world—he wrote primarily in Scots Gaelic—until the 1970s, when it began to receive wider circulation. The turning point was probably the bilingual edition of *Reothairt is Contraigh* (*Spring Tide and Neap Tide*). Maclean's work combines elements of popular song, the lyrical quality of earlier generations of Gaelic poetry, and the muscular strength and solemnity of the Presbyterian psalm tradition.

For many years Maclean lived in the Braes district of Skye, in a house where his great-grandmother's family once lived, overlooking the Sound of Raasay. Possessing a strong sense of place and promoting a kind of local loyalty was very important to him.

Sorley Maclean died in November 1996, and with him went a part of Scotland as well. He was the last of a particular kind of Gaelic poet. His work transcended time and language and national boundaries. We surely will not see his like again.

REFLECTION

For many years, the Gaelic language was met with official disapproval, with sneers and contempt, especially from outsiders. Poets like Sorley Maclean lent their considerable stature to the tradition, stressing individual dignity and self-respect. Have you ever been made to feel that your heritage and family traditions were unworthy? What have you done to help change attitudes?

FOR FURTHER READING

Angus Peter Campbell, ed. *Somhairle: Dain is Deilibh (A Celebration on the 80th Birthday of Sorley MacLean* (Stornoway: Acair, 1991).

Thomas Rain Crowe with Gwendal Denez and Tom Hubbard, eds. *Writing the Wind: A Celtic Resurgence: The New Celtic Poetry* (Cullowhee, NC: New Native Press, 1997).

Sorley Maclean, George Campbell Hay, Iain Crichton Smith, Derick Thomson, Donald MacAuley. Introduction by Donald MacAuley. *Nua-Bhardachd Ghaidhlig: Modern Scottish Gaelic Poems: A Bilingual Anthology* (Edinburgh: Canongate Publications, 1987).

ꞳRchíꞴꞲlꝺ mꞳcLeíꞩh

POET
(1892-1982)

Only the old know time: they feel it flow
like water through their fingers when the light
ebbs from the pasture and they wade in night.
It frightens them.
> ARCHIBALD MACLEISH
> ("Conway Burial Ground")

rchibald MacLeish was born on May 7, 1892, in Glen-
coe, Illinois, to Andrew MacLeish, the Glasgow-born
president of Carson Pirie Scott and Company,
Chicago's famous department store. MacLeish would eventually
become the unofficial poet laureate of his day.

MacLeish grew up in a mansion, by the vast expanse of Lake
Michigan, called Craigie Lea, which his father named after an old
Scottish ballad. Andrew MacLeish was a very reserved man—he
kept his emotions in check. "My father came from a very old
country in the north and far away," MacLeish recalled, "and he
belonged to an old strange race, the race older than any other. He
did not talk of his country, but he sang bits of songs with words
he said no one could understand anymore. When he spoke to his
collies they crawled with bellies on the ground."

MacLeish was educated at Yale and the Harvard Law School.
Later, he became a writer for *Fortune* magazine. Eventually, in 1933,

he was awarded the Pulitzer Prize for poetry. His most public position, though, was when President Franklin Roosevelt chose him as the librarian of congress. After World War II, MacLeish became Boylston Professor at Harvard University, where he taught for some fifteen years.

MacLeish wanted to serve some purpose in life. He wanted to do good. But most of all, he wanted to write poetry. He thought that by putting words down on paper he could make a difference.

After trying his hand at practicing law and teaching, MacLeish decided to change course—drastically. One night while walking home—he strolled across Boston Common and all the way to Harvard Square in Cambridge and further yet to his house beyond—he concluded that now, at the age of thirty, was the time to see if he really had the makings to be a writer, a poet. He decided he would go to Paris to live the life of a true artist.

It was a great risk, of course, but MacLeish felt, with the support of his wife, that it had to be done—and that he could do it. Although they had planned to stay one year, they stayed five, and during those prolific years, he wrote and wrote. His poems were published in the pages of the *Atlantic*, the *New Republic*, the *North American Review*, and other publications.

The fear of loss and the fleeting passage of time are common themes in MacLeish's work. His poetry speaks across the generations.

> There is no dusk to be,
>   There is no dawn that was,
> Only there's now, and now,
>   And the wind in the grass.
> FROM "An Eternity"

His perspective changed, however, over the years. The world that once looked like a miserable place at the age of twenty, stops the poet in his tracks at age sixty, overwhelmed as he was by the wonders of it all and how it could so easily drift from his fingers.

MacLeish also spoke of parents outliving their offspring, such as the death of the MacLeish's oldest son—Archibald's younger brother—Kenneth to cancer. And in the elegiac "Hebrides," about the family's ancestral home on the island of Barra, the children have gone over the ocean and all the parents have left is each other.

> "It is the human season," he once wrote.
> On this sterile air
> Do words outcry breath: the sound goes on and on.
> I hear a dead man's cry from autumn long since gone.
>
> I cry to you beyond upon this bitter air.
>
> FROM "Immortal Autumn"

And when his beloved mother died at the age of ninety-one in 1947, MacLeish felt somehow reassured: she had not left him, she was with him still.

> You think a life can end?
> Mind knows, nor soul believes
> How far, how far beyond
> The shattering of the waves,
> How deep within the land,
> The surge of sea survives.
>
> FROM "For the Anniversary of My Mother's Death"

MacLeish's most obviously religious work was the successful play, *J. B.*, an interpretation of the story of Job and the meaning of life. To MacLeish, the meaning of life could be distilled into one word, *love*: "It is in man's love that God exists and triumphs: in man's love that life is beautiful: in man's love that the world's injustice is resolved." *J. B.* was nothing less than a modern parable crafted from the Bible.

Much of MacLeish's poetry is imbued with a gentle spirituality, a quiet wisdom that travels down through the ages and speaks poignantly of the coming of the eternal night. He never did discover the answers to life's mysteries, just questions, or, in the words of his son, journalist and author, William H. MacLeish, "What are we to make of ourselves in the presence of this incomprehensible cosmos?"

Long before Archibald MacLeish died on April 20, 1982, a few weeks short of his ninetieth birthday, he had become a cultural icon, the old man of letters, the nation's sage. His words did, indeed, mean something. His life did, indeed, have meaning.

REFLECTION

Archibald MacLeish felt that in order to live a good life, a meaningful life, one had to perform a public service, whether writing a piece of poetry or serving the country. What is your definition of a meaningful life?

FOR FURTHER READING

Scott Donaldson. *Archibald MacLeish: An American Life* (Boston: Houghton Mifflin, 1992).

Archibald MacLeish. *Collected Poems, 1917–1982* (Boston: Houghton Mifflin, 1985).

William H. MacLeish. *Uphill with Archie: A Son's Journey* (New York: Simon & Schuster, 2001).

αlistαiR ɳacleod

WRITER
(1936-)

And what is the significance of ancestral lands
long left and never seen?
ALISTAIR MACLEOD
("The Road to Rankin's Point")

listair MacLeod was born in Saskatchewan in 1936, where he lived until he was ten years old, when his parents moved back to the family farm on Cape Breton Island, Nova Scotia.

MacLeod taught at Indiana University from 1966 to 1969, and then at the University of Windsor, where he remains professor of English and Creative Writing. To make ends meet during his lean undergraduate years, he worked as a logger, a miner, and a fisherman, and all of these professions make appearances in his work.

Until the publication of his first novel, *No Great Mischief* in 1999, MacLeod's stellar reputation as a writer's writer rested solely on two short story collections, *The Lost Salt Gift of Blood* and *As Birds Bring Forth the Sun and Other Stories* (in the United States, all of his short stories have been gathered in one collection, *Island*). In these stories he managed to capture the essence of a people—the Scottish Highlanders who had emigrated to Cape Breton Island in the nineteenth century and their descendants in the New

World—with an economy of words that at times seems quite astonishing. For despite the brevity of his work, MacLeod has created a literary landscape that is worthy of anything produced by the likes of a Hardy, a Faulkner, or a Joyce.

MacLeod's tales describe life in a harsh climate, a world where the sea is omnipresent. The sea serves another purpose, too. It both separates and brings together the past with the present—for the Scottish ancestors who crossed the ocean generations earlier are still very much a living, breathing part of the current inhabitants, continuing to sing the music and songs of their Scots pioneers. And if they no longer speak the old Gaelic tongue on a daily basis, it is, nevertheless, an essential element of their collective psyche.

MacLeod writes in a simple, straightforward manner and yet his lyricism is evident throughout, the rhythm between words and sentences almost echoing the water that laps against the Cape Breton shore. The narrator in "The Road to Rankin's Point" has returned home to die because he does not know where else to go but, not one to share his feelings, he chooses not to tell his parents of his fatal condition. And so he relies further and further upon memory: "I feel myself falling back into the past now, hoping to have more and more past as I have less and less future." During this same visit his grandmother has died and the house where she once lived is now silent: "For the first time in the centuries since the Scottish emigrations, there is no human life at the end of this dark road."

In "The Closing Down of Summer," the miner and his mates find a warm reassurance, "the privately familiar," in the Gaelic songs they sing over and over again in the darkness of the mines. Like the language that is losing ground, the protagonist knows, too, that his profession—mining—will also soon be a relic of the past. "Our sons will go to the universities to study dentistry or law and to become fatly affluent before they are thirty." The narrator is preoccupied with leaving something worthwhile behind, although he fears everything he has done will be utterly forgotten.

All of these fragile beings try to hold on, as long as possible, to the good things in life. MacLeod's characters often walk, literally, in the footsteps of the original Scots settlers. "[W]e carry certain things within us. Sometimes there are things within us which we do not know or fully understand and sometimes it is hard to stamp out what you can't see."

MacLeod laments, too, the gap of knowledge between the generations, as later descendants sing the words of a strange language without fully understanding their meaning. And so sometimes all that remains are ghostly shadows of a culture reduced to long-departed voices on a tape recorder.

MacLeod writes about families and the emotional and physical ties that bind us, whether separated by generations or by the vast expanse of ocean. A common theme is the loss of family, sometimes the people we know and love, and sometimes of family members we never met, yet the sorrow remains. MacLeod's characters resurrect memories from a place they have never seen. Thus, the legacy of emigration carries through the centuries, the old family photographs fading more with each passing year. The people who populate his fiction wish to stop time, if only they could, to preserve what they have left before it, too, drifts away from their fragile fingertips.

And so stories of earlier generations are told over and over again. The repetition becomes a sort of Celtic litany, a reassuring chanting of memories from the past. These are stories, such as the tales spun by MacDonald clan in *No Great Mischief*, where authentic memories from one's life become mixed up with other people's stories, and does it even matter? For, in the end, they all become one story.

These are stories, too, where the characters live with great sorrow in their hearts, although they do not know why, for they cannot identify the source. "I think of my grandparents a great deal and, as in the manner of the remembered Gaelic songs, I do not do so consciously." Memories of the deceased drift in and out of their consciousness.

And no matter how long "away," home remains the place where they do not live. Thus, their duty in life seems to be able to reconcile their past (the country of their ancestors) with the present (the country where they make their living). The struggle continues.

REFLECTION

The theme of uncertainty runs through the work of Alistair MacLeod. His characters take nothing for granted, as if they somehow acknowledge that they are mere pawns in the great game called life. Alexander MacDonald's wife says, "We never know what lies ahead of us. There is never time enough." And yet they do their best to carry on. Do you take your loved ones for granted? Do you think you have all the time in the world and so put off until tomorrow what you should be doing today?

FOR FURTHER READING

Alistair MacLeod. *As Birds Bring Forth the Sun and Other Stories.* Afterword by Jane Urquhart (Toronto: McClelland & Stewart, 1992).

___. *Island: The Complete Stories* (New York: W. W. Norton & Co., 2001).

___. *The Lost Salt Gift of Blood.* Afterword by Joyce Carol Oates (Toronto: McClelland & Stewart, 1989).

___. *No Great Mischief* (Toronto: McClelland & Stewart, 1999).

George MacLeod

Presbyterian Minister
(1895-1991)

Nearer are you than breathing,
closer than hands and feet.
GEORGE MACLEOD

ike the Celts of centuries ago, George MacLeod, founder of
the ecumenical Iona Community, believed that God was
everywhere, both visible and invisible, at home and at work,
in the day and during the night. There is not a moment, he maintained, when God's presence cannot be felt. With abiding opti-
mism and even greater enthusiasm, MacLeod merged an older
form of Celtic spirituality with modern Presbyterianism, combin-
ing both the mystical and the practical.

Born in 1895, MacLeod was the grandson of the great Scots
preacher Norman MacLeod. He attended Winchester and
Oxford, studied theology at Edinburgh University, and served as
an officer with the Argyll and Sutherland Highlanders in World
War I, where he witnessed firsthand much bloodshed on the
Western Front. It was an experience that had a profound effect
on him.

Indeed, MacLeod returned from the war a broken man, con-
suming massive quantities of whisky and smoking almost fifty cigarettes a day. But then, one day, something happened. Kneeling
in a railway compartment on a moving train, he promised to

devote the rest of his life to Christ. He began training for the ministry and became the Assistant Minister at St. Giles Cathedral in Edinburgh, and then held another prestigious position at the Church of St. Cuthbert's, also in Edinburgh.

Throughout his conversion and the days beyond, MacLeod became increasingly aware of the dichotomy within the nation—the great divide between rich and poor. But rather than just pay lip service to his conflicted emotions, he chose to do something about it by agreeing to serve in the ravaged parish of Govan, the shipbuilding area of Glasgow that had been devastated by depression and wracked by severe unemployment.

During this period, MacLeod began moving toward a more fluid spirituality, one that did not abide by strict rules and regulations. It was, in fact, an active brand of spirituality that MacLeod wholeheartedly embraced. His goal was to help humanity as much as humanly possible, to shed some light on the darkness of contemporary life, and to relieve the suffering of the poor and those unfortunate people that society had rejected. Rather than turning away from the messiness of daily life, MacLeod's spirituality led him to dig deeper and to become even more involved in practical matters. Because his spirituality was rooted in the hard earth, MacLeod wasn't afraid of getting his hands dirty, literally and metaphorically.

In 1938 Macleod made a decision that would change his life and the lives of everyone around him forever. He decided to rebuild the then-ruined abbey on the island of Iona, long considered the cradle of Scottish Christianity, and make it once again a center for Christian worship. That first crucial summer several young ministers from the Church of Scotland and a number of unemployed craftsmen built basic housing—huts surely reminiscent of the beehives of their Celtic ancestors—where they lived, ate, and slept. For the next eighteen years or so these "huts" served as homes for these spiritual vagabonds, as the party went about the often tedious and very time-consuming task of rebuilding this ancient monument. Working every summer under MacLeod's guidance, they gradually renovated most of the monastic buildings.

Many people on the mainland thought MacLeod was mad to want to carry out his plan. And yet, over the years, the work went on—and somehow from somewhere the funds came rolling in.

MacLeod was a pacifist during World War II, which, not surprisingly, brought him his share of critical jabs. But he was also a popular radio preacher, his authoritative voice broadcast throughout the British Empire.

MacLeod became moderator of the General Assembly of the Church of Scotland in 1957 and, ten years later, he was appointed to the House of Lords. In 1988, several years before his death, he visited the MacLeod Centre for International Reconciliation, named on his behalf.

MacLeod believed in the essential goodness of humanity and in the essential goodness of the Lord. Christ, in his view, bridged the material with the spiritual world. And yet, because evil resides in the world, in many forms, he felt it his duty to combat it whenever possible.

George MacLeod died in the summer of 1991 at the age of ninety-six. The community he established—his "strange little experiment" grounded on hope and a will to succeed—so many decades ago, continues to flourish. Today there are about 200 Members, 1400 Associates, and more than 1500 Friends who promote peace and social justice, combat racism, and encourage an interfaith dialogue. The Iona Community continues to be an ecumenical and internationally recognized spiritual center, and the doors to the refurbished abbey remain open to all.

REFLECTION

When everyone else thought he had lost his senses, George MacLeod soldiered on, knowing in his bones that he was doing the right thing. How does the opinion of your peers affect your decision-making process? Once you make a decision, do you stick to it?

SITES ASSOCIATED WITH GEORGE MACLEOD

Iona Community
Community House
Govan, Glasgow, Scotland
Administrative headquarters of the Iona Community on the mainland. The Wild Goose Resource and Worship Group promotes new approaches to worship throughout the United Kingdom and abroad. The Community's publishing wing, Wild Goose Publications, produces books relating to the Community.

Iona Abbey
Isle of Iona, Argyll, Scotland
The restored Iona Abbey, originally a Benedictine institution, welcomes up to fifty guests each week from all over the world, as well as thousands of secular and spiritual pilgrims during the summer. Guests and staff share meals, daily worship, activities, chores, and social events.

FOR FURTHER READING

Ronald Ferguson. *George MacLeod* (London: Collins, 1990).
George MacLeod. *The Whole Earth Shall Cry*, Ronald Ferguson, ed. (Glasgow: Wild Goose Publications, 1985).
T. Ralph Morton. *The Iona Community Story* (London: Lutterworth Press, 1957).
J. Philip Newell. *Listening for the Heartbeat of God: A Celtic Spirituality* (Mahwah, NJ: Paulist Press, 1997).

Margaret of Scotland

QUEEN OF SCOTLAND
(c.1046-1093)

. . . through her devotion to justice, piety, mercy, and love,
we contemplate in her, rather than miracles,
the deeds of the ancient fathers.
TURGOT (Historian)

Scotland's first canonized saint and the wife of Malcolm III of Scotland, Margaret was an outsider looking in. It didn't take long for the Scots to warm to this woman of mixed English and German parentage and Hungarian birth, however, and when they did, they took to her wholeheartedly.

Margaret was born in 1046, the daughter of an Anglo-Saxon prince and a German princess. She spent her childhood years in Hungary and England, receiving a rigorous religious education. At one point she wanted to become a nun. In 1068, two years after the Norman Conquest, Margaret, her mother, and her brother Edgar fled to the safety of the court of Malcolm III of Scotland. Margaret was young, lovely, pious, and quite learned, and Malcolm became smitten with her.

Unlike many in their day, Margaret and Malcolm married out of both love and convenience, but mostly it was love. Margaret found her true purpose in life by serving the poor and attending to the sick, and her surprisingly enlightened husband supported his wife's many causes and less than conventional behavior. It wasn't unusual to see beggars, at her invitation, actually dining at the royal table. Like Jesus, she even washed the feet of her poor but appreciative guests.

Margaret was a peacemaker at heart. Although a "foreigner," she learned just enough Gaelic to communicate with the people, and made an effort to reach out to her constituents. In fact, she did what she could to encourage both Scots and English to live together peaceably. Although she was not always successful, she did try. She was also very much involved in church administration in Scotland, providing generous grants to the Culdees, for example, who believed mightily in church reform. She also presented endowments to various churches and worked indefatigably at reforming clerical abuses. Some even say she was the guiding force behind the rebuilding of Iona. What's more, she objected to particular practices within the Celtic church, namely the control of churches and the lack of sacraments.

In 1070 Margaret founded Dunfermline Abbey in the ancient capital of Scotland, although it was because of the work of her son, David I, that it owes much of its wealth and prestige.

Margaret and Malcolm died in the same year, 1093; Malcolm at the Battle of Alnwick, and Margaret of a broken heart just four days later. She was only forty-eight years old.

Margaret was renowned for her devotion to justice, her piety, and her compassion. She has the honor of being the only Scottish royal saint, canonized in 1250 and, in 1673, named a patron of Scotland. Margaret's canonization made Dunfermline a popular pilgrimage center for many centuries.

REFLECTION

Margaret was an outsider, and yet she went out of her way to make people feel welcome. Have you ever been made to feel uncomfortable by someone because of the way you look, talk, or act? What have you done or how would you recommend others handle a poor first impression?

SITES ASSOCIATED WITH MARGARET OF SCOTLAND

Dunfermline Abbey and Palace Visitor Centre
Monastery Street, Dunfermline, Scotland
Founded by Margaret's son David I in 1128. The Romanesque nave is considered one of the finest in Britain. It is the burial place of King Malcolm III.

The Abbot House
Maygate, Dunfermline, Scotland
Administrative headquarters of the first Benedictine abbey in Scotland. Tells the story of Margaret, her marriage to Malcolm, and her canonization.

Martin of Tours

BISHOP
(c. 316–397)

*I am a soldier of Christ
and it is not lawful for me to fight.*
SAINT MARTIN

Martin was born the son of a military official in an area of what is now Hungary. Considered one of the early fathers of Christian monasticism in Europe, Martin believed that the rigors of the monastic life would bring a much-needed discipline to the religious communities of the continent.

According to Roman law of the time, Martin was required to enter the Roman army—he was only fifteen. But Martin was not a typical citizen of the Roman Empire. He rejected the call to arms, knowing that even at this tender age he would not and could not resort to violence. Consequently, his rebellious act led to his being forcibly inducted.

On a cold winter night, while serving in Amiens in France, Martin met a man dressed in rags begging for alms. But because Martin had no money, he graciously offered the warmth of his heavy cloak instead. With his sword, he cut the garment in half: one half for the shivering beggar, the other to keep for himself to withstand the elements. Later that evening, something remarkable occurred. He dreamed that he saw Jesus wearing the part of the cloak that he had given away to the beggar. This experience had a profound effect on him. Humbled, the next morning he resolved to convert to the Christian faith.

"I am a soldier of Christ," Martin proclaimed, "and it is not lawful for me to fight." Not surprisingly, the Roman authorities were not amused. Later, when he was accused of being a coward, he volunteered to go to the front lines—unarmed, protected only by the mercy and good graces of Christ—but his offer was not accepted. Instead, he was incarcerated, to be released only after the war ended. He then traveled to Poitiers, where he became a disciple of the holy bishop Hilary, and later joined the monastery at Solesmes. About a decade later he was asked to become Bishop of Tours, where he served for twenty-five years, until his death in 397.

Martin had studied the life of Saint Antony, one of the Desert Fathers. It is more than likely that Martin, and others like him such as Saint John Cassian, first introduced Antony's ascetic teachings on the European continent. These teachings eventually reached the Celtic monks. It's been said that Martin of Tours met the Celtic saint Ninian when Ninian was on his way home from a pilgrimage to Rome. Thus, Martin greatly influenced Celtic monasticism.

REFLECTION

If you had nothing but the perennial clothes on your back, would you give over your last earthly possessions into the arms of a stranger?

William Maxwell

WRITER AND EDITOR
(1908-2000)

*Where the understanding of other men differs from ours
there is just as good a chance that we are in the presence
of truth as of opinion.*
WILLIAM MAXWELL (*Ancestors*)

illiam Maxwell was an editor's editor. Born on August 16, 1908, in Lincoln, Illinois, a descendant of hardy Scots pioneers, he lived the early years of his life in Lincoln. When he was ten years old, his mother became ill with influenza and died shortly thereafter—and his world literally collapsed overnight. Eventually his father remarried, sold the house, and moved the family to Chicago, where Maxwell attended high school.

Like many a Midwestern young man, Maxwell moved to New York with literary stars in his eyes. His dreams came true when he interviewed for a staff position with *The New Yorker*, and the magazine's founding editor, Katharine White, hired him. That was 1937. He remained there until his retirement as fiction editor some four decades later. During his tenure, he edited the work of J. D. Salinger, John Cheever, John O'Hara, John Updike, Harold Brodkey, and many others. From 1969 to 1972 he was president of the National Institute of Arts and Letters.

Clearly, Maxwell enjoyed a prestigious career, and yet, at heart, he remained a humble and extremely private figure. Maxwell felt the editor's role was to be unobtrusive. "As a writer I don't very much enjoy being edited. As an editor I tried to work so slightly on the manuscript that ten years later the writer would read his story and not be aware that anybody was involved but him."

In addition to his position at *The New Yorker*, Maxwell was a prolific writer himself. His first novel, *Bright Center of Heaven* was published in 1934. Included among his many other works are the story collections *Billie Dyer* and *Over by the River,* and the highly acclaimed novel *So Long, See You Tomorrow*, which won the American Book Award. His fiction often revolved around particular and recurring themes: the fragility of life, the uncertainty of the world, the loss of innocence, the crushing of a child's dreams.

Although Maxwell was not a spiritual writer in the traditional sense, his work is luminous and eloquent. He was a great stylist and elegant composer of words. In his most heartfelt work, *Ancestors: A Family History,* he captures a vanished world as he retraces the history of his family from pioneers to itinerant preachers to small-town businessmen. This American of Scottish ancestry ("I have always liked my name," he writes. "[E]verything Scottish—kilts, plaid, bagpipe music, the accent, the coloring—produces a mysterious, unthinking pleasure in me") assembles a genealogical detective story, piecing together bits and bobs until some kind of picture, albeit a fragmented one, comes into view.

Maxwell offers many insights along the way, noting, for example, that we often lose sight of where we come from. Indeed, it doesn't take particularly long for one generation to lose touch with another, sometimes within a matter of years. Can you imagine the difficulty, then, in making sense of a family's life over generations? It takes considerable energy and goodwill for families to stick together, never mind trying to determine where one's relative is situated on the family tree. And so, ancestors often disappear from our memory, as if they never existed—gone, leaving just the skeletal remains of shadowy figures. Unless, that is, we bear witness. Unless words and thoughts are recorded in a journal. Unless some physical evidence of a life becomes apparent to us. Unless someone had the presence of mind to write down details that will serve as a connecting link from one generation to the next.

The past, after all, is messy and confusing, and the mind can play tricks on us. For example, we don't always remember the way things really happened: events twist and turn, according to the whims and limited memory of the person involved. Once a loved one dies, many of us want to wipe the slate clean, to put the deceased person's life and business into a neat, orderly box. Or, as Maxwell remarks, "The past is forever being swept away in the interest of neatness and order."

And yet death, as life, is not orderly or neat. It takes tremendous effort to come to terms with an intangible past, with a past that we cannot always make sense of. And so, in *Ancestors*, Maxwell uses everything at his disposal—his vivid literary imagination, his persistent need to uncover the truth, his exquisite skill with the written word—to bring the past into clear focus and to allow long-departed shades to emerge from the darkness.

To know our future we need to know our past, goes the old adage. By retracing the history of the Maxwell family tree, William Maxwell has not only done his own family a great service, but he has done us all a huge favor. His story is the story of many small-town folk who traveled along the nation's roads and byways in search of a better life, in search of the perennial Promised Land. Some found it. Some did not. But like life itself, the search continues.

William Maxwell's own search ended on July 31, 2000, when he passed away at the age of ninety-one at his home in

New York City.
REFLECTION

Usually one person in the family takes on the role of "family historian," keeping the links alive through the generations. Who plays that role in your family? How important is it for you to know where you come from?

FOR FURTHER READING

William Maxwell. *Ancestors: A Family History* (New York: Vintage, 1995).

Ninian

ABBOT
(?-c.432)

Thither, thither I must go, that leaving my country,
my kindred, and my father's home, I may be deemed worthy
in the land of vision to perceive the will of the Lord
and to find shelter under the roof of His temple.
NINIAN

I t's hard to believe now, but the small Scottish village of Whithorn was once a center of international trade and worship. For almost eleven hundred years the shrine of St. Ninian was a prominent pilgrimage site.

Even today not much is known about Ninian. Recent evidence indicates that he might have lived in the early sixth century, not the fifth as previously thought. All we can say for certain is that he was born in Cumbria and was later ordained a bishop. Some accounts say he arrived at the Isle of Whithorn, in southwestern Galloway, where he built a church, called the Candida Casa or "shining white house." According to the Venerable Bede, the church was built "in a manner to which the Britons were not accustomed." Some accounts say that from here, in Galloway, Ninian and his disciples preached the gospel to the southern Picts, an early Celtic peoples then living in the area.

Some historians believe that Ninian dedicated this church to Saint Martin of Tours; others say he was trained in Rome; and still others describe him crossing the Alps en route to Rome. It is possible, according to these accounts, that he visited Martin at Tours. If so, it was but a short visit, and then he left for Scotland, bringing with him a band of stonemasons provided by Martin.

At least one scholar, Daphne Brooke, suggests that Ninian modeled his church after Martin's monastery, so impressed was he with Martin's solitary contemplation and prayer life and the way he evangelized the people of the countryside. Brooke theorizes that Whithorn was not only reminiscent of Martin's community in France, but that it was actually an extension of that community.

Not too many stories exist about Ninian. Once, though, on a journey with one of his disciples, Ninian rested, took out a Psalter, and began to read a psalm—just as it started to rain. Everything quickly became soaked except Ninian and his book—until, that is, he took his eyes off the book and began thinking "inappropriate" thoughts. Only then did Ninian and his Psalter get wet. When his companion gently admonished him, Ninian resumed his reading—and the rain immediately stopped altogether.

Whatever the truth of the historical Ninian, we can say that a cult of Saint Martin had materialized by the beginning of the sixth century, and Ninian was one of his greatest advocates. Ninian was considered a holy man and miracle worker, held in great reverence by Christian populations.

The medieval Knights of St. John established hostels for pilgrims traveling along the main routes to Whithorn, and the pilgrims lent prosperity and a robust life to the town. There were pilgrims from Scotland, England, Ireland, the Isle of Man, and France, as well as nobles and beggars, bishops and peasants, abbots and street peddlers. James IV came almost annually to Whithorn, climaxed by a royal procession through the streets.

The relics of Saint Ninian consisted of a full set of bones, the saint's clothing, his staff, bell, and psalm book. Because Ninian was said to have been a healer of lepers and the blind, the cult of Saint Ninian is strongly associated with healing. Even Robert the Bruce, King of Scots, was said to have made the long journey to Whithorn in 1329, just months before his death. By the early sixteenth century, the cult of Saint Ninian had reached its zenith.

Although no longer a popular stop on most pilgrimages—sacred or secular—Whithorn remains an important Christian heritage site within the larger Celtic world.

REFLECTION

Ninian had earned a reputation over the years as a great healer, and yet he remains an enigmatic figure—elusive, distant, and lost somewhere in time. What can we learn from such a person?

SITES ASSOCIATED WITH NINIAN

Whithorn Priory and Museum
Main Street, Whithorn, Scotland
The ruins of a twelfth-century priory stand on the site where Ninian built his small stone church, the first Christian church in Scotland. The small museum contains early Christian crosses, considered by many to be the finest collection of carved stone crosses in southern Scotland.

The Whithorn Discovery Center
45–47 George Street, Whithorn, Scotland
The center tells the story of Scotland's first Christian settlement. Discoveries from over a decade of excavations are on display.

St. Ninian's Chapel
Whithorn, Isle of Whithorn, Scotland
Located three miles southeast of Whithorn (follow the sign-posted footpath from the village to the headland), the thirteenth-century roofless chapel served the community and those pilgrims coming from Ireland and the Isle of Man.

FOR FURTHER READING

Mosa Anderson. *St. Ninian: Light of the Celtic North* (London: The Faith Press, 1964).

Daphne Brooke. *Wild Men and Holy Places: St. Ninian, Whithorn and the Medieval Realm of Galloway* (Edinburgh: Canongate Press, 1994).

Alan MacQuarrie. *The Saints of Scotland: Essays in Scottish Church History A.D. 450–1093* (Edinburgh: John Donald, 1997).

flannery O'Connor

WRITER
(1925-1964)

*I think there is no suffering greater than what is caused
by the doubts of those who want to believe.*
FLANNERY O'CONNOR

In yourself right now is all the place you've got.
HAZEL MOTES (*Wise Blood*)

orn Mary Flannery O'Connor in Savannah, Georgia, on
March 25, 1925, O'Connor was that rarest of literary
achievements: a Catholic writer in the deep heart of the
Protestant South. She was not particularly prolific, but what she
did write—some thirty-two short stories and two novels—was profoundly influential.

O'Connor attended the Georgia State College for Women.
After graduating in 1945, she received her master's from the
University of Iowa two years later. She devoted the rest of her life
to pursuing the written word, living on her mother's dairy farm
in Milledgeville, Georgia, and writing as her strength permitted,
usually several hours in the morning before surrendering to the
limitations of the debilitating illness, lupus, that would eventually
kill her.

O'Connor belonged to the rich Southern Gothic tradition.
Her works were populated by grotesque characters who often

found themselves in morbidly funny and yet quite violently brutal situations. "When a Southerner wants to make a point, he tells a story; it's actually his way of reasoning and dealing with experience," she once said.

Mary Flannery O'Connor believed strongly in the mystic tradition within the Catholic Church. (She dropped her first name because, as she remarked to critic Richard Gilman, "Who was likely to buy the stories of an Irish washerwoman?") Considering herself a "conscious Catholic," she was particularly influenced by the work of two French Catholics, Francois Mauriac and Georges Bernanos.

"People make a judgment of fanaticism by what they are themselves," she mused.

> To a lot of Protestants I know, monks and nuns are fanatics . . . And to a lot of monks and nuns I know, my Protestant prophets are fanatics. For my part, I think the only difference between them is that if you are a Catholic and have this intensity of belief, you join the convent and are heard no more; whereas if you are a Protestant and have it, there is no convent for you to join and you go about the world getting all sorts of trouble and drawing the wrath of people who don't believe anything much at all down on your head.

Not a moralist in the slightest, O'Connor freely admitted to having preoccupations with the notions of belief, death, grace, and the devil, "because I'm a Catholic."

"I'm a born Catholic and death has always been brother to my imagination," she offered by way of explanation. "I can't imagine a story that doesn't properly end in it or in its foreshadowings."

Among her most important works is the novel *Wise Blood* (1952), about a street-corner preacher named Hazel Motes who attempts to establish a church without the benefit of Christ.

Donning a bright blue suit and a black preacher's hat, he traipses through the languid Southern landscape trying to help others see the light—dim though it may be—but fails to find redemption within his own insular, Christ-created world.

The Violent Bear It Away (1960) is about the tortured relationship between a grandfather and his equally selfish and mean-spirited granddaughter. It takes its cue from the biblical phrase: "From the days of John the Baptist until now, the kingdom of heaven suffereth violence, and the violent bear it away."

O'Connor was also considered one of the finest of short story writers. In 1955 she published *A Good Man Is Hard to Find and Other Stories*, which contains such O'Connor classics as "The Life You Save May Be Your Own" and "The Artificial Nigger." Her second collection of short stories, *Everything That Rises Must Converge*, was published posthumously in 1965, and *The Complete Short Stories* appeared in 1971. She was also a prolific letter writer. Her correspondence was published under the title of *The Habit of Being* in 1979.

O'Connor wrote about backwoods prophets and fallen angels, with an odd and disturbing mixture of Christian symbolism laced with violence. Her tales often ended in apocalyptic chaos, and yet even her darkest words retained an aura of mystery about them. Christian dualism was a common O'Connor theme, as was the concept of original sin and a new birth. O'Connor's characters often stripped bare their identity, like a snake shedding its old skin. Her works are full of spiritually troubled people who either reject Christ or mock him and, in the end, usually pay the price for their transgressions. Many of her characters pursued an idiosyncratic form of Christianity, or at least their own peculiar interpretation of it.

Only true Christianity, in O'Connor's worldview, could offer the promise of salvation and the hope for redemption. Her stories are in a sense modern morality plays, involving a "road company" of itinerant preachers and life's assorted misfits culled from the marginal people of the rural South, people on the fringe of society, the ordinary folk of the vast Southland. Some are latter-day Christ figures who shun conventional society to seek solace and company in the soothing arms of like-minded soul mates. Just as Jesus confronted people directly—flaws and all—O'Connor's preachers also extend their hand to society's outcasts and losers, looking for the kingdom of Christ on an earthly plain.

Like most of us, her characters don't always know where they are going. They are just as frightened and uncertain about their fate. And yet, amidst their suffering, there often comes a stranger. The messianic figure that arrived on the scene some two thousand years ago appears in modern form in O'Connor's work. We may not always recognize him, we may not always admire him—indeed, we may even come to loathe him—but he is there nevertheless. In fact, her backcountry characters—apocryphal figures reaching across the millennia—can be traced back to Christ's own time.

O'Connor's short life ended on August 3, 1964, when she died of lupus in Milledgeville, Georgia, at the age of thirty-nine. And yet what a literary legacy she left behind. Catholic, Christian, and proudly Southern, she was one of the most original voices to emerge from the South.

REFLECTION

Grace was a powerful theme in the writing of Flannery O'Connor. She felt it was her purpose as a writer to reveal the mystery of God's grace in everyday life. Have you experienced the power of grace in your own life? What triggered it? How did it make you feel?

SITES ASSOCIATED WITH FLANNERY O'CONNOR

Flannery O'Connor Childhood Home Foundation
207 East Charlton Street, Lafayette Square, Savannah, Georgia
O'Connor lived in this house until 1938. Now it is part memorial and part literary center for the city of Savannah.

FOR FURTHER READING

Robert Coles. *Flannery O'Connor's South* (Athens, GA: University of Georgia Press, 1993).

Rosemary M. Magee, ed. *Conversations with Flannery O'Connor* (Jackson, MS: University Press of Mississippi, 1987).

Flannery O'Connor. *The Habit of Being,* Sally Fitzgerald, ed. (New York: Farrar, Straus & Giroux, 1979).

John O'Donohue

WRITER
(1956-)

We are always on a journey from darkness into light.

At birth you appear out of nowhere,
at death you disappear to nowhere.
JOHN O'DONOHUE

With his gentle demeanor and soothing personality, John O'Donohue has come to epitomize the best characteristics of modern Celtic spirituality. He has become popular on both sides of the ocean for explaining the ancient wisdom of the Celts in contemporary terms, so that whether you are a homemaker or a scholar, his words find their way to each and every heart.

In works such as *Anam Cara: A Book of Celtic Wisdom* and *Eternal Echoes: Exploring Our Yearning to Belong*, he explores such themes as the mystery of friendship, solitude, work, aging, and death; in other words, universal themes that apply to us all.

O'Donohue defines the Celtic concept of soul friend, or *anam cara*, as "a person to whom you could reveal the hidden intimacies of your life." In the early Celtic church, this person acted as a teacher, companion, or spiritual guide—a soul friend with whom all pretenses vanish, leaving only the truth. With your *anam cara,* you could truly be yourself, without fear of reprisals, without fear of misunderstandings.

From this as a foundation, O'Donohue offers commonsense wisdom steeped in a Celtic sensibility, yet he also quotes liberally from the Bible. "Some of the most beautiful writing on love is in the Bible," he notes, citing Paul's First Letter to the Corinthians: "Love is patient and kind; love is not envious or arrogant or rude" (13:4–5).

He discusses the fickle nature of love, the way it can change from affection and trust to bitterness and resentment almost overnight. The spirituality of the senses then come into play. "To be sensual or sensuous is to be in the presence of your own soul," he writes.

O'Donohue laments the loss of ritual in our lives. In our nonstop attempt to cram every waking moment with activity, we no longer sit down to enjoy a meal with our loved ones. Rather, we eat on the run, downing liquid vitamins to compensate for the absence of time.

Silence is another victim of modern culture, notes O'Donohue. We are afraid of silence. We can't handle it. It makes us uncomfortable. We need to plug the gaps with noise and empty words—anything, in fact, to fill the silence. By doing this, we lose the sense of the poetic. "Poetry is the place where language in its silence is most beautifully articulated," he says. "Poetry is the language of silence." Indeed, according to O'Donohue, "to be genuinely spiritual is to have great respect for the possibilities and presence of silence."

Of course, O'Donohue comments on the spiritual hunger of our day, the longing for something eternal, something permanent in an impermanent world despite "the divine restlessness" that resides in the human heart. Most of us would like to think that we are here for a reason, that our life has meaning. O'Donohue insists that "each of us has something to do here that can be done by no one else." If, according to Descartes, "I think therefore I am," in the Celtic pantheon, it would be more accurate to say, "I am in everything and everything is in me," since the Celts believed in the interrelatedness of nature.

O'Donohue discusses the soulless, anonymous quality of much of the work many of us do. We work in order to eat, in order to survive. But countless people get no pleasure in the eight or so hours they spend in the office or wherever the workplace happens to be located. Rather than being seen as a person, as an individual with his or her own wants and needs, too often the employee is dismissed as a means to an end, mere functionaries, cogs in the perennial machine.

Work, says O'Donohue, doesn't have to be that way. We can be happy at what we do. In order to feel satisfied, we simply must find a way of expressing ourselves, of truly bringing our talents and skills to bear on our daily lives. Most people work for persons or entities that have an inordinate power over us, or so we think. They have the power to fire us, to belittle us, to humiliate us—if, says O'Donohue, we give them that power. "People have power over us because we give our power away to them."

We always want something. We are always longing, yearning, for the ineffable, for the elusive, for that intangible something that is forever outside our reach. That is the struggle of life; that is the joy and pleasure of life. The ancient Celts saw the world from a circular perspective. The beginning leads to the end, the end to the beginning, and on and on and on. Notes O'Donohue, "In eternal time all is now; time is presence."

REFLECTION

Think of the place where you work. Is it caring? Does it offer a kind atmosphere? Does it nurture creativity? Now think of your time spent after work. Are you surrounded by supportive and loving people? Or, is daily life, like work, a constant struggle? Consider the ways that you can take the power that is within you back where it belongs.

FOR FURTHER READING

John O'Donohue. *Anam Cara: A Book of Celtic Wisdom* (New York: HarperCollins Publishers, 1997).

____. *Eternal Echoes: Exploring Our Yearning to Belong* (New York: HarperCollins Publishers, 1999).

John Ogilvie

JESUIT PRIEST AND MARTYR
(1579-1615)

Whether Christ or the King is rather to be obeyed, judge you.
JOHN OGILVIE

John Ogilvie was a man who spoke his conscience, indeed, a man who sacrificed his life for his faith.

Born in 1579 near Keith in Banffshire in the north-east of Scotland, Ogilvie left home at the age of thirteen to study on the continent, mostly in Belgium. In 1596 he entered the Scots College at Louvain.

Although raised a Calvinist, Ogilvie converted to Catholicism and then transferred to the Benedictine College at Ratisbon before joining the Jesuits when he was seventeen. He became a novice of the Society of Jesus in 1599, and was ordained a priest, in Paris, in 1610 or 1613. At his own request, he was sent home to Scotland in November 1613. It was a dangerous time for a Catholic to be in Scotland where, after the Reformation, the Catholic faith was all but outlawed. The government had actually prohibited the celebration of Mass, and those who violated the laws were hunted down and sent to the gallows.

And yet, Ogilvie willingly chose to return, chose to risk his life to minister to the few remaining Catholics. He conducted most of his missionary work in Edinburgh and Glasgow, disguised at times as a horse dealer or a soldier, and brought back to the Church many errant Catholics.

Ogilvie spent a scant nine months offering solace to these lost souls before he was arrested on the streets of Glasgow the following year, betrayed by a nephew of the sheriff, Adam Boyd, who pretended he wanted to be reconciled back to the Catholic Church. Authorities, searching Ogilvie's room at the inn where he was staying, found in his possession "three little books containing directions for receiving Confessions" and a relic of Saint Ignatius, the founder of the Jesuits. Initially imprisoned in the Glasgow Tolbooth, Ogilvie was then sent to Edinburgh for additional interrogation. During the questioning, the young Jesuit earned the grudged respect of his adversaries for his patience, bravery, and good sense of humor, even in the face of impending danger.

Ogilvie refused to name other Catholics and to admit to the supremacy of the king over the pope. Like his English counterpart, the martyred Sir Thomas More, he remained stoic and accepted his fate without complaint or tears, enduring interminable hours of torture, primarily in the form of sleep deprivation. Pricked by needles, his incarcerators forced him to stay awake for eight days and nine nights.

Ultimately, Ogilvie was condemned as a traitor and taken to the gallows to be hung on March 10, 1615, at Glasgow Cross. Even while on the scaffold, he once again declared his loyalty to the king. His pending death, he said, had everything to do with religion, not disrespect toward the monarch. He embraced the hangman and offered his forgiveness before saying his final prayers, first in Latin and then in English. Because of his stature, he was not quartered—the usual fate for traitors—but rather buried in the churchyard of Glasgow Cathedral.

Ogilvie was declared venerable in the seventeenth century, beatified by Pope Pius XI on December 22, 1929, and canonized in 1976 by Paul VI.

In 1965, in a remarkable coda to a remarkable life, a Glasgow man by the name of John Fagan was diagnosed with inoperable cancer. While on his deathbed, someone pinned a medal of Blessed John Ogilvie to his nightshirt, and the man soon recovered from his illness and was back at work. No satisfactory medical explanation was ever given for the complete and rapid remission of the man's illness.

REFLECTION

Buoyed by an absolute belief in his faith, John Ogilvie was not afraid to speak his mind. He paid the ultimate price for his honesty, however. Have you ever been in a position where standing up for your convictions led to conflict and discord? How did you handle the situation?

FOR FURTHER READING

George Anderson, SJ. "John Ogilvie, SJ: A Martyr of Scotland." *Company* (Winter 2000).

Laurence O'Toole

BISHOP
(c.1128–1180)

Laurence O'Toole was totally dedicated to God:
indefatigable in his prayer,
stern in his bodily penances,
unstinting in his almsgiving.
POPE HONORIUS III

orn in 1128 in County Kildare, Laurence O'Toole was the son of an Irish chieftain. He spent many of his childhood years as the hostage of Diarmait Mac Murchadha (Dermont MacMurrough), king of Leinster and a noted rival family. This period of enforced incarceration caused the young man to turn inward and to trust no one but God.

Years later, in 1140, O'Toole entered the monastery at Glendalough, where he became abbot in 1153, at the age of twenty-five. While Kevin may have been the founder of the monastic community of Glendalough, O'Toole did more than anybody to encourage its growth and foster there a spirit of camaraderie.

O'Toole's strength of character and devout piety impressed his superiors. He was also a popular figure among the ordinary folk. In 1162 he was selected to be Archbishop of Ireland, becoming the first Irish archbishop of the country. While in that position he concentrated on building churches. For example, he is considered the founder of what is now called Christ Church in Dublin. He also introduced the Augustinian order to Ireland, with their emphasis on prayer, fasting, and poverty. Because of O'Toole's efforts, many poor people received a daily meal and hundreds of orphaned and hungry children were offered both physical and spiritual shelter and protection.

When O'Toole was made the papal legate of Ireland in 1179, his growing influence on the Irish Church began to disturb his rival Henry II. The dispute was short-lived, however. On his return journey home to Ireland from the continent, O'Toole fell ill and died on November 14, 1180, in the Augustinian monastery at Eu in Normandy.

The process for O'Toole's canonization began in 1191, and was finally concluded on December 11, 1225. O'Toole's heart is preserved at Christ Church Cathedral in Dublin.

Learning well the lessons offered at Glendalough, O'Toole was devoted to the people for whom he served. Indeed, the simple lifestyle and austere living conditions kept him in good stead throughout his adult life. Unlike some clergy, O'Toole was down to earth—he lived in community with other members of his cathedral community and he had no airs about him. Every Lent he would return to Glendalough for peace and solitude and to better commune with God.

REFLECTION

O'Toole's incarceration changed his outlook on life completely. From that point forward, he became determined to rely only on himself and his God. Do you think this to be a wise decision? What would you have done?

Patrick

APOSTLE OF IRELAND
(390?-461?)

I arise today
through strength in the sky:
light of sun
moon's reflection
dazzle of fire
speed of lightning
wild wind
deep sea
firm earth
hard rock.
PATRICK ("The Deer's Cry")

he is the most famous of Celtic saints and yet, in some very profound ways, he is the most enigmatic. For Patrick, Ireland's patron saint, is at once a paradoxical figure and a victim of unusual circumstances. Taken as a youth, against his will, to a strange country, he willingly returned years later to that same country. Entertaining though it may be, the Patrick of legend—he of the green shamrock in hand as he chases the snakes out of Ireland—bears little resemblance to the historical Patrick.

Born during the latter days of the fourth century in Roman Britain—it is not certain where—Patrick was kidnapped by Irish pirates and sold into slavery; he was only sixteen years old at the time. During his period of incarceration, this most uncertain of youths became close to God, finding the strength he needed by turning inward, by embracing prayer. According to the words that flowed from his own pen, he made "as many as a hundred prayers in a single day."

Patrick came from wealth—his father was a tax collector and a deacon. His grandfather was also a priest. Not particularly religious as a youth nor much of a scholar, his life changed drastically when he was kidnapped by Irish pirates and sold into slavery—and for the next six years he served as a lonely shepherd in exile. In an instant, this young man lost everything that he had ever known. Separated from his loved ones and taken from the familiar countryside that had been his constant companion, he felt bereft and absolutely alone. And with nowhere else to turn, he looked toward God for some kind of respite, some indication that all would be well. "It was he who strengthened me," Patrick confessed, "consoling me just as a father comforts his son."

Patrick eventually returned to his British homeland, seizing an opportune moment to flee his Irish captors and traveling some two hundred miles to board a ship bound for the continent. From there—probably in Gaul—he slowly made his way back home. But he was not the same Patrick who left, and particularly vivid dreams beckoned him back to Ireland. ("We beseech thee to come and walk once more among us," pleaded the Irish voices.)

And so he again returned to the land where he was once a stranger but now seemed very much like home. This time, though, Patrick returned as a bishop. And it was he who, more than anyone, is credited with firmly establishing Christianity in Ireland. A true and wise believer ("a slave in Christ," he once described himself), he carried the Spirit with him as he traveled the length and breadth of the land. He not only brought with him an infectious love of learning but, more importantly, a profound and sincere love of God. And it is this legacy that remains to this day.

Unlike most of the early Celtic saints, Patrick left behind concrete examples of his writing, namely, *Letter to Coroticus* and his *Confession*. His writing is redolent of the Bible. Virtually every line written by his pen contains some biblical allusion. Indeed, the Bible is so much an integral part of his very being that his writing style seems to echo the rhythm of the good book itself.

The first work, *Letter to Coroticus*, was addressed to an obstreperous British chieftain, and served as a plea for mercy for a group of young Christian men and women who were taken prisoner by pagan pirates. Patrick wrote the letter in Latin, with the hope that it would be read in public and, hence, pillory the chieftain into feeling some kind of shame.

Patrick's *Confession*, autobiographical in nature, essentially is a summary of his life. Written "after the fact," so to speak, when Patrick's life work was already done, when he was an old man, this work has been described by more than a few scholars as Patrick's *de facto* last will and testament. Perhaps, too, it was Patrick's attempt to prove to the world, and indeed to himself, that he was worthy of the position awarded him.

Patrick is the most human of Celtic saints, a deeply flawed man who delved deep within himself to emerge anew. If he were living in modern-day America, he would have likely said that he had reinvented himself. Like most of us, he questioned his purpose in life and occasionally pondered his own competence. Thus, at times, he felt woefully ill prepared to handle the ongoing struggles of daily living. And yet, he persevered—as we all must, if we wish to see the light of another day.

Years later, in old age, Patrick looked back at a youth spent in ignorance of the greater mysteries of the earth. Even as a presumably wiser yet still tongue-tied adult, he continued to fear that his perceived inadequacies would be brought to light. And so he shouldered on, confronting if not overcoming his fears, knowing that the "Spirit of the living God" would always be there to comfort him and catch him should he fall. Toward the end of his accomplished life, Patrick remained a man humbled yet supremely grateful of the gifts of the Spirit bestowed upon him.

Like many of us today, Patrick knew well the tricks that the mind can play. He experienced the emotional turmoil of uncertainty, felt the sting of rejection, and questioned his abilities. Yet, he was generous to a fault and remained a self-effacing, obedient servant of God. More than this, he committed himself to serving his people; he submitted to his calling with absolute devotion.

Perhaps Patrick's greatest gift to humanity is his selflessness. Like the Christ figure that he admired so dearly, Patrick willingly sacrificed his own personal freedom for the sake of a greater good. Clearly, most of us will not—cannot—relinquish what we hold most precious, but we can all do more to share the spirit of goodness that resides in us. We can, for example, choose to offer our support to someone in need. We can extend our love. We can simply be there to listen. Quite often, our presence is all that is required. We can, in other words, choose to make a difference.

REFLECTION

Think about difficult times you have experienced. How did you overcome them? How can you help others overcome their self-doubts?

SITES ASSOCIATED WITH PATRICK

Croagh Patrick
Murrisk, County Mayo, Ireland
In 441 Patrick is said to have fasted here for forty days and nights. Legend has it that it is from this summit that he expulsed the snakes from Ireland. A statue of Patrick stands at the foot of the mountain. Modern-day pilgrims descend on this holy site on the last Sunday in July in honor of the celebrated saint.

Downpatrick Cathedral
Downpatrick, County Down, Northern Ireland
A stone marks the purported burial site of Saint Patrick.

Hill of Slane
Near Drogheda, Ireland
Historic site marks the spot where Patrick lit a paschal (Easter) fire in 433 to symbolize the triumph of Christianity over paganism.

Station Island
Lough Derg, County Donegal, Ireland
Pilgrimage of St. Patrick's Purgatory attracts thousands of pilgrims each summer from June to mid-August. A visitor's center in the nearby village of Pettigo tells Saint Patrick's story.

St. Patrick Heritage Centre
Downpatrick, County Down, Northern Ireland
Contains exhibits on the life of Saint Patrick.

St. Patrick's Trian Visitor Complex
40 English Street, Armagh, Northern Ireland
This modern visitor center includes a small library, visitor genealogical service, and books on genealogy.

FOR FURTHER READING

Joseph Duffy. *Patrick In His Own Words* (Dublin: Veritas, 1972)

John Skinner, trans. *The Confession of Saint Patrick* (New York: Image Books, 1998)

Greg Tobin. *The Wisdom of St. Patrick: Inspirations from the Patron Saint of Ireland* (New York: Ballantine Books, 1999).

Lesley Whiteside. *The Spirituality of St. Patrick* (Harrisburg, PA: Morehouse Publishing, 1996).

Píran

PATRON SAINT OF CORNWALL
(circa sixth century)

*[N]othing now will deprive me
of . . . the true case of my flock!*
DONALD RAWE

Piran arrived in Cornwall through a circuitous route. One stormy day in Ireland a band of ruffians, who were afraid of Piran's power and authority because of his great goodness, chained him to a millstone, dragged him to the nearest cliff, and threw him into the stormy sea, ostensibly to his death below. But Piran was no ordinary person. As he fell, the winds diminished and the sea became tranquil and calm. Later, as the sun broke through the clouds, Piran was sitting peacefully on the millstone itself, which floated down the waters and eventually deposited him on the Cornish shore at the village of Perranporth. The day was March 5, and it became known as his feast day.

Piran wasted no time in erecting a chapel on the site where he landed—possibly the oldest site of Christian worship in Britain. Before he could build the chapel though, he lived in a temporary shelter—the ubiquitous Celtic hut—for forty days and forty nights, fasting and praying.

Many Celtic saints enjoyed a special relationship with animals. Piran, in particular, befriended foxes, badgers, boars, and calves. But he also loved the earth's natural elements, such as the

181

colorful stones and pebbles found along the Cornish coast. In fact, some credit Piran with the development of the process of tin-making. For centuries tin was the major industry in Cornwall and the unusual shape of the tin mines—sort of an upside-down hat—dotted the Cornish landscape for generations. In fact, only fairly recently has the tin industry fallen on hard times. It is not surprising, then, that the Cornish miners adopted Piran as their patron saint. But more than this, the Cornish people themselves took a special liking to the saint. The Cornish flag—a white cross on a black background—is commonly known as Saint Piran's cross.

Many Celtic saints lived to a grand old age, and if one was to believe the stories surrounding Piran, then his death at 206 must certainly be one of the oldest.

REFLECTION

Piran had a number of enemies who tried to do great harm to him, both physically and mentally, and yet his spirituality kept him strong. Can you think of a time when your own inner and outer demons were so troublesome that they almost got you down and yet, somehow, you were able to miraculously rally from the depths?

Joseph Mary Plunkett

POET AND REVOLUTIONARY
(1887-1916)

I see his blood upon the rose
And in the stars the glory of his eyes,
His body gleams amid eternal snows.
His tears fall from the skies.
JOSEPH MARY PLUNKETT
("I See His Blood Upon the Rose")

oseph Mary Plunkett lived a short, intense life. One of the signers of the Proclamation of the Irish Republic, he was also the composer of deeply mystical poetry and lovely sonnets.

Born in November 1887 in Dublin and educated in Catholic schools, Plunkett grew up with a strong appreciation of Irish history and Irish folklore. Its mythic heroes in particular cast a spell on the young Plunkett. For a brief time he was editor of the *Irish Review* and, along with Edward Martyn and Thomas MacDonagh, he was a founder of the Irish Theatre.

As a member of the Irish Volunteers, Plunkett was the mastermind behind the 1916 Easter Rising, which called for a military attack against the British government on Easter Sunday, April 23, 1916. The rebels seized the General Post Office and almost captured Dublin Castle. Ultimately, the plan failed and Plunkett surrendered to the British army. He was imprisoned in

Dublin's Richmond Barracks and executed on the morning of May 4, 1916, along with fourteen additional members of the Rising. He was only twenty-eight years old.

A few hours before Plunkett's death, he married Grace Gifford in his prison cell. His friend, colleague, and mentor, Thomas MacDonagh, had been executed the day before, while his father and his brother had their death sentences commuted to ten years' service.

Plunkett's dream was to see an Ireland "Gaelic as well as free." In his mind's eye, he saw revolution as an act of salvation and sacrifice. Thus, his death would not be in vain, for the blood of Irish martyrs, he believed, would cleanse the Irish soul and help rid the country of alien influences. Moreover, the executions changed the rebels' stature, almost overnight, from cowardly traitors and hooligans—the common man and woman on the street did not support the rebellion since many Irish were already fighting with the British in France during the height of World War I—to martyred heroes. Plunkett, in death, had fashioned at least a partial victory over his enemies.

A profound mystic, Plunkett was influenced by the writings of Saint John of the Cross, Saint Teresa of Avila, and Saint Francis. He published a volume of poetry, *The Circle and the Sword*, in 1911; his *Complete Poems* were published after his death.

In structure and content, Plunkett's poetry recalls the vision, or aisling, poems of the Irish tradition, where a mythical figure represents the spirit of Ireland.

> The claim that has the canker on the rose
> Is mine on you, man's claim on Paradise

To Plunkett, both Christ and the Irish martyrs shared a common fate:

The sun rose up at midnight
The sun rose red as blood,
It showed the Reaper the dead Christ

Upon his cross of wood.

For many live that one may die
And one must die that many live—

His poetry also is reminiscent of the nature poetry of earlier generations of Irish poets, wherein the natural elements take on human characteristics and the poet himself becomes one with nature. It is a typically Celtic way of looking at the world.

I am a wave of the sea
And the foam of the wave
And the wind of the foam
And the wings of the wind.

My soul's in the salt of the sea
In the weight of the wave
In the bubbles of foam
In the ways of the wind.

REFLECTION

Joseph Mary Plunkett died for a cause he firmly believed in. Short of giving up your own life for something or for someone, how strong are your convictions? At what price would you be willing to surrender everything?

Olíver Plunket

BISHOP AND MARTYR
(1625–1681)

[T]hen Jesus told his disciples, "If any want to become my followers,
let them deny themselves and take up their cross and follow me.
For those who want to save their life will lose it,
and those who lose their life for my sake will find it."
MATTHEW 16:24–25

And death is the reason to begin again,
without letting go.
JAY WRIGHT (from "Death as History")

Oliver Plunket was considered the last Catholic to be put to death for his faith at Tyburn, and the first of the Irish martyrs to be beatified.

Born in County Meath in 1625, Plunket attended the Irish College in Rome to study for the priesthood. He was ordained a priest in 1654 and in 1657 became a professor of theology at the college.

The persecution of Catholics in Ireland reached its zenith with the arrival of Oliver Cromwell in 1649. His influence spawned anti-Catholic legislation, such as the dispossession of Catholic landowners and the outlawing of Catholic priests. To avoid persecution, Plunket petitioned to remain in Rome.

When anti-Catholicism lessened, Plunket was able to return to Ireland. In 1657 he became Archbishop of Armagh and went about trying to undo the damage of the Cromwell legacy.

Plunket was an enthusiastic promoter of the faith, establishing schools, ordaining priests, and confirming thousands of his fellow Catholics during this period. For example, he established a school of boys in Drogheda, Ireland. His ministry extended even as far as Gaelic-speaking Catholics in the Highlands and Islands of Scotland.

But Plunket had to undergo considerable hardship to serve the faithful. He sought out people in the mountains and the woods, often administering the sacraments in the open air and enduring the full brunt of the elements.

In 1673, when Ireland experienced renewed religious persecution—chapels were closed and priests were once again hunted down—Plunket was forced to go into hiding. But he refused to abandon his faith or his people. Essentially it became a crime to be a Catholic in Ireland.

In 1679 Plunket was arrested and falsely accused of being involved in the so-called Popish Plot to overthrow the government. He was imprisoned in Dublin Castle and tried for treason, where he was declared innocent by an all-Protestant jury. The authorities were not happy with the decision, however, and thus had him transferred to London for another trial. Because of the suddenness of the decision and the distance involved, there was not sufficient time for Plunket to make arrangements to bring witnesses from Ireland to England.

The first trial was inconclusive but the second essentially amounted to a kangaroo court. Based on perjured testimony, Plunket was convicted of high treason "for promoting the Catholic faith," and was sentenced to be hanged, drawn, and quartered at Tyburn Hill in London.

On July 1, 1681, the day of execution, as a crowd gathered along the way, Plunket calmly prepared for his death as he stood on the gallows. He could have saved himself by giving false testimony against his fellow priests, but he refused; he also rebutted the charges of treason. What's more, on the scaffold he publicly forgave anyone who had anything to do with his death.

Plunket was beatified in 1920 by Pope Benedict XV and canonized on October 12, 1975, by Pope Paul VI. His feast day is July 1.

REFLECTION

Oliver Plunket exhibited grace and forgiveness at the moment of death, even though the charges against him were unjust. Could you be so forgiving of your enemies? Or should some things not be forgiven?

John Duns Scotus

SCOTTISH FRANCISCAN THEOLOGIAN
(1266-1308)

Of realty the rarest-veinèd unraveller; a not
Rivalled insight, be rival Italy or Greece.
GERARD MANLEY HOPKINS
("Duns Scotus's Oxford")

e don't know much about the brief life of the medieval theologian John Duns Scotus. Born in 1266 in the Scottish Border town of Duns (then known as Littledean), he was considered one of the greatest medieval theologians, on a par with none other than Thomas Aquinas.

Scotus was tutored by his uncle, Elias Duns, a Franciscan friar, in Dumfries in the southwest corner of Scotland. In 1291, at the age of fifteen, he was admitted to the Franciscan order, was later ordained a priest, studied at Oxford and Paris, and taught in Paris and Cologne.

Scotus lived a quiet life, commenting and writing mostly on the Bible and the works of Aristotle, discussing many of the same themes as his rival, the Dominican Thomas Aquinas. Scotus tried to prove the existence of God from a philosophical perspective. He believed in the absolute significance of the individual and of the importance of free will. Every human life was unique and special, while conforming to a larger whole, which, in his view, pointed to the existence of a Creator who created individuality within a rich pattern of uniformity. Both plains could exist at the same time without causing havoc and without being inconsistent.

Scotus explained the spiritual realm from a practical and purely logical perspective. Thus, since most reasonable human beings could agree that all things required a cause for their existence, he concluded that this "prior existence"—which some call God—owes its existence to existence itself. To Scotus, God represented infinite love and the goodness of the universe. His theories relied more on what could be proved through reason and logic rather than miracles or revelation.

Scotus was given the nickname of Doctor Subtle (or Doctor Subtilis), primarily for the subtleness and grace of his writings and the way in which his thoughts flowed effortlessly on the printed page. He had a marvelously inventive mind—he never stopped learning, never stopped constantly questioning his own theories and his own assumptions—and for this he was admired by his fellow Franciscans and Dominicans alike. However, in less charitable moments, critics of Scotus and his philosophy referred to his followers as "Dunses," for their obstinacy and traditionalism. Through the centuries, the word has come to us as *dunces*, an ironic linguistic twist given the intellectual rigor that Scotus always applied to his work.

Scotus died suddenly in Cologne on November 8, 1308, at the age of forty-two.

In recent years, Scotus has been an admired figure among a number of twentieth-century intellectuals. Poet Gerard Manley Hopkins, in particular, was impressed by his practical theories and straightforward common sense and, above all, by a strong sense of awe and mystery that runs through his work.

REFLECTION

To John Duns Scotus, God was love. God represented the mystery of the universe, the mystery of life itself. What does life mean to you? Do you take it for granted, until something tragic occurs to force you to reconsider, or do you value every moment of the day as a precious gift?

SITES ASSOCIATED WITH JOHN DUNS SCOTUS

Scotus Statue
Duns, Borders, Scotland
A statue of Duns's famous son stands in the town's public park.

John Millington Synge

PLAYWRIGHT AND POET
(1871–1909)

Is it a storm of thunder is coming, or the last end of the world?
MARTIN DOUL (In *The Well of the Saints*)

along with Sean O'Casey, John Millington Synge is perhaps the best-known playwright to emerge from Ireland during the twentieth century. His plays are still being performed today, particularly his masterpiece, *The Playboy of the Western World*.

Born in 1871 in Rathfarnham in south Dublin, the son of the Anglo-Irish aristocracy, Synge was a sickly child. And yet he grew up with a fondness for nature and the pastoral glories of the Irish countryside. Studying at Dublin's Trinity College, he later spent a few unfocused years in Paris. Although he considered himself an atheist, he did have his mystic side, reveling in the fantastic stories of fairies and ghosts that haunted his homeland.

Like fellow Irishman James Joyce, Synge focused on one subject and one subject alone: Ireland. He was especially interested in the west of Ireland and its remote islands off the coast. And even more specifically, he was fascinated by the Irish-speaking inhabitants of those wildest of Celtic fringes, the Aran Islands.

Aran has had spiritual associations for centuries. Saint Enda, for example, reportedly came here in the late fifth century and founded a monastery that became recognized throughout

Europe. It's been said that Columba of Iona and Ciaran of Clonmacnoise studied under Enda.

The peak population of the islands around the time of the Great Famine of 1845–1849 when it reached some 3,500. By the time Synge visited, the numbers had dwindled to just under 3,000. Today it is approximately 1350.

During the so-called Celtic Twilight period of the late nineteenth century and into the twentieth, Aran was transformed into this mythic place, a Celtic Garden of Eden, whose humble residents embodied the epitome of Celtic purity and goodness. Poets and playwrights, archeologists and folklorists, painters and academics, descended on the islands in search of venerable wisdom. Because one of the core principles of the newly formed Gaelic League was the revival of the Irish language, people turned to places like Aran and the Blasket Islands and other pockets of Gaelic culture such as Connemara and Donegal for cultural sustenance.

Synge's friendship with the great Irish poet William Butler Yeats changed his life forever. Because they shared common interests and common cultural goals for Ireland, Synge listened to Yeats when he exhorted his friend to leave Paris behind and return to Ireland. "Go to the Aran Islands," Yeats told him. "Live there as if you were one of the people themselves; express a life that has never found expression."

Synge spent several weeks on Aran between 1898 and 1902. He devoured the windswept landscape with eyes wide open and a mind that fell in love with the stories and legends. The people and the sites captured his imagination. "The sense of solitude was immense," he wrote. "I could not see or realize my own body, and I seemed to exist merely in my perception of the waves and of the crying birds, and of the smell of seaweed." He transferred his experiences into art in the from of plays (*The Shadow of the Glen* in 1905, *The Well of the Saints* in 1905, *The Playboy of the Western World* in 1907, *The Tinker's Wedding* in 1908, and *Deirdre of the Sorrows* in 1910) and in prose (*The Aran Islands* in 1907 and *In*

Wicklow, West Kerry, and Connemara in 1911). He wrote of lonely cottages in the shadow of a glen; of village roadsides after dark; of weather-beaten blind beggars and wandering friars, sorrowful queens, and loyal servants. A ruined medieval chapter on the islands inspired the story of the holy well in *The Well of the Saints*. In fact, many of the folktales and legends that he heard were prominently featured in his work. He also managed to find the time to collect folksongs. Hence, the ancient legend of the Children of Uisneach would become the foundation for *Deirdre of the Sorrows*.

From Connaught came the story of a local man who killed his father with a spade in a moment of passion and then fled to the Aran Islands to the safety of family members, which formed the basis of what would become *The Playboy of the Western World*. Synge attributed this Irish tendency of protecting the criminal to a general aversion to authority. "If a man has killed his father, and is already sick and broken with remorse," he theorized, "they can see no reason why he should be dragged away and killed by the law."

Referring to a time when a feeling of immense admiration overcomes him as he rowed with the men of Inishmann, one of the Aran Islands, Synge commented on the men's ancient Gaelic that seemed "so full of divine simplicity that I would have liked to turn the prow to the west and row with them forever." At other times, though—Synge was subject to prolonged melancholy spells—he felt utterly alone. "On some days I feel this island as a perfect home and resting place; on other days I feel that I am a waif among the people."

In particular, there was something about the purity of the language spoken in Aran that profoundly moved Synge, even when he understood little of what was being said. He would become awestruck by the grandeur of nature and made to feel weak and feeble in its tumultuous grip.

> A week of sweeping fogs has passed over and given
> me a strange sense of exile and desolation. I walk
> round the island nearly every day, yet I can see
> nothing anywhere but a mass of wet rock, a strip
> of surf, and then a tumult of waves.

He was overwhelmed, too, by the "inarticulate chant" of the wild keening, or the Irish cry for the dead, which he calls a combination of "Catholic grief" and "pagan desperation." The harrowing lament for the dead becomes not so much a personal loss as an outpouring of collective grief for all the islanders "who feel their isolation in the face of a universe that wars on them with winds and seas."

Throughout, his language is heightened, a combination of Gaelic lyricism with English practicality. Tim Robinson has called Synge a "romantic atheist," which somehow seems strangely appropriate and, truth be told, highly ironic given his family history (his ancestors originally came from England and spawned a number of clergy for the Protestant Church in Ireland, while an uncle had been a Church of Ireland minister in Aran in the 1850s). And yet, what appealed to Synge most was the archetype, the lonely figure—in this case, usually an Aran fisherman or farmer—who represented the mythic and noble Ireland of his imagination. "Synge's language," writes Robinson, "is the translation into English not of an Irish text but of the Irish language itself."

Many observers have commented on Synge's somber appearance, of the gravity from which he approached life. He had a haunted look about him, as if judgment day and the wrath of God lay just around the corner. This haunting fatalism colored much of his work, so that even when he wrote about a lighthearted subject, there was always a dark cloud hovering perilously above. His plays have been referred to as fantastic realism, where the dead and the living share close quarters. Fate, in fact, is a common theme, especially in *Riders to the Sea*, where the vast ocean and its uncaring waves tragically took the lives of so many young men over the centuries.

Synge's world is uniformly dangerous and unpredictable, lost to the unfathomable rhythms of the elements. His characters find little solace in religion or in authoritative clerical figures. Rather, they are forced to rely on their own inner resources—to locate their own inner compass—and yet they all remain part of a wider and ineffable world and just as subject to its willy-nilly forces.

Synge died at the prematurely young age of thirty-eight of Hodgkin's disease.

The twentieth century has been blessed with the presence of many magnificent playwrights from Ireland, especially Hugh Leonard, John B. Keane, Stewart Parker, and Brian Friel. But Synge's legacy most obviously lives on in the work of the young Anglo-Irish playwright Martin McDonagh, the son of a Connemara father and a Sligo mother.

McDonagh's trilogy of Aran Island plays (*The Cripple of Inishmann*, *The Lieutenant of Inishmore*, and *The Banshees of Inisheer*) and his Connemara Trilogy (*The Beauty Queen of Leenane*, *A Skull in Connemara*, and *The Lonesome West*) are full of the poetic playfulness (what McDonagh himself has called "a core strangeness of speech"), structural devices, and not always flattering characterizations that are so much associated with Synge. But McDonagh's often cruel and violent world of rogue eccentrics and wanton grotesques in rural Ireland is a far cry from the primitive romanticism of Synge.

Synge remains a unique voice in Irish literature, a creator of words who discovered poetry in one of the most ancient of cultures and exulted in its savage beauty.

REFLECTION

Synge had mixed emotions about nature; he often felt overwhelmed by its destructive forces and yet he was acutely attracted to it, in a deeply spiritual way. How do you feel about nature? Does its elemental power frighten you at times? Or do you find a sense of peace and tranquility in its timeless beauty?

FOR FURTHER READING

J. M. Synge. *The Aran Islands*. Edited with an introduction by Tim Robinson (London: Penguin Books, 1992).

John Millington Synge. *Plays, Poems and Prose*. Introduction by Micheál Mac Liammóir (New York: Everyman's Library/ Dutton, 1958).

RECOMMENDED VIEWING

Man of Aran (1934). The famous documentary by the American filmmaker Robert Flaherty is still considered a classic of the silent era.

teilo

WELSH SAINT
(?-c.580)

His learning shone like the sun.
ANONYMOUS

eilo was one of the most important of the Welsh saints. He was born into a pagan family at Penally, in western Wales, and was taught by a disciple of King Arthur. Later Teilo befriended David. When conflict erupted with the Irish, Teilo, along with David and another man named Padarn, left Wales altogether to embark on a pilgrimage to holy Jerusalem.

According to the story, the trio went to a great church in the heart of the city where three chairs stood. Two were decorated with precious metals, while the third consisted of humble cedar wood. David and Padarn chose the elegant chairs, but Teilo decided to sit on the plain one. Later he was told that this was the very same chair that Christ chose, and so Teilo, too, felt obligated to preach the gospel. As a token for their long journey, the church authorities gave David an altar; Padarn, a staff; and Teilo, a bell that had special qualities. The bell was later transported to his shrine at Llandarff Cathedral in Wales.

The three men eventually returned to Britain. Teilo, though, went not to Wales, but to Cornwall. Later, he was forced to leave when, in 547, a yellow fever epidemic raged through the land, leaving thousands of people homeless or dead in its wake. Many families fled to the safety of Brittany, which was spared the terrible plague. Teilo was among the many clergy who chose to go there. Once on safe ground, he stayed with Samson, a fellow countryman, at the monastery at Dol.

In the seven years and seven months that Teilo remained at the monastery, he and Samson became fast friends and comrades in faith. Like many Celtic saints, Teilo felt a special connection to nature; he loved to plant fruit trees and enjoyed the freedom of riding with the stags.

When Teilo finally returned to Britain he had earned a reputation as a wise and good man. Once, when asked, "What is the greatest wisdom in a man?" he reportedly replied, "To refrain from injuring another when he has the power to do so." Helping others was more important to him than bettering himself or raising his station in life. He did his utmost to come to the aid of humanity. Sometime in the sixth century, Teilo founded a church at Llandaff, and today that cathedral still stands.

Teilo died at Llandello Fawr in Carmarthenshire, Wales, but was buried at his ancestral home in Penally.

REFLECTION

Teilo was a modest man with humble tastes. If, everything being equal, you were given a choice between selecting a plain object or a fine one, which would you choose? Why?

SITES ASSOCIATED WITH TEILO

Llandaff Cathedral
Llandaff, Wales
Said to have been founded by Teilo in the sixth century, the cathedral was rebuilt in 1120 in the Norman style. In the nineteenth century, the pre-Raphaelite artists Edward Burne-Jones, Dante Gabriel Rossetti, and colleagues of William Morris were commissioned to create new stained glass windows and decorative panels. Whole sections of the cathedral were destroyed during

World War II but additional restorations were completed in 1960. A tenth-century Celtic cross is the only pre-Norman relic.

William Butler Yeats

POET AND PLAYWRIGHT
(1865-1939)

Cast a cold eye
On life, on death.
Horseman, pass by!
WILLIAM BUTLER YEATS
("Under Ben Bulben")

Who else but William Butler Yeats could earn the honor of the greatest English-language poet of the twentieth century? Who else created such exquisitely crafted poetry and some of the most memorable lines?

"Down by the Salley Gardens." "The Lake Isle of Innisfree." "When You Are Old." "The Wild Swans at Coole." "Easter 1916." "The Second Coming." "Sailing to Byzantium."

He was like no other. He was not typically anything. An elusive, enigmatic figure, Yeats hovered in the shadows of Irish public life even when he was a major part of it. And yet, he stood apart.

Born in Dublin on June 13, 1865, Yeats spent his youth mostly in London until returning to Dublin to finish high school. Even as a young man, he had the poetic instinct. He knew he would devote his life to poetry and to the pursuit of cultivating the literary imagination.

Yeats had spent many summers as a child in County Sligo, where he soaked up the rural atmosphere and committed to memory many of the stories he had heard from ordinary men and women who brought the ancient tales to life. Fascinated by folklore and old songs, he read translations of the Celtic sagas and his heart swooned at the possibilities. Here in his own country was an authentic tradition that anyone could proudly claim his or her own. The ancient Irish literature and Gaelic mythology fired his imagination and convinced him that Ireland could—must—develop its own indigenous literature far removed from the influences of London and the continent.

Yeats was deeply spiritual by inclination, although highly skeptical of established religion. In effect, he, this descendant of Anglo-Irish Protestant clergymen, created his own religion carved serendipitously from disparate parts—clairvoyance, the occult, mysticism, folklore, theosophy, spiritualism, the works of Blake, Swedenborg, and Boehm—until he finally arrived at his own particular vision of spiritual truth.

Yeats's writings brought together both pagan and Christian elements. For example, *The Celtic Twilight*, originally published in 1893, was based mainly on conversations he had with ordinary folk in Sligo and concentrated almost exclusively on the supernatural. By this time, too, he had compiled *Fairy and Folk Tales of the Irish Peasantry* and *Irish Fairy Tales*. His poetry recreated Irish heroic themes while interspersed with the earthy folk traditions of the Irish peasantry. Ancient Irish kings and Irish place names populate his poetry. Yeats's decision to turn to the heroic and mystic side of the distant Irish past for his subject matter was an intentional attempt to prove to the skeptical Irish people that they, in fact, had a past and, hence, a literature, worth celebrating. Most of all, he wanted Ireland to wake up to the sound of its own voice.

Yeats earned a reputation as a poet who wrote eloquently about love in all of its manifestations. He fell deeply in love with the elusive Maud Gonne, an actress and fiery Irish nationalist who was a fierce advocate of Irish independence. At the time, though, Yeats was but a poor, struggling journalist, and all he could offer was his love—and his words.

> But I, being poor, have only my dreams;
> I have spread my dreams under your feet;
> Tread softly because you tread on my dreams.
> > "He Wishes for the Cloths of Heaven"

Yeats's love for Maud Gonne was never fully reciprocated, however. He proposed to her several times, and each time she rejected him. Many of his so-called "Rose poems" were written for her. For example, in poems such as "The Secret Rose" and "The Rose of the World," he uses Gaelic mythology to describe his mixed feelings toward her: love mixed with several parts of anger and frustration. In his words, though, Maud's elusive beauty transcends the mere physical to approach the spiritual realm. She is, essentially, forever beyond reach. "All that's beautiful drifts away / Like the waters," he once wrote.

Yeats also wrote many plays, although very few are performed today. With Lady Gregory and Edward Martyn, he founded the Irish Literary Theatre in 1899, which would eventually evolve into the famous Abbey Theatre. Included among his early works is a play inspired by Maud Gonne, *The Countess Cathleen*. Other plays include *The Land of Heart's Desire*, *Cathleen ni Houlilan*, *On Baile's Strand*, *At the Hawk's Well*, *Purgatory*, and the so-called Cuchulain cycle, *The Green Helmet* in 1910, *The Only Jealousy of Emer* in 1919, and *The Death of Cuchulain* in 1939.

Increasingly, Yeats attempted to strip bare his plays to their most essential ingredients. (He had no interest in the popular theatre.) Above all, he sought simplicity, whether in acting or stage design. He created a series of plays—such as *Four Plays for Dancers* and *The Player Queen* and, perhaps most effectively, *The Dreaming of the Bones*—inspired by the Japanese Noh tradition. Formal, structured, highly stylized, with very little dialogue, it was the kind of theatre that suited his interpretation of dramatic form. Rather than traditional narrative technique, he turned to a set of motions and symbols, choreographed movement, that used masks and gesture to tell a story. It all fit in with his increasingly esoteric worldview.

Yeats's interest in spiritualism and mysticism culminated in the publication of a complex prose work called *A Vision*, that used an elaborate series of symbols employing the phases of the moon—it was essentially his own private theory for the collapse of the world made public—that lamented what he considered the destruction of Western civilization.

At heart, Yeats remained an idealist who longed to transcend the cruelties of life. He turned to nature and to the Irish myths to escape from the tawdriness and pettiness of the outside world, and he used the distinctive rhythms of Gaelic speech, its peculiar inflections and intonations, to convey his message to the public.

Yeats's career went through several major phases: the dreamy and romantic poet of his early years; to a more vigorous and muscular style inspired by the dreams and struggles of Irish nationalism; to a metaphysical period, where he experimented with different kinds of rhythms and employed an increasingly complex system of symbols; and finally the period of the mature Yeats where, reaching his masterly stride, he is fully in control of his art. Ironically, despite a lifetime of searching, he has more questions than he has answers. This is the Yeats that explores in his own idiosyncratic style the timeless questions of purpose and meaning, of love and hate, the transience of things, and of the very nature of art itself.

"Man can embody truth but he cannot know it," he wrote toward the end of his life.

Yeats won the Nobel Prize for Literature in 1923, and the previous year he became a senator of the new Irish state. He died of heart failure on January 28, 1939, in the south of France, and was buried there. In 1948 his remains were returned to Ireland where he was interred, as per his wishes, at Drumcliffe churchyard in the shadow of Ben Bulben, in his beloved County Sligo.

The great poet had wished to attain spiritual immortality. At the very least, he had hoped to find the answer to his lifelong quest, What is the meaning of existence? Alas, it eluded even him.

REFLECTION

As a poet, Yeats addressed the fundamental issues that confront the human condition: love and death, meaning and purpose. He turned to art to try to come to terms with what it means to be a human being. Where or to whom do you turn in your own struggle to find meaning in the experience of being human?

SITES ASSOCIATED WITH WILLIAM BUTLER YEATS

Sligo County Museum and Art Gallery
Sligo, County Sligo, Ireland
The museum houses a small selection of Yeats memorabilia; the gallery includes paintings by Yeats's brother, Jack, and several portraits by his artist-father, John B. Yeats.

FOR FURTHER READING

Richard Ellmann. *Yeats: The Man and the Masks* (New York: W. W. Norton & Co., 2000).

Frank Tuohy. *Yeats: An Illustrated Biography* (New York: New Amsterdam, 1991).

RECOMMENDED LISTENING

Now and In Time To Be: A Musical Celebration of the Works of W. B. Yeats (Grapevine). Van Morrison, Christy Moore, the Waterboys, the Cranberries, and others offer musical interpretations of such Yeats classics as "Down by the Salley Gardens," "The Song of Wandering Aengus," and "The Stolen Child," among others. Includes a recording of Yeats himself reciting probably his most famous poem, "The Lake Isle of Innisfree."

Bibliography

Adam, David. *Border Lands: The Best of David Adam's Celtic Vision* (Franklin, WI: Sheed & Ward, 2000).

____. *The Holy Island: Pilgrim Guide* (Norwich: Canterbury Press, 1997).

Adomnan of Iona. *Life of St. Columba.* Translated by Richard Sharpe (London: Penguin Books, 1995).

Anderson, Father George, SJ. "John Ogilvie, SJ: A Martyr of Scotland." *Company* (Winter 2000), pp. 23–25.

Anderson, Mosa. *St. Ninian: Light of the Celtic North* (London: The Faith Press, 1964).

Athanasius. *The Life of Antony and The Letter to Marcellinus.* Translated by Robert C. Gregg. Classics of Western Spirituality (New York: Paulist Press, 1980).

Attwater, Donald, with Catherine Rachel John. *A Dictionary of Saints* (New York: Penguin Books, 1995).

Backhouse, Janet. *The Lindisfarne Gospels: A Masterpiece of Book Painting* (London: The British Library, 1995).

Beaumont, John W. *Saint Andrew and St. Andrews* (Lathones, Fife: S.McK. Fox, 1995). Booklet.

Bergman, Susan, ed. *Martyrs: Contemporary Writers on Modern Lives of Faith* (Maryknoll, NY: Orbis Books, 1996).

Bitel, Lisa. *Isle of the Saints* (Ithaca, NY: Cornell University Press, 1990).

Bolster, M. Angela, RSM. *Catherine McAuley: Venerable for Mercy* (Dublin: Dominican Publications, 1990).

Bradley, Ian. *Celtic Spirituality: Making Myths and Chasing Dreams* (Edinburgh: Edinburgh University Press, 1999).

____. *Columba: Pilgrim and Penitent* (Glasgow: Wild Goose Publications, 1996).

Brett, Donna Whitson, and Edward T. Brett. *Murdered in Central America* (Maryknoll, NY: Orbis Books, 1988).

Brooke, Daphne. *Wild Men and Holy Places: St. Ninian, Whithorn and the Medieval Realm of Galloway* (Edinburgh: Canongate Press, 1994).

Brown, George Mackay. *For the Islands I Sing: An Autobiography* (London: John Murray Publishers, 1997).

____. *Magnus* (Glasgow: Richard Drew Publishing, 1973).

——. *Portrait of Orkney* (London: John Murray Publishers, 1988).

Cahill, Thomas. *How the Irish Saved Civilization*: The Untold Story of Ireland's Heroic Role from the Fall of Rome to the Rise of Medieval Europe (New York: Doubleday, 1995).

Campbell, Angus Peter, ed. *Somhairle: Dain is Deilibh (A Celebration on the 80th Birthday of Sorley MacLean)* (Stornoway: Acair, 1991).

Carmichael, Alexander, ed. *Carmina Gadelica*. With a Preface by John MacInnes (Edinburgh: Floris Books, 1992).

——, ed. *The Sun Dances: Prayers and Blessings from the Gaelic*. Introduction by Adam Bittleston (Edinburgh: Floris Books, 1993).

Carney, James Guadalupe. *To Be a Revolutionary: The Autobiography of Father James Guadalupe Carney* (New York: Harper and Row, 1987).

Chadwick, Nora. *The Celts* (London: Penguin Books, 1971).

Chiffolo, Anthony F., comp. *At Prayer with the Saints* (Liguori, MO: Liguori, 1998).

Clancy, Thomas Owen, and Gilbert Markus. *Iona: The Earliest Poetry of a Celtic Monastery* (Edinburgh: Edinburgh University Press, 1995).

Coffey, Michael, and Terry Golway, eds. "The Great Famine: Between Hunger and the White House." In *The Irish in America* (New York: Hyperion, 1997).

Coles, Robert. *Flannery O'Connor's South* (Athens, GA: University of Georgia Press, 1993).

Crowe, Thomas Rain, ed., with Gwendal Denez and Tom Hubbard. *Writing the Wind: A Celtic Resurgence* (Cullowhee, NC: New Native Press, 1997).

D'Arcy, Mary Ryan. *The Saints of Ireland* (Cork: Mercier Press, 1985).

Davies, Oliver, and Fiona Bowie, eds. *Celtic Christian Spirituality: An Anthology of Medieval and Modern Sources* (New York: Continuum, 1999).

Delaney, Frank. *The Celts* (Boston: Little, Brown, 1986).

De Waal, Esther. *The Celtic Way of Prayer: The Recovery of the Religious Imagination.* (New York: Doubleday, 1997).

Donaldson, Scott. *Archibald MacLeish: An American Life* (Boston: Houghton Mifflin, 1992).

Doyle, Dennis and Paula. *Songs of Celtic Christianity* (Pacific, MO: Mel Bay Publications, 1995).

Duffy, Joseph. *Patrick In His Own Words* (Dublin: Veritas, 1972).

Ellmann, Richard. *Yeats: The Man and the Masks* (New York: W. W. Norton & Co., 2000).

Ellsberg, Robert. *All Saints: Daily Reflections on Saints, Prophets, and Witnesses for Our Time* (New York: Crossroad, 1997).

Farmer, David Hugh. *The Oxford Dictionary of Saints* (Oxford: Oxford University Press, 1978).

Ferguson, Ronald. *George MacLeod* (London: Collins, 1990).

France, Peter. *Hermits: The Insights of Solitude* (New York: St. Martin's Press, 1996).

Friedenberg, Richard, with an Introduction by Robert Redford. *A River Runs Through It: Bringing a Classic to the Screen* (Livingston, MT: Clark City Press, 1992).

Gibson, Rob. *Highland Clearances Trail* (Evanton, Scotland: Highland Heritage, 1996). Booklet.

Hawkes, Jane. *The Golden Age of Northumbria* (Morpeth, Northumberland: Sandhill Press, 1996).

Hoy, Suellen. "Walking Nuns: Chicago's Irish Sisters of Mercy." In *At the Crossroads: Old Saint Patrick's and the Chicago Irish*. Edited by Ellen Skerrett (Chicago: Wild Onion Books, 1997).

Hughes, Kathleen, and Ann Hamlin. *Celtic Monasticism* (New York: Seabury Press, 1981).

Joyce, Timothy. *Celtic Christianity: A Sacred Tradition, a Vision of Hope* (Maryknoll, NY: Orbis Books, 1998).

Kerrigan, Catherine, ed. *An Anthology of Scottish Women Poets* (Edinburgh: Edinburgh University Press, 1991).

Lacey, Brian. *Colum Cille and the Columban Tradition* (Dublin: Four Courts Press, 1997).

Laxton, Edward. *The Famine Ships: The Irish Exodus to America* (New York: Henry Holt, 1996).

Lynch, Thomas. *Bodies in Motion and At Rest: On Metaphor and Mortality* (New York: W. W. Norton & Co., 2000).

———. *Still Life in Milford: Poems* (New York: W. W. Norton & Co., 1999).

———. *The Undertaking: Life Studies from the Dismal Trade* (New York: Penguin Books, 1998).

Macdonald, Iain, ed. *Saints of Northumbria: Cuthbert, Aidan, Oswald, Hilda* (Edinburgh: Floris Books, 1997).

———, ed. *Saint Magnus* (Edinburgh: Floris Books, 1993).

McFarland, Ron, and Hugh Nichols, eds. *Norman Maclean*. American Authors Series (Lewiston, ID: Confluence Press, 1988).

Mackey, James, ed. *An Introduction to Celtic Christianity* (Edinburgh: T. T. Clark, 1989).

Maclean, Norman. *A River Runs Through It and Other Stories* (Chicago: University of Chicago Press, 1976).

———. *Young Men and Fire* (Chicago: University of Chicago Press, 1992).

Maclean, Sorley. Introduction by William Gillies (Edinburgh: National Library of Scotland, 1981). Booklet.

Maclean, Sorley, George Campbell Hay, Iain Crichton Smith, Derick Thomson, Donald MacAuley. Introduction by Donald MacAuley. *Nua-Bhardachd Ghaidhlig: Modern Scottish Gaelic Poems: A Bilingual Anthology* (Edinburgh: Canongate Publishing, 1987).

MacLeish, Archibald. *Collected Poems, 1917–1982* (Boston: Houghton Mifflin, 1985).

MacLeish, William H. *Uphill with Archie: A Son's Journey* (New York: Simon & Schuster, 2001).

MacLeod, Alistair. *As Birds Bring Forth the Sun and Other Stories.* Afterword by Jane Urquhart (Toronto: McClelland & Stewart, 1992).

——. *Island: The Complete Stories* (New York: W. W. Norton & Co., 2001).

——. *The Lost Salt Gift of Blood.* Afterword by Joyce Carol Oates (Toronto: McClelland & Stewart, 1989).

——. *No Great Mischief* (Toronto: McClelland & Stewart, 1999).

MacLeod, George. *The Whole Earth Shall Cry.* Edited by Ronald Ferguson (Glasgow: Wild Goose Publications, 1985).

Macleod, John. *Highlanders: A History of the Gaels* (London: Sceptre, 1996).

Macquarrie, Alan. *The Saints of Scotland: Essays in Scottish History AD 450–1093* (Edinburgh: John Donald Publishers, 1997).

Magee, Rosemary M., ed. *Conversations with Flannery O'Connor* (Jackson, MS: University Press of Mississippi, 1987).

Maher, Michael, ed. *Irish Spirituality* (Dublin: Veritas Publications, 1979).

Maxwell, William. *Ancestors: A Family History* (New York: Vintage, 1995).

Mayers, Peter. *Listen to the Desert: Secrets of Spiritual Maturity from the Desert Fathers and Mothers* (Liguori, MO: Liguori Publications, 1996).

Meehan, Bernard. *The Book of Kells* (London: Thames and Hudson, 1996).

Miller, Kerby, and Paul Wagner. *Out of Ireland: The Story of Irish Emigration to America* (Washington, D.C.: Elliott & Clark, 1994).

Mitton, Michael. *The Soul of Celtic Spirituality in the Lives of Its Saints* (Mystic, CT: Twenty-Third Publications, 1996).

Moreton, Cole. *Hungry for Home: Leaving the Blaskets: A Journey from the Edge of Ireland* (New York: Viking, 2000).

Morton, Tom. *Going Home: The Runrig Story* (Edinburgh: Mainstream Publishing, 1991).

Morton, T. Ralph. *The Iona Community Story* (London: Lutterworth Press, 1957).

Muir, Edwin. *An Autobiography* (London: Chatto & Windus, 1980).
_____. *Collected Poems* (London: Faber and Faber, 1984)

Munro, Donnie. "Dreams from Hard Places: A Lecture" (Glasgow: Sabhal Mor Ostaig and Scottish Television, 1996). Booklet.

Neeson, Eoin. *The Book of Irish Saints* (Cork: Mercier Press, 1967).

Newell, J. Philip. *Listening for the Heartbeat of God: A Celtic Spirituality* (Mahwah, NJ: Paulist Press, 1997).
——. *Echo of the Soul: The Sacredness of the Human Body* (Harrisburg, PA: Morehouse Publishing, 2001).

O'Connor, Flannery. *The Habit of Being.* Edited by Sally Fitzgerald (New York: Farrar, Straus, and Giroux, 1979).

Ó Criomhthain, Tomás. *The Islandman.* Translated by Robin Flower (London: Oxford University Press, 1978).

O'Donohue, John. *Anam Cara: A Book of Celtic Wisdom* (New York: HarperCollins Publishers, 1997).
——. *Eternal Echoes: Exploring Our Yearning to Belong* (New York: HarperCollins Publishers, 1999).

O'Driscoll, Robert, ed. *The Celtic Consciousness* (New York: George Braziller, 1981).

Ó Fiaich, Tomás. *Columbanus: In His Own Words* (Dublin: Veritas, 1990).

O'Flaherty, Liam. *Famine* (New York: The Literary Guild, 1937).

O'Meara, John J. *The Voyage of Saint Brendan: "Journey to the Promised Land."* Translated from the Latin (Gerrards Cross, Buckinghamshire, England: Colin Smythe Limited, 1991).

Ó Riordáin, John J. *The Music of What Happens: Celtic Spirituality, a View from the Inside* (Dublin: Columba Press, 1996).

____. *A Pilgrim in Celtic Scotland* (Dublin: Columba Press, 1997).

O'Rourke, Daniel, ed. *Dream State: The New Scottish Poets* (Edinburgh: Polygon, 1994).

O'Sullivan, Maurice. *Twenty Years A-Growing.* With an Introductory Note by E. M. Forster (Nashville: J. S. Sanders, 1998).

Palsson, Hermann, and Paul Edwards, trans. *Orkneyinga Saga: The History of the Earls of Orkney* (London: Penguin Books, 1981).

Parker, Michael. *Seamus Heaney: The Making of the Poet* (London: Macmillan, 1993).

Pemberton, Cintra. *Soulfaring: Celtic Pilgrimage Then and Now* (Harrisburg, PA: Morehouse Publishing, 1999).

Pennick, Nigel. *The Celtic Saints: An Illustrated and Authoritative Guide to These Extraordinary Men and Women* (New York: Sterling Publishing, 1997).

Plummer, Charles, ed. *Lives of Irish Saints* (London: Oxford University Press, 1922).

Prendergast, Mark J. *Irish Rock: Roots, Personalities, Directions* (Dublin: O'Brien Press, 1987).

Prebble, John. *The Highland Clearances* (London: Penguin Books, 1963).

Rabey, Steve. *In the House of Memory: Ancient Celtic Wisdom for Everyday Life* (New York: Dutton, 1998).

Richards, Eric. *The Highland Clearances: People, Landlords and Rural Turmoil* (Edinburgh: Birlinn, 2000).

——. *Patrick Sellar and the Highland Clearances* (Edinburgh: Polygon, 1999).

Rodgers, Michael, and Marcus Losack. With a Foreword by Esther de Waal. *Glendalough: A Celtic Pilgrimage* (Harrisburg, PA: Morehouse Publishing, 1996).

Sawyers, June Skinner, ed. *Quiet Moments with Patrick and the Celtic Saints: 120 Daily Readings* (Ann Arbor, MI: Servant Publications, 1999).

Sayers, Peig. *An Old Woman's Reflections*. Translated by Seamus Ennis (London: Oxford University Press, 1978).

Sellner, Edward C. *Wisdom of the Celtic Saints* (Notre Dame, IN: Ave Maria Press, 1993).

Severin, Tim. *The Brendan Voyage* (London: Little Brown, 1996).

Severin, Tim. *The Brendan Voyage*. Modern Library Exploration. Series Editor: John Krakauer. With an Introduction by Malachy McCourt (New York: The Modern Library 2000).

Sheldrake, Philip. *Living between Worlds: Place and Journey in Celtic Spirituality* (London: Darton, Longman, and Todd, 1995).

Simpson, Ray, comp. *Celtic Blessings: Prayers for Everyday Life* (Chicago: Loyola Press, 1999).

Skinner, John, trans. *The Confession of Saint Patrick* (New York: Image Books, 1998).

Smith, Iain Crichton. *Consider the Lilies* (Edinburgh: Canongate Publishing, 1987).

Stagles, Joan and Ray. *The Blasket Islands: Next Parish America* (Dublin: O'Brien Press, 1988).

Stegner, Wallace. "Haunted by Waters." In *Where the Bluebird Sings to the Lemonade Springs: Living and Writing in the West* (New York: Random House, 1992).

Stokes, Niall. *Into the Heart: The Stories Behind Every U2 Song* (New York: Thunder's Mouth Press, 1997).

Synge, John Millington. *The Aran Islands*. Edited with an Introduction by Tim Robinson (London: Penguin Books, 1992).

——. *Plays, Poems and Prose*. Introduction by Micheál Mac Liammóir (New York: Everyman's Library/Dutton, 1958).

Thurston, Herbert, and Donald Attwater, eds. *Butler's Lives of the Saints*. 4 vols. (Westminster, MD: Christian Classics, 1980).

Tobin, Greg. *The Wisdom of St. Patrick: Inspirations from the Patron Saint of Ireland* (New York: Ballantine Books, 1999).

Toulson, Shirley. *The Celtic Alternative* (London: Century, 1987).

Tuohy, Frank. *Yeats: An Illustrated Biography* (New York: New Amsterdam, 1991).

Waddell, Helen, translator with an introduction. Preface by M. Basil Pennington. *The Desert Fathers*. Vintage Spiritual Classics (New York: Vintage, 1998).

Wallace, Martin. *Celtic Saints* (San Francisco: Chronicle Books, 1995).

Walsh, Michael, ed. *Butler's Lives of the Saints* (San Francisco: Harper San Francisco, 1991).

Webb, J. F., trans. *The Age of Bede*. Edited with an Introduction by D. H. Farmer (London: Penguin Books, 1998).

Whiteside, Lesley. *In Search of Columba* (Dublin: Columba Press, 1997).

——. *The Spirituality of St. Patrick* (Harrisburg, PA: Morehouse Publishing, 1996).

Woodham-Smith, Cecil. *The Great Hunger: Ireland 1845–1849* (New York: Penguin Books, 1991).

Woods, Richard J. *The Spirituality of the Celtic Saints* (Maryknoll, NY: Orbis Books, 2000).

Woodward, Kenneth L. *Making Saints: How the Catholic Church Determines Who Becomes a Saint, Who Doesn't, and Why* (New York: Simon & Schuster, 1990).

Vendler, Helen. *Seamus Heaney* (Cambridge, MA: Harvard University Press, 1998).

Yeoman, Peter. *Pilgrimage in Medieval Scotland* (London: Batsford/Historic Scotland, 1998).